The Younger Pitt

PROFILES IN POWER

. . . .

THE
YOUNGER PITT

Michael Duffy

Longman

An imprint of **Pearson Education**

Harlow, England · London · New York · Reading, Massachusetts · San Francisco
Toronto · Don Mills, Ontario · Sydney · Tokyo · Singapore · Hong Kong · Seoul
Taipei · Cape Town · Madrid · Mexico City · Amsterdam · Munich · Paris · Milan

Pearson Education Limited

Edinburgh Gate
Harlow
Essex CM20 2JE
England

and Associated Companies around the world

Visit us on the World Wide Web at
www.pearsoneduc.com

First published in Great Britain in 2000

© Pearson Education Limited 2000

ISBN 0 582 05278 5 CSD
ISBN 0 582 05279 3 PPR

British Library Cataloguing-in-Publication Data
A catalogue record for this book can be obtained from the British
Library

Library of Congress Cataloging-in-Publication Data
Duffy, Michael, 1944–
    The younger Pitt / Michael Duffy.
        p.   cm. — (Profiles in power)
    Includes bibliographical references (p.   ) and index.
    ISBN 0–582–05278–5 (cased : alk. paper) — ISBN 0–582–05279–3 (pbk. : alk. paper)
        1. Pitt, William, 1759–1806. 2. Great Britain—Politics and government—1760–1820. 3.
    Prime ministers—Great Britain—Biography. I. Title. II. Profiles in power (London,
    England)

    DA522.P6 D84 2000
    941.07′3′092—dc21
    [B]   00–032708

10 9 8 7 6 5 4 3 2 1
06 05 04 03 02 01

Typeset by 35 in 11/13pt Janson
Produced by Pearson Education Asia Pte Ltd.
Printed in Singapore

CONTENTS

LIST OF ABBREVIATIONS

Add. MSS	British Library, Additional Manuscripts
BL	British Library
C.C.GIII	Duke of Buckingham and Chandos (ed.), *Memoirs of the Courts and Cabinets of George the Third*, 4 vols (1853–55)
EHR	*English Historical Review*
HJ	*The Historical Journal*
HMC	Historical Manuscripts Commission
Holland	This common contemporary abbreviation has been employed instead of the full title of the Dutch republic: the United Provinces of Holland, Zeeland etc.
L.C.GIII	A. Aspinall (ed.), *The Later Correspondence of George III*, 5 vols (Cambridge, 1962–70)
NRS	Navy Records Society
PH	*Parliamentary History*
Parl. Hist.	W. Cobbett (ed.), *The Parliamentary History of England from the Earliest Period to the Year 1803*, 36 vols (1806–20)
Pitt/Rutland Corresp.	Earl Stanhope (ed.), *Correspondence between the Rt. Hon. William Pitt and Charles, Duke of Rutland . . . 1781–1787*, with Introduction by the Duke of Rutland (1890)
PRO	Public Record Office, London
Speeches	W.S. Hathaway (ed.), *The Speeches of the Rt. Hon. William Pitt*, 4 vols (1806)

The place of publication for works cited is London unless otherwise stated.

CHRONOLOGY

1759	Pitt born 28 May
1773–9	At Cambridge. American Declaration of Independence and war 1776; death of father 1778; France (1778), Spain (1779) and Holland (1780) enter war against Britain
1780	Called to the Bar as a recognised trial lawyer; general election, defeated for Cambridge University seat
1781	MP for Appleby, takes seat 23 January, first speech 26 February
1782	Fall of Lord North's Ministry (March); introduces parliamentary reform motion (May); becomes Chancellor of the Exchequer in Shelburne's Ministry (6 July)
1783	Shelburne defeated on peace preliminaries and Pitt resigns (February); declines King's invitations to form a government; visits France; encourages King to defeat Fox's India Bill and appointed First Lord of the Treasury and Chancellor of the Exchequer (19 December)
1784	Struggle to win supremacy in the Commons (January–March); general election; MP for Cambridge University; passes own India Act and begins tax reforms
1785	Defeated on Westminster Scrutiny, parliamentary reform proposals, Irish Commercial Propositions; presses administrative economic reforms
1786	Richmond's fortifications bill defeated; start of the two years that made Pitt's reputation as a Minister; Sinking Fund scheme to eliminate National Debt; Commercial Treaty with France
1787	Consolidation of customs duties; supplants French influence over the Dutch; first opposes repeal of religious Test Acts
1788	'Triple Alliance' with Prussia and Holland; Regency Crisis (November 1788–February 1789)

1789   Outbreak of revolution in France

1790   Nootka Sound crisis with Spain; general election

1791   Negotiations with Opposition (February–March); defeated in Ochakov crisis with Russia; Church and King riots in Birmingham; Tom Paine's *Rights of Man* stimulates formation of radical reforming societies

1792   Extends Sinking Fund; proclamation against seditious writings; forces resignation of Lord Chancellor Thurlow; failed negotiations with Portland Whig Opposition; accepts King's offer of Wardenship of Cinque Ports; autumn crises over internal disturbances and radicalism and over external threat of French to the Austrian Netherlands and Holland; encourages loyalist association movement (November)

1793   Outbreak of war with France (1 February); opposes Grey's parliamentary reform motion; negotiates First Coalition of European powers; initial successes followed by defeats at Dunkirk (September) and Toulon (December)

1794   Scares from threat of invasion and agitation for a convention by radical clubs; first call for home defence volunteers; suspension of Habeas Corpus (May); Glorious First of June naval victory but defeat in Netherlands; union with Portland Whigs (11 July); imperial successes (West Indies) checked

1795   Fall of Holland; ministerial reshuffle (December 1794–January 1795); crisis with Lord Lieutenant of Ireland, Earl Fitzwilliam (February); Prussia and Spain make peace with France, and Dutch join French against Britain; corn scarcity and radical agitation; attack on King's carriage (November); 'Two Acts' against treasonable practices and seditious meetings (November–December); announces willingness to make peace with lasting French government

1796   General election; abortive peace overtures to France (February, September–December); Spain joins war against Britain

1797   Pitt's *annus horribilis*: abandons courtship of Eleanor Eden; run on banks and suspension of cash payments (February); Austria defeated and withdraws from war; mutinies in fleet (April–May); Cabinet divisions on peace overture (June); unsuccessful negotiations with France (July–September); death of Eliot (September); naval victory at Camperdown (October); unpopular assessed taxes proposals

1798   Renewed invasion threat; encourages volunteers and patriotic subscription; duel with Tierney (27 May); rebellion in

Ireland suppressed (May–June); naval victory at the Nile
(August); negotiations to renew Coalition against France;
incomes tax enacted

1799   Renewal of continental war; banning of named subversive
societies; repulse of expedition to Holland, and Russian
defeat in Switzerland

1800   Union of Britain and Ireland enacted (to start 1 January
1801); corn scarcity and rioting; collapse of continental war;
forces Egyptian expedition through Cabinet

1801   Determines to resist Armed Neutrality of Baltic Powers;
resigns over royal opposition to Catholic Emancipation
(14 March); but supports successor Addington in making
peace with France

1802   Peace of Amiens with France (March); general election;
Pitt severely ill in autumn, delays taking seat

1803   Attempts to persuade Pitt to enter Ministry; renewal of war
with France (May); returns to Commons but defeated on
Patten's motion (June); leads volunteer movement against
invasion threat

1804   Joins attack on Addington's conduct of war, and becomes
First Lord of the Treasury again when Addington resigns
(10 May); Treasury reforms; union with Addingtonians
(December)

1805   Negotiations to form a third European Coalition; defeated
over Melville (May); withdrawal of Addingtonians from
government (July); renewal of European war; naval victory
at Trafalgar, but allies defeated at Ulm and Austerlitz

1806   Dies 23 January

. . . .

INTRODUCTION

True Patriotism in the times of public peace and tranquillity . . . consists in a sober and steady obedience to the laws, and observance of the constitution; in mild and moderate endeavours to rectify whatever disorders and corruptions may have crept into either . . . ; in a firm support without respect to names and parties, or private connections of whatever administration may happen to be then established in points wherein they are right, in a firm though a calm opposition to them, in matters wherein they may be wrong; but above all, it consists in providing for the contingencies of war during the times of peace, in increasing the revenue without burthening trade, in discharging the public debts, and in promoting arts, science, agriculture, manufactures and population throughout the kingdom.

Indeed, it is only in times of public and national distress, . . . that real Patriotism becomes bustling and active, and makes a noise in the world.

Anon., *Essay on Patriotism and on the character and conduct of some late famous pretenders to that virtue*, pp. 12–13 (London, 1768).

It has become customary to trace Pitt's political career chronologically in two unequal parts: the years of peace and reform, followed by the years of war and repression. This I have tried to avoid, since I am inclined to agree with Pitt's much abused 'official biographer', George Pretyman Tomline, that 'Mr Pitt's administration forms a consistent whole, and all its various parts are founded on the same principle, and give a force and support to each other.'[1] Historians have debated the particular principle that moved Pitt, but it seems to me that his life and speeches echo the sentiments expressed in the extract above, which represent the Patriot ideal of the mid-eighteenth century. Ironically they were enunciated in a pamphlet attacking Pitt's father, whereas it was from his father that Pitt acquired his Patriot inspiration. When the Younger Pitt spoke of his ambition for 'character', it was a character as a virtuous Patriot statesman that he had in mind.[2]

I have chosen to take primarily a thematic rather than a chronological approach, as the best way to show the fields of power in which Pitt operated and how he operated, as well as the continuities between the customarily divided parts of his career. It also helps to show the sheer range of his activity, operating across far more areas, for a far longer length of time, than any of his most powerful eighteenth-century predecessors, or for that matter, any of his successors. Not only was he Britain's youngest ever head of a government, but his hold on office was also phenomenal. For four-fifths of his 25-year political career he was in government (and for all except eight months of this was leader of the government). In 1801 an admiring Cabinet colleague, the Duke of Portland, declared that 'Pitt and Office cannot be separated'.[3] The career of William Pitt the Younger is undoubtedly a profile in power.

First claim to my gratitude for their patience and support in preparing this study must go to my family. I am also indebted to advice, encouragement and information supplied by many individuals, and particularly Jeremy Black, John Ehrman, Charles Fedorak, Piers Mackesy, Anthony Smith, Elizabeth Sparrow and David Wilkinson. Ideas have been honed under the critical scrutiny of many cohorts of special subject students at Exeter to whom I am eternally grateful. The helpful services and permission to publish of many libraries and archives must be acknowledged and notably the Bodleian Library, Oxford; the British Library; Buckinghamshire County Record Office; Cambridge University Library; the William L. Clements Library, Ann Arbor, Michigan; Kent Archives Office; Leeds Central Library (the Harewood Estate); the National Library of Scotland; the National Maritime Museum, Greenwich; Nottingham University Mss Dept; the Public Record Office, London; the John Rylands Library, Manchester; the Scottish Record Office; Sheffield Central Library; and the Suffolk Record Office.

· · ·

NOTES AND REFERENCES

1 Lord Rosebery (ed.), 'Tomline's Estimate of Pitt', *The Monthly Review*, vol. 12: August (1903), p. 21.
2 Earl of Malmesbury (ed.), *Diaries and Correspondence of James Harris, Earl of Malmesbury* (1845), vol. 4, p. 78.
3 *Ibid.*, p. 44.

Chapter 1

'SUPERIOR EVEN TO CHARLES FOX':

THE SHORT PATH TO POWER

. . .

GREAT CHATHAM'S SON

In any reckoning of British politics and government the rapidity of William Pitt the Younger's rise to power is unique and will probably remain so. On 28 May 1780 he came of age on his twenty-first birthday. Within seven months he was elected a Member of Parliament; within two years and two months he was Chancellor of the Exchequer and a member of the Cabinet; within three years and seven months he was First Lord of the Treasury and leader of the government.

The least astonishing part of this extraordinary progression was his election to the House of Commons at such an early age. The unreformed eighteenth-century electoral system gave youth its chance. One in six of all members of the Commons which Pitt entered were under the age of thirty, though few were as young as he. Entrance was available if the youth could find a patron with a predominant influence over a parliamentary seat, either through family or political connection or by having a famous father with whose reflected glory a patron would wish to be associated. The Younger Pitt fell into the latter category. He was the second son of the great Earl of Chatham (William Pitt the Elder) who had been the most dazzling and turbulent political comet of the mid-eighteenth century. His inspirational leadership had helped guide the nation to victory in its most successful war – the Seven Years War (1756–63). William Pitt the Younger was born in the so-called Year of Victories of 1759 when his father's fame stood at its zenith.

As influential on him as this success, however, was the fact that the Younger Pitt grew up amidst the decline of his father's reputation. The Elder Pitt stood as a Patriot statesman, acting disinterestedly for the national good, independent of party rancour or faction, and hostile to all forms of mismanagement resulting from the corruption and jobbery of eighteenth-century politics. He was the enemy of aristocratic domination of the House of Commons and of titles, pensions and sinecures offered by governments to win their majorities. But by 1768 he was being assailed in publications such as the anonymous *Essay on Patriotism*, which introduces this book, denouncing him as a 'patriotic imposter'. He was alleged to have put pride before service to his country by resigning in 1761, when his Cabinet colleagues would not approve his plans for war with Spain, and refusing support for their subsequent conduct of the war. His reputation as the incorrupt 'Great Commoner' was severely shaken when, after his resignation, he accepted a £3,000 per annum pension and a peerage for his wife and, still more, when he became Earl of Chatham on briefly returning as Prime Minister in 1766–8. His Premiership, an experiment in the Patriot ideal of a non-party Ministry based on support for 'measures not men', collapsed amidst Cabinet recriminations and power struggles when illness removed him as its unifying force. Chatham's subsequent espousal of parliamentary reform regained him some popular and independent support (though it also separated him from other major politicians), but he lost touch with the national mood on foreign and imperial policy which had formerly been his greatest strength. He urged war on an unreceptive country over the Spanish occupation of the Falkland Islands in 1770, and he unavailingly pressed peace and reconciliation with America on an impatient country between 1774 and his death in 1778.

The relationship between the Younger Pitt and his father was a strong one. His cousin, William Grenville, later remarked that Pitt 'always spoke of Lord Chatham with affection, and no wonder; for there never was a father more partial to a son'.[1] This relationship made it virtually inevitable that the Younger Pitt would go into politics at the earliest possible opportunity. Not only had Chatham trained his son for public speaking from childhood, but there was a pressing filial obligation to restore the Patriot, Great Commoner, reputation of his dead father. He should carry forward in the House of Commons the torch of Patriot principles which his father had espoused – though with the lessons before him (which he did not forget) of his father's mistakes. Yet it was a bold venture, since he launched his political career from precarious financial foundations. Chatham died heavily in debt and Pitt was left dependent on a grant of £600 a year from his elder brother, and what he could borrow against his expectation when his father's estate was eventually cleared of creditors. For an independent income of his own he had to turn to one of the professions open to gentlemen. In 1779–80 he served his terms at Lincoln's Inn and in the summers of 1780 and 1781 he practised as a lawyer on the Western Circuit. This was however an uncertain financial existence, and, since Members of Parliament were not paid and his Patriot ideals precluded a pension or sinecure, he really needed an active, paid government office to sustain an effective political career.

In these early years of his career he was extraordinarily lucky in the way events unfolded in the most favourable way for him, though much still depended on his own capacity to exploit his good fortune. As the War of American Independence (1775–83) worsened, with France and Spain joining in against Britain, Chatham's opposition to the breach with America was seen in a more favourable light. The floundering conduct of the war by Lord North's government highlighted Chatham's vigorous and successful conduct of the previous war, while the Ministry's mismanagement was blamed on that corruption and excessive Crown influence which Chatham had so often attacked in the past. The materials were thus at hand for a vindication of his father's name, and the opportunity for access to the appropriate forum came within months of his coming of age, when Parliament was dissolved and a general election called in September 1780.

In standing forward to vindicate his father's name and principles, however, Pitt was also handicapped by those very principles. Idealistically he sought to be even purer than his father. He could not turn to any existing party or connection to help bring him forward but, like his father, advertised himself as an 'independent Whig'.[2] This meant being independent of party, but committed to maintaining the mixed and balanced constitution which contemporaries believed had been established by the Whigs in the Glorious Revolution of 1688 and which he believed to be in jeopardy from encroachments on the independence of Parliament by the King, George III, and his government. The Younger Pitt carried his independence so far as to reject early offers of nomination to pocket boroughs, even though the proffering patrons were his relatives Earl Temple and Thomas Pitt, and even though his father had entered Parliament in this way. Instead he sought election by an open and independent constituency and turned to Cambridge University which he had entered, after a private domestic education, in 1773 at the age of fourteen. At Cambridge he took his MA without examination (as he was entitled to do as the son of a peer) in 1776, in which year his mother described him as 'perfectly well at Cambridge, and follows the exercise of his mind, and that of his Horse, with an equal Ardor, which I confess I think for Him the perfect Thing'.[3] During three years of further study and hard riding there, his high spirits, playful wit and quick repartee among those of his acquaintance enabled him to build up a strong circle of friends and potential supporters. A seat for his University he described as 'of all others the most desirable, as being free from expense, perfectly independent, and I think in every respect extremely honourable'.[4] He began working up an interest on his behalf before he left Cambridge in 1779, but the general election, called unexpectedly early by the government, came before his canvassing had built up much momentum, and he came bottom of the poll.

Necessity therefore compelled him to accept the good offices of a Cambridge friend, the Duke of Rutland, whose contacts with the great northern borough-monger, Sir James Lowther, got Pitt returned for Appleby in Westmorland on terms which Pitt felt satisfied his need for independence. 'Judging from my father's principles,' Pitt told his mother of Lowther, 'he concludes that mine would be agreeable to his own.' Lowther imposed no specific terms but expected Pitt to vacate the seat should their lines of conduct become opposite.[5]

The snap early election caught all opponents of government unprepared, and a temporary upturn in the war and Treasury influence enabled Lord North's Ministry to secure a majority. Consequently the new member for Appleby, like his father, took his place on the side of the Opposition. He made his maiden speech barely a month after taking his seat, on 26 February 1781, in support of an Opposition bill to reallocate money from the King's Civil List to the public service. His chance came unexpectedly, but he was ready for it thanks to his father's coaching and his own attendance to hear his father's later speeches and subsequent debates (his close friendship with William Wilberforce stemmed from the frequency with which they found themselves listening in the strangers' gallery before each was elected to the Commons). Pitt spoke impromptu, with composure and assurance, to points made by former speakers in the debate. Even Lord North generously declared it the best first speech of a young man that he had ever heard. His father's reputation gave him a ready hearing and inevitably there were comparisons with his father. Edmund Burke reportedly asserted that he was 'not a chip of the old block: he is the old block himself'. It may be that his father's fame helped sway judgements in his favour. George Selwyn, who came to the House especially to hear his third speech on 12 June, judged that 'if the matter and expression had come without that prejudice, or wrote down, all which could have been said was, that he was a sensible and promising young man'.[6]

Nevertheless his father's renown could only advance his career so far. He needed his own abilities to take full advantage of this flying start, and after his first speech in the autumn session, even Selwyn admitted that 'Mr Pitt's speech today had made a great noise'. After his next speech the veteran Horace Walpole recorded that 'young William Pitt took to pieces Lord North's pretended declaration, which he had minuted down, and exposed them with the most amazing logical abilities, exceeding all the abilities he had already shown, and making men doubt whether he would not prove superior even to Charles Fox'. On New Year's Day 1782 another of his audience wrote of him that 'He is wonderful in all respects, but in nothing so much as in the regular and rapid improvement he makes: I have heard him speak three times only, and each speech was much better than the former.'[7]

Despite the verbal battery from a glittering display of Opposition talent, in which Pitt joined his voice to those of Charles Fox, Burke, Sheridan and others, Lord North had held his own in the spring session of 1781, sturdily seconded by the Scottish Lord Advocate, Henry Dundas. Pitt's advance would have been halted without another twist of circumstances in his favour. The surrender of a British army at Yorktown catastrophically wrecked the war in America and destroyed confidence in the Ministry. In March 1782, with his majority collapsing, Lord North resigned.

The disintegration of North's long-established government reduced the political world to a series of fragmented groupings. In these circumstances it was not just Pitt's speaking powers that gave him weight. His ready wit and conviviality, particularly with acquaintances of his own age in Parliament, made him a leading figure in a young members' club called Goostree's. It largely consisted of old Cambridge friends: amongst whom were John Jeffreys Pratt and Lord Euston, the sons respectively of Earl Camden and the Duke of Grafton, former prominent supporters of his father. Edward Eliot and Henry Bankes he also knew from Cambridge. Wilberforce had also been at Cambridge but did not make Pitt's acquaintance till they met in London, as did Richard Pepper Arden who shared a staircase with him at Lincoln's Inn. The banker Robert Smith became connected with him after he entered Parliament. Two other Cambridge acquaintances, William Lowther and the Duke of Rutland (who controlled six Commons seats), might also be included in this close circle. Many of these were older than Pitt – Arden fifteen years, Smith seven, Rutland five, Bankes three, Euston and Eliot a year – and it says much for his attractive personality that he was able to win their affection and eventual support.

As yet Pitt had an influence with them rather than their guaranteed firm votes, but it was noticed: Selwyn wrote in March 1782 that 'Young Pitt will not be subordinate; he is not so in his own society. He is at the head of a dozen young people, and it is a corps separate from that of

Charley's [Fox]; so there is another premier at the starting post, who, as yet, has never been shaved.' Ten days earlier a scheme by Dundas to prop up North's flagging Ministry included bringing in Pitt as Treasurer of the Navy 'with a seat at the Treasury, Admiralty and Trade, to some of his young friends'. Already Pitt was seen as attracting his own support.[8]

Inexperience however led him into overplaying his hand. In expectation of offers when a new government was constructed, he determined never to accept a subordinate situation and he told the Commons so on 8 March. Horace Walpole considered it a great indiscretion:

> so arrogant a declaration from a boy who had gained no experience from, nor ever enjoyed even the lowest post in any office, and who for half a dozen orations, extraordinary indeed, but no evidence of capacity for business, presumed himself fit for command, proved that he was a boy, and a very ambitious one and a very vain one. The moment he sat down he was aware of his folly, and said he could bite his tongue out for what he had uttered.[9]

It left him without bargaining power and dependent on the goodwill of the senior politician with whom he most associated – the Earl of Shelburne, who had inherited leadership of a residue of Chatham's former followers. Shelburne applied to the Earl of Rockingham to whom, as leader of the largest Opposition grouping, the formation of the new government had been entrusted. Rockingham was prepared to offer the minor post of Vice-Treasurer of Ireland, worth £5,000 a year, but Pitt rejected it out of concern for consistency after his public declaration and for fear of having his image of Patriotic virtue tainted by a quasi-sinecure office of profit (again seeking to be purer than his father whose first office it had been). Shelburne had too many other prior claims that he needed to satisfy to be able to press for a Cabinet post for Pitt, and so the new government was formed without him.

With his political progress apparently stalled again, Pitt quickly found the means to keep himself before the public eye. The expense and mismanagement of the American War had stimulated demand for parliamentary reform to make Parliament better representative of propertied national opinion. From London radicals it spread to the county gentry, and in 1779 the Reverend Christopher Wyvill formed the Yorkshire Association as an extra-parliamentary pressure group to campaign for reform, with other counties setting up Associations in imitation. Pitt's father had been a convert to the cause of parliamentary reform, and in October 1780 Pitt was elected to the committee of the Kent Association of which his enthusiastic brother-in-law, Lord Mahon, had become chairman.

The movement hit a setback with North's election victory, but their hopes revived at his fall. In April 1782 reformers, including Wyvill and Pitt, met at the London house of the Duke of Richmond and agreed that Pitt should move in the Commons for a Select Committee to consider the state of the representation. He introduced this motion – his first – on 7 May, in a speech of one and a half hours urging calm revision of principles and a moderate reform of defects. Though it was rejected by 161–141, he successfully established himself as the leading Commons spokesman for parliamentary reform, with direct contact with reformers outside the House. A further meeting twelve days later agreed to launch a national petitioning campaign to enable Pitt to renew the question in the next session.

. . .

SHELBURNE'S CHANCELLOR OF THE EXCHEQUER

In fact Pitt's career advanced rapidly before this, as once more fortune turned his way. The new government split into feuding parts in a power struggle between Shelburne and Fox. Pitt's absence from office enabled him to escape being tarnished by it, and he was free to stand forward when Rockingham suddenly died in July and Fox and his friends resigned after the King turned to Shelburne to head the ministry. With vacant Cabinet places to fill and a need for someone who might stand up to Fox in the Commons, Pitt's claim for high office made in March now unexpectedly paid off. Having been on the point of setting off to earn his living on the Western Circuit, he could scarcely refuse Shelburne's offer of the post of Chancellor the Exchequer with a seat in the Cabinet. Of his friends, Arden became Solicitor-General, while Eliot and Pratt were given seats on the Treasury and Admiralty Boards.

Remarkable as his advancement was, Pitt's position was a weak one in a weak Ministry. He was not yet able to demand a specific post and what was offered to him was at the mercy of the need to satisfy others. The King and Shelburne originally intended him as Home Secretary of State, but Thomas Townshend, a useful speaker with more experience, eventually received that office and the leadership of the government in the Commons. Townshend and at least two others turned down the Exchequer, so that Pitt got it by default. It was not to be an office of power, for Shelburne as First Lord of the Treasury intended to keep financial matters firmly in his own hands. Both Pitt and Shelburne had much still to prove. Even a future friend and follower of Pitt, the Earl of

Mornington, wrote in horror on hearing the first rumours of the new Ministry: 'W. Pitt Secretary of State! and Lord Shelburne Premier! surely the first cannot be qualified for such an office, and the last is, in my opinion, little to be depended upon.'[10]

Pitt's first government appointment was directly into a Cabinet office, but his first share in power lasted barely nine months, and only two long parliamentary recesses stopped it being shorter. Shelburne was far from popular. Clever and well informed by talented private advisers, he was nevertheless inherently secretive and had a reputation for duplicity. Moreover although he had won the King's goodwill, this was presently of diluted value, since George III's prestige was at a low ebb at this moment of defeat in the American War which he had so zealously espoused. It was reckoned that in the Commons, Shelburne's supporters and the King's Friends could muster 140 votes, Fox 90 and the fallen Lord North (who had 'made' the sitting House in 1780) 120, the remainder being without firm commitment. Much therefore depended on the wider support Shelburne could attract for his policies. Here however he faced the need to settle what would inevitably be adverse peace terms with America and its European partners and which would draw odium on the government that agreed them. Shelburne in fact extricated the nation from the war with some skill, but the concessions he had to make ultimately fragmented his Cabinet and enabled his opponents to rally a majority against him in the Commons.

It was only after Parliament reassembled in December 1782 to discuss the peace that Pitt began to develop an effective power-role for himself. The vast preponderance of Treasury patronage lay with Shelburne, and Pitt was dependent on whatever the First Lord was prepared to lay off to him. When, for example, a rearrangement in the office created five vacancies, Shelburne kept two for his own disposal and granted one each to his two Treasury Secretaries, Orde and Rose, and the other to Pitt. The young Chancellor of the Exchequer attended the Treasury Board conscientiously, but Shelburne seems to have worked directly with expert revenue officials, his own private advisers and the Treasury Secretaries. Pitt was involved in his schemes for the administrative reform of the Treasury, being given responsibility for putting two bills through the Commons, one to reform the customs and the other to regulate the public offices. There are however at least two indicators that Pitt was not in Shelburne's inner circle on Treasury business. One is the little surviving correspondence between the two, particularly when Shelburne was at his country seat at Bowood in the autumn of 1782; the other is the testimony of one of the Treasury Secretaries, George Rose, that although he met Pitt at the Board and sometimes at dinner at

Shelburne's, he did not become closely acquainted with the Chancellor of the Exchequer until after they left office.[11]

Similarly, although Pitt was present at all recorded meetings of the Cabinet, the role of that body was limited. Shelburne kept a direct control over the peace negotiations by private meetings with foreign emissaries, by sending personal representatives and corresponding privately with British envoys, as well as by using the two Secretaries of State. In reports of the Cabinet debates Pitt is anonymous. Others such as the Duke of Richmond and Lord Keppel emerge as the ones forcefully expressing their views and complaining at the lack of proper Cabinet consultation. In the short life of the Shelburne Ministry power unquestionably lay in the hands of the Prime Minister, and whatever Pitt learned from the style, there is little to suggest that he established any cordial relationship with him. When, two years later, Shelburne sent an emissary to discuss Pitt's offer of an elevation in the peerage, the former Premier remarked that 'I know the coldness of the climate you go into, and that it requires all your animation to produce a momentary thaw.'[12]

Only when Shelburne's hold on power became threatened in the House of Commons did Pitt's role become more prominent and in-fluential. Pitt's greatest asset to any government was still his speaking ability and he rapidly came to speak with more authority than the other Cabinet Ministers in the Commons, General Conway and Thomas Townshend. He was however by no means free from blunders. In the initial debates on the peace negotiations on 6 December he wrongly asserted, and continued to assert when challenged, that the peace with America was unconditional on the results of further peace negotiations with France, contradicting what Shelburne himself said in the Lords. The King blamed it on inexperience: 'It is no wonder that so young a man should have made a slip!'[13] Another error became renowned. In the first debate on the final peace treaties on 17 February 1783, Pitt responded to Sheridan's criticisms by sarcastically declaring that his sallies were better reserved for the stage – only to bring on himself the withering reply from the playwright that were he to do so, he might be tempted to try an improvement on one of Ben Jonson's best characters, the Angry Boy in *The Alchemist*![14]

Nevertheless Pitt's debating skills became the most reliable and indis-pensable support to Shelburne in the Commons. Pitt was consequently a major influence when the Premier looked to strengthen his shaky Ministry. When Richmond resigned his Cabinet seat and Lord Carlisle the Lord Stewardship over the peace terms, Shelburne gave both to Pitt's friend Rutland – even though this precipitated the resignation of another Cabinet member, the Duke of Grafton, over lack of consultation.

The crucial decision was whether to seek a safe majority by accommodation with North or with Fox. Pitt was adamantly against sitting in any Cabinet with Lord North, so that even though Shelburne made soundings for North's support (apparently without Pitt's knowledge), these inevitably stalled on the Premier's inability to offer high office to North himself. Pitt was authorised to explore his own preference of an approach to Fox for reconciliation among the former Opposition, but Fox refused to come in on any terms while Shelburne remained, and Pitt would not abandon the Premier, so that this overture too collapsed. Fox and North then approached each other and, against expectations, these former determined opponents reached terms for a coalition which enabled them to defeat the Ministry's peace proposals in successive debates in the Commons on 17 and 21 February, inducing Shelburne three days later to announce his intention of resigning.

For Pitt, the speech he made in the last of these two debates was the most important of his life, and the real making of his immediate pretensions to head the government. He knew that the Ministry was doomed, and he had to extricate himself from the wreck. He had to show himself as a power in his own right, independent of the doomed Shelburne, but he had to do so without appearing to be disloyally deserting the Premier in this final trial. In a two and three-quarter hours' speech he adroitly solved all his problems by giving the House a discourse on Patriotism. One Opposition supporter described it as 'upon the highest stilts that ever his father was mounted'.[15]

He maintained that the peace terms were the best that could be obtained after North's mismanagement of the war. He accused the Opposition of attacking them not out of any consideration of the national interest, but simply as a vehicle to eject Shelburne. Their self-seeking was shown by the unnatural coalition of two groups, those of Fox and North, whose principles had been wholly opposite: 'if this ill-omened marriage is not already solemnized, I know a just and lawful impediment, and, in the name of public safety, I here forbid the banns'. Shelburne, their intended victim, he praised for 'acting an honest and honourable part' in difficult circumstances.

From a resolute defence of the peace terms and of Shelburne's virtues, he moved to a personal statement of his own principles and separate political associations. The Chatham name was recalled and vindicated by contrast to present misfortunes:

> I feel, Sir, at this instant, how much I had been animated in my childhood by a recital of England's victories:– I was taught, Sir, by one, whose memory I shall ever revere, that at the close of a war, far different indeed

from this, she had dictated the terms of peace to submissive nations. This in which I place something more than a common interest, was the memorable aera of England's glory.

Having linked himself to a matchless mentor far above Shelburne or any of his rivals, he pressed the point again near the close of his speech:

My earliest impressions were in favour of the noblest and most dis-interested modes of serving the public: these impressions are still dear, and will I hope, remain for ever dear to my heart: I will cherish them as a legacy infinitely more valuable than the greatest inheritance. On those principles alone I came into parliament, and into place.

This Chathamite legacy and principles were those of the Patriot: 'I have ever been most anxious to do my utmost for the interest of my country; it has been my sole concern to act an honest and upright part'; nothing could be imputed to his official conduct 'which bears the most distant connection with an interested, a corrupt, or a dishonest intention'. He declared his future candidacy for power by admitting his ambition and his unashamed pursuit of high situation and great influence, but he coupled this with the Patriot qualification 'whenever they can be acquired with honour, and retained with dignity'. When he left office he would not resort to an indiscriminate opposition to his successors to try to get back into power, but, so long as they governed with a view to the real and substantial welfare of the community at large, he promised them his 'uniform and best support on every occasion, where I can honestly and conscientiously assist them'.

Appealing for recognition of his integrity and consistency of political conduct, he came to his climax:

you may take from me, Sir, the privileges and emoluments of place, but you cannot, and you shall not, take from me those habitual and warm regards for the prosperity of Great-Britain, which constitute the honour, the happiness, the pride of my life; and which, I trust, death alone can extinguish. And with this consolation, the loss of power, Sir, and the loss of fortune, though I affect not to despise them, I hope I soon shall be able to forget.

This was rounded off by a Latin quotation from Horace: 'I praise her [Fortune] while she abides. If she flutter her swift wings for flight, I renounce her gifts . . . and woo honest dowerless poverty.'[16]

It was blatant self-propaganda, openly addressed 'to the independent part of the house, and to the public at large',[17] and it might be dismissed as Patriot cant which the Commons had heard from so many politicians seeking self-justification in the eighteenth century. It was spoken however with a conviction which came not just from youthful idealism, but from realisation that a character for integrity and consistency was the only sure protection to a political career for a man without fortune like himself, seeking to make his way as an independent Whig. To his audience what he said about wooing 'honest dowerless poverty' appeared patently true. He earned enough from his time at the Exchequer to afford a two-month holiday in France in the autumn of 1783, but he had sought no provision against leaving office, and expected to return to the bar again to earn his living. The speech could not save Shelburne's Ministry, but it saved the advancement of Pitt's career. One of those listening on the opposite benches, Thomas Pelham, noted that 'even his enemies or rather opponents unanimously acknowledged it to be the finest speech that ever was made in Parliament'.[18]

The first results of this personal triumph were soon apparent. Two days later, Shelburne broached the idea of Pitt as his successor to his astute political manager of Scotland, Henry Dundas, who responded enthusiastically next day that Pitt's qualities were obvious and, moreover:

> in place of being an objection his youth appears to me a very material ingredient in the scale of advantages which recommend him. There is scarce another political character of consideration in the country to whom many people from habits, from connexions, from former professions, from rivalships and from antipathies will not have objections. But he is perfectly new ground against whom no opposition can arise except what may be expected of that lately allied faction.[19]

Shelburne put the proposal to the King, who approached Pitt at once.

It was the first of three offers of the leadership to Pitt which he declined before finally accepting the fourth in December. His refusals show a great degree of political maturity and judgement in being able to control his ambition. He had set his criteria for taking high office in his 21 February speech – that it would be acquired with honour and retained with dignity. He told the King that only the moral certainty of a majority in the Commons would induce him to accept. His father's old colleague, Earl Camden, warned that he would be too dependent on the Court. He himself told Dundas that he would be at the mercy of North and his friends not continuing to oppose and 'in point of honour to my own feelings, I cannot form an administration trusting to the hope that it will be supported, or even will not be opposed, by Lord North . . . The first moment I saw the subject in this point of view, from which I am sure I cannot vary, *unalterably* determined me to decline.'[20] This persistent antipathy to North contrasts with all Pitt's assertions of the principle of 'measures not men', of putting national interests before personal animosities. But he held North responsible for the misuse of Crown influence to corrupt Parliament, and for the confrontation with the colonies which had hastened the death of his father, who had exhausted himself in battling against it, and resulted in the loss of America.

Rejection of the King's offer in fact strengthened rather than weakened Pitt's position, since it revealed the complete lack of any viable alternative to save the King from surrender a second time to Charles Fox, for whom the monarch had developed a personal antipathy even stronger than Pitt's towards North. While former Crown servants like Earl Gower might be induced to come forward in the Lords, there was an indispensable need for an able leader to face Fox in the Commons. But Townshend quickly moved out of the heat by taking a peerage as Lord Sydney, and Dundas was short of social standing. Pitt's cousins the Grenvilles were considered, but William Grenville described his cousin James as having no health and still less spirits for so arduous an undertaking and himself as 'too little versed in the navigation of that tempestuous sea, to venture out in such a hurricane as this'. North was approached separately, but would not serve without Fox. Gower suggested another Pitt cousin, Thomas, and a desperate George III retorted, 'Mr Thomas Pitt or Mr Thomas anybody', but Thomas Pitt declared himself 'certainly unequal to a task like this',[21] and Thomas anybody did not emerge as the Fox–North Coalition kept the pressure on by withholding passage of the annual votes of supply and the Mutiny Act for the armed forces. The King was forced to open negotiations with the Duke of Portland as nominal leader of the Coalition. When, however, on 20 March, Portland indicated disagreement between the partners over the distribution of offices, George III eagerly turned to Pitt again.

Pitt would only accept the government if it was shown that the Coalition was divided, for he might then be seen to be honourably seeking to save the country from anarchy. On these tenuous grounds the King broke off negotiations with Portland. Pitt however deferred acceptance until he saw the position in a debate on 24 March. But if he was hoping to find the Coalition disunited, and a spontaneous independent demand for him to take the lead, then he was disappointed. The Coalition rallied against its opponents and the independents stayed silent. Without their support, Pitt told the Marquis of Carmarthen, 'he should think it inconsistent with his duty to the King or to the public service, as well as highly detrimental to his own character as well as his future views, to undertake under the present aspect of affairs so weighty a charge as the government of the country'. Old Horace Walpole thought him wise. However glorious it would be 'to obtain the chariot for a day' at his age, and even though it would put him at the head of a party, in or out of place, he would have been doomed to failure since no supplies would have been granted by the hostile majority.[22] This second refusal was decisive. Shelburne finally went on 26 March and Pitt too resigned on the 31st, after which the King finally admitted defeat and accepted a Coalition government.

. . .

THURLOW AND TEMPLE'S CO-CONSPIRATOR

For Shelburne, resignation was regarded as writing an end to his political career, but Pitt emerged with his reputation enhanced, and former Shelburne supporters moved to his banner. Dundas now attached himself firmly to Pitt, while the Marquis of Carmarthen wrote to him that 'I am proud to own my conduct should be regulated by yours'. There was widespread recognition, as Thomas Pitt told the King on 28 March:

> that extraordinary as it was, a youth of twenty-three had from a variety of causes attracted the attention and expectations of the whole Kingdom while he was happy in H.M.'s good opinion; and that therefore it was to him alone that we must look up for such a system as I had alluded to when the moment should be ripe for it, and that he had friends and connections who I did not doubt in such a cause would stand forward to support him.[23]

As in the previous year, Pitt did not remain idle on the back benches. He furthered his reforming reputation by pushing the administrative reform measures prepared with Shelburne through the Commons (they were defeated in the Lords), and on 7 May he moved proposals for parliamentary reform which would have added a hundred new MPs to the counties and the London metropolis, counterbalancing the rotten boroughs whose numbers would have fallen as they were convicted of corrupt practices. On this occasion he lost heavily by 293–149, but his name remained in the public eye, and he highlighted the differences within the Coalition between the reformer Fox and the anti-reformer North.

The extent to which Pitt was mindful of his reputation clearly emerges from his response to a further overture from the King. George III had taken his defeat hard. He refused to grant peerages to the Coalition and raged against the extent of their proposed financial settlement for his dissolute son (and Fox's friend), the Prince of Wales, on his coming of age. The Monarch poured out his resentment to Pitt's cousin, Lord Temple, newly returned from being Shelburne's Lord Lieutenant of Ireland. On 19 July Pitt himself was approached by the ex-Lord Chancellor and King's Friend, Lord Thurlow, in what he interpreted as an attempt to see whether he could be drawn into a government 'more on the foundation of the old politics of the Court'. He 'treated as out of the question any idea of measures being taken to extend influence' though 'such means as are fairly in the hands of Ministers' might be employed. He told Thurlow that he and Temple were ready to act whenever they could form 'a permanent system, consistent with our principles, and on public ground', and he reasserted his support for parliamentary reform which he would give on every seasonable occasion. Pitt expected an offer from the King whenever affairs were ripe, but hoped to have 'put the business on such a ground as can alone make it advisable and honourable'.[24]

What Pitt did not suspect was how quickly affairs would become ripe. Far from plotting to take over government, he spent the summer holidaying in Brighton and then on his two-month tour in France – the only time he ever left England. He returned to London for the meeting of Parliament on 11 November, but even then there was no inkling of what was to follow. Thurlow advised his friend Gower that 'people are much dissatisfied in the present, and very hopeless of the future', and there was no reason to hurry to Parliament.[25] Two days later Pitt received an offer from Fox to join the Coalition which he immediately rejected. He should perhaps have wondered why. The reason emerged on 18 November when Fox introduced his India Bill into the Commons.

Something had to be done about India, where the financially hard-pressed East India Company administered a population larger than that of Britain itself. The issue was sensitive since a potentially vast field of patronage was at stake, and decisions were repeatedly deferred during the equally contentious American crisis. The Coalition now made a genuine attempt to resolve the problem, but it did so in a way which took management and patronage out of the hands of the East India Company and into those of commissioners appointed initially by the Coalition-controlled Parliament and irremovable for four years, providing the Coalition with a major patronage resource beyond the next election.

The political and constitutional implications of this measure were not lost on Pitt, as he frantically appealed to supporters to get to Parliament as quickly as possible:

The bill which Fox had brought in relative to India will be, one way or other, decisive for or against the coalition. It is, I really think, the boldest and most unconstitutional measure ever attempted, transferring at one stroke, in spite of all charters and compacts, the immense patronage and influence of the East to *Charles Fox, in or out of office.*[26]

Fox sought to overcome the contentiousness of his proposals by rushing the bill through quickly, relying on the traditional slow arrival at the start of a session of those not subject to the government whip. By 27 November Pitt was desperately seeking means to delay its progress by challenging its financial necessity and calling for papers so as to buy time in which laggard opponents of the bill might reach London. It was a weak ploy, in which Pitt was out-argued and outvoted by Fox.

With the rapid passage of the India Bill through the Commons apparently unstoppable, its opponents took stock. They had a potentially powerful outside ally in the reaction of the City of London. The East India Company formed a defence committee and Pitt was in close contact with two of its leaders, George Johnstone and Richard Atkinson. Also a meeting of the City's Common Council on 26 November voted to petition against the bill which both interfered with the chartered rights of a City company and was blamed for a fall in the value of India stock which threatened financial confidence more widely. The sensation however had not yet spread far outside London, and this was reflected by the reluctance of country MPs to come up to Parliament before the New Year. Parliament was indeed where the main battle would have to be fought. There the various opponents of the Coalition finally threw their lot in together on 25 November when the Crown's supporters, Thurlow and the Duke of Chandos, dined with Pitt's allies, the Duke of Richmond and Earl Temple. Pitt should have been there too but was detained in the Commons. They were reinforced by the arrival of Dundas on the 27th. Not only did he have an alternative plan of East Indian reform, but he also had access to a valuable former colleague, North's political manager and maker of the present Parliament, the former Treasury Secretary, John Robinson. Robinson had strong qualms about the conduct of the Coalition in forcing the King's hand. Early on 30 November Dundas left Robinson's Harwich home, carrying 'some minutes . . . for *both* houses', to attend meetings due that day in London. It was probably at these meetings that the decision was taken to seek the King's intervention to defeat the bill in the House of Lords by making known his opposition to the measure. Next day Thurlow took to George III a memorandum to this effect drawn up by himself and Temple.[27]

It was long denied by Pitt's biographers that Pitt himself had any knowledge of this plot, the constitutional propriety of which was extremely dubious. This denial no longer holds up against the evidence which John Cannon set out in 1969 in *The Fox–North Coalition*, though Cannon's portrayal of Pitt as master-schemer has in turn been challenged by Paul Kelly, arguing that 'Pitt himself seems to have taken few decisions affecting his appointment to office, allowing himself to be propelled along by initiatives taken by others and by events'.[28] However this would have been out of character, for events earlier in the year hardly show Pitt allowing himself to be propelled along by others. Pitt was essential to the formation of any replacement ministry after the India Bill was defeated. As John Robinson had recognised as early as March, 'without him nothing can be made up',[29] and since Pitt had already declined two direct offers and side-stepped a third via Thurlow, his assent could not be simply taken for granted. George III recognised this by sending an intermediary to check with Pitt himself before agreeing to the Thurlow–Temple plan, and it is inconceivable that the latter two would have approached the King in the first place without Pitt's backing. Because he was so much the key player it was impossible for Pitt to take too public a part in the initiatives without alerting the Coalition. Those who acted in his place were natural intermediaries because of their connections: Thurlow with the King; Dundas with Robinson.

Skilful though Fox's management of the India Bill had been in the Commons, Pitt was now better placed to force a successful conclusion than at any time previously. He had an issue on which he could honourably oppose the Coalition and not appear merely factious. That issue was attracting outside support as on 3 December the Common Council of the City of London instructed the City's MPs to vote against the India Bill, and two biting cartoons by James Sayers on 25 November and 5 December (the latter portraying Fox as 'Carlo Khan', an oriental despot) caused a sensation which even Fox admitted did him immense damage. Robinson's detailed forecast of the state of the Commons, delivered between 6 and 9 December, indicated potential support for an anti-Coalition government as 253 against 305 in the present Parliament and 369 against 189 after an election, and Dundas was able to show several MPs as being more favourable than Robinson's predictions. Pitt himself told Rutland on the 6th that 'The closet [i.e. King] will do everything, as far as I can judge, in fair co-operation and concert, if the crisis is found to be ripe, which I think it will.'[30]

After his humiliating defeat in March, however, George III wanted confirmation of Pitt's readiness to act before committing himself, and, on his behalf, the Earl of Clarendon saw Pitt on 9 and 11 December. In between the two interviews, on the 10th, Pitt consulted with Temple, Richmond, Thurlow and Gower at the latter's house on what should be done. The result was to repeat the advice to use the King's name to rally opposition against the India Bill in the Lords, where it had its first reading on the 9th. The advantage of this option, rather than direct dismissal of the Ministry, was that it enabled a prior test of opposing strengths, and defeat might cause the Ministry to divide and dissolve of itself without further Crown intervention. Moreover it was necessary to prevent the issue becoming a direct constitutional battle between King and Parliament: the Lords had to be shown as differently minded from the Commons. It was also considered important that petitions from the East India Company and the City of London be presented prior to a vote, to influence the Lords and to 'fill important corporations as well as individuals with apprehensions and disgust' at the tendency of the bill, so providing a plausible and solid reason for the Coalition's dismissal. All this decided the King who authorised Temple to tell peers that whoever voted for the India Bill 'was not only not his friend, but would be considered by him as an enemy'.[31] The peers took the warning. On 15 December they adjourned its second reading and on the 17th they threw it out by 95 votes to 76.

· · ·

THE KING'S MINISTER

If the course of events had apparently gone to plan, this good fortune did not survive the defeat of the India Bill. Very quickly Pitt was plunged into fighting for his political life amidst the greatest constitutional crisis of the century. Within days any hope of a smooth and rapid transfer of power was in tatters as the Coalition held together and fought back strongly.

Pitt had hoped that the Coalition would break up on the defeat of the India Bill, enabling him to attract from its ranks sufficient members of the old opposition alliance against North to sustain government on independent Whig lines. He had no wish to be the puppet leader of a royal coup which restored government 'on the foundation of the old politics of the court'. This was certainly his motive in seeking to get prestigious Whig names, like Grafton (whom he approached via an inter-mediary on 14 December) and Camden, into a new Ministry: as he said when still pursuing them nearly a year later, to give the Cabinet 'so clear a Whig complexion' as their accession would make it.[32]

Such hopes, which depended on Pitt's ability to exploit events as they occurred, explain why there was no previously prepared strong succession or well-formed future plan before the Coalition Ministry was dismissed, and why he was so embarrassed when he could not exploit events his way. For the Coalition did not dissolve of itself. On the same day as the India Bill was defeated in the Lords, the Coalition secured 2–1 majorities in the Commons for motions attacking the use of the King's name and those who advised its use in the Lords. When on the 18th the Coalition leaders still did not resign, the impatient King sent messengers at midnight to Portland, Fox and North, requiring them to surrender their seals of office. Next day Pitt's appointment as First Lord of the Treasury was announced along with that of Temple as Secretary of State and Gower as Lord President of the Council. The Coalition benches received the news with loud laughter.

Pitt had speculated on a fall-back position in which the authors of the India Bill were dismissed but their followers were left to themselves either to resign or to desert the Coalition. Even this alternative however failed to produce favourable results, as within a few days 55 ministers and office-holders resigned their posts in solidarity with their leaders. When on the 21st Pitt at last made an overture to Fox via Earl Spencer, an old Cambridge friend of Pitt but present supporter of Fox, it was rejected. Pitt declared his readiness to go as far as he creditably could to secure an accommodation, but that he would not sit in Cabinet with Lord North nor could he accept the India Bill to the extent proposed. Fox consulted his friends but declared the first condition perfectly inadmissible.

Kelly has accused Pitt of naive optimism in expecting that all might go well in these events,[33] but Pitt had good grounds for his hopes. Memories of former co-operation remained strong, and there was still much that many of North's former opponents had in common, as in their desire for reform, as well as in personal connections like Spencer, or Temple's brother Tom, who linked both camps. Attempts had been made to restore co-operation by both sides: by Pitt in February (and the obstacle then – Shelburne – had since been removed) and by Fox in November. It was only after 21 December that the split at last appeared more permanent.

Pitt was in danger if the breach with his former Opposition colleagues could not be repaired, for Fox had retained a powerful weapon with which to wreck attempts to form a new government. A land tax bill had to be passed to meet large payments by government on 5 January, but when Coalition Ministers first began to suspect secret moves against the India Bill, they had delayed its passage as a precaution, and it was still awaiting its third reading until after the Commons debated events in the Lords. In this way not only was government held in suspense while an attack was launched on the new Ministers, but their only way of escape, through a dissolution of Parliament, was closed. There was no time for a general election, to try to secure a majority to pass a new land tax bill, before payments depending on it had to be made.

Caught in this stranglehold, Pitt was forced into major concessions to buy time. To secure the passage of the land tax bill he had to surrender his strongest potential weapon by pledging that there would be no immediate dissolution if it passed. He also had to watch the sacrifice of his cousin, Earl Temple, who in recent months had become his closest political ally. As the man who took the King's message around the peers, Temple would be the focus of attack, and, without the escape of a dissolution, he would be a continuing political liability. Whether out of fear, or to take the pressure off Pitt, or both, he resigned on the 21st. Both of these steps were announced in the Commons on the 22nd, and on these terms Fox allowed the land tax bill through and agreed to a short recess until 12 January. He had shown the Coalition's strength, scored two substantial triumphs and was in a position to play the same game again in the spring, when the annual supplies and the Mutiny Bill had to be voted – if the Ministry had not collapsed before then.

These setbacks undoubtedly hit Pitt hard. His Cambridge tutor and friend, George Pretyman, recorded Temple's resignation as the only public event that ever gave the Premier a sleepless night. Nevertheless next morning he was resolved 'not to abandon the situation he had undertaken, but to make the best stand in his power, though very doubtful of the result'. The Ministry was reconstructed around Pitt, Richmond, Thurlow and Gower. Thurlow was restored as Lord Chancellor, the Duke of Rutland became Privy Seal, Earl Howe First Lord of the Admiralty, and Lords Sydney and Carmarthen Home and Foreign Secretaries – both, according to Robinson, '*pro tempore* to *give room* for *arrangements*'. There was a feeling that matters were improving and that, as Robinson bluntly said and 'felt it acknowledged by Mr. Pitt's best friends (and that it was even his thoughts too) that the resignation of Ld T_ was a relief of a millstone, cut off, which was round his neck'. Pitt, however, was still cautious. In reporting the formation of the new Cabinet to Temple on the 23rd he added that 'for how many days or weeks remains to be seen'.[34]

Many scarcely expected the new Ministry to survive the Christmas recess – the political hostess Mrs Crewe dubbed it 'a mince-pie administration'[35] – but the Parliamentary adjournment gave the King and his ministers time to fill the remaining offices and strive to rally support. Among the most assiduous was the King himself, who regarded this battle as the decisive moment of his reign. Frustrated in his efforts to give the Ministry a pronounced 'Whig complexion' by refusals from Fox, Grafton, Camden and others, and with even Richmond, who took the Ordnance, initially declining to sit in the Cabinet, Pitt was reduced to some galling necessities, above all in the mass lobby for the votes commanded by Viscount Sackville who, as Lord George Germain, had been the Secretary of State responsible for the military conduct of the disastrous American War. Nevertheless Pitt held out against appointing those King's Friends most notoriously associated with the 'old politics of the Court', including Robinson and Charles Jenkinson, nor did he bring into his Ministry his unpopular predecessor Shelburne.

By the time Parliament reassembled, almost all government posts had been filled by a motley collection of Pitt's 'young friends', former Shelburnites and others of the old Opposition to North who had not joined Fox, ex-Northites and King's Friends. To many it seemed a shaky foundation for a successful government. An opponent, William Eden, commented that 'They are in desperate straits even for old men and boys to accept situations'. Benjamin Keene, who declared he never was a friend to the Coalition, wrote that 'The present ministry, not having the prospect of a long continuance, can hardly expect the support of persons unconnected as I am.'[36] Lack of confidence in the Ministry's survivability was reflected in the number of peerages said to have been offered and refused over the recess. One only was announced, to an established supporter, Thomas Pitt, named Lord Camelford on 29 December. Yet Pitt's defeat in having to pledge not to dissolve Parliament in December may have been a blessing in disguise, for the Ministry had much to prove before it could overcome the hostility of independents to the expense of an early election and could attract the support of borough patrons who expected patronage from a lasting Ministry in return for placing seats at the government's disposal. Despite Robinson's predictions, an early election might not have produced the usual government majority.

Pitt, above all, had still to prove himself. Was the Coalition jingle composed by Captain Morris right, that 'Billy's too young to drive us'? One outraged independent abused him as a 'stripling' in November for demanding the attendance of members by a call of the House. In the formation of the new Ministry, concern at such reactions was reflected by the packaging of his name with those of older politicians: Gower and Temple on the 19th, Gower, Thurlow and Richmond on 23 December; indeed Dundas may have thought that Gower should have been nominal head of the Ministry. Nevertheless Pitt intended to lead and Dundas told Orde on the 18th, in explaining Shelburne's exclusion, that 'This young man does not choose to suffer it to be doubtful who is the effectual Minister.' But was he up to that responsibility? Robinson described him as 'a delicate high spirited mind, beset by Boys, Theoreticks and prejudiced persons'. Could he rise above the youthful enthusiasm and idealism of his entourage? To another potential supporter, the Shelburnite Benjamin Vaughan, Pitt's record showed 'a want of powers in business' – in his handling in the Commons of the peace and of the India Bill – and that he wanted coolness. Such unfavourable impressions of the 'Angry Boy' remained to be overcome. Pitt had to demonstrate an ability to survive if he was to secure a general confidence.[37]

Over the recess Pitt and his colleagues decided that their best strategy for survival was to fight on their own ground, by bringing forward their own India Bill, rather than simply defend against the inevitable Foxite attacks. Dundas had long been interested in India and had a ready-made plan which could be presented as a positive alternative to Fox's bill and, moreover, had the support of the East India Company. Since everyone recognised something had to be done about India, this was the strongest ground to maximise support, and, after all the lobbying done over the recess, Pitt seems to have gone to the Commons on 12 January 1784 confident of a majority.

His optimism was blown away, however, by the accident that he could not be present at the start of business because of the requirement to submit himself for re-election on being appointed to office. Fox therefore had the floor when Pitt was admitted as a newly re-elected member, and the former successfully maintained his claim to precedence in a desperate battle for the initiative that followed. The first debate was consequently on Fox's terms, and Pitt had to defend himself desperately against charges of using secret influence. He brazened it out, relying on that reputation for personal integrity which he had done so much to nurture.

> He declared he came up no backstairs [to the King's closet]; . . . that he knew of no secret influence, and that his own integrity would be his guardian against that danger: but the House might rest assured, whenever he discovered any, he would not stay a moment longer in office.[38]

It was a disingenuous defence; not an outright lie but decidedly economical with the truth. He had indeed not gone up the royal backstairs; the King's emissary had gone up his. Secret influence was denied by resorting to its meaning as expressed in Burke's famous *Thoughts on the Causes of the Present Discontents* (1770) in which a double Cabinet allegedly existed, with secret advisers imposing their will on the official ministers. That was not the case on this occasion, when those who advised were now fully responsible as public ministers too: repeatedly Pitt asserted that he would 'never condescend to be the instrument of any secret advisers whatever'.[39]

His reputation saved him from personal condemnation, but he had to suffer the passage by majorities of 39 and 54 of a string of resolutions condemning the unconstitutional use of the King's name, throwing obstacles in the way of a dissolution, and demanding an administration which had the confidence of the Commons and the public. Disappointed of his hoped-for majority, Pitt lost heart. At a Cabinet dinner next day he 'even hinted at giving the thing up'.[40] He had to be urged into continuing by his colleagues, amongst whom Richmond now volunteered to join the Cabinet, and by the King, who sent a strong letter of support. Pitt still had his India Bill up his sleeve, and hopes rose again on the 16th when it was given an unopposed first reading. That day was indeed a good one for the young leader. The Coalition pressed too far in criticising the King's prerogative in choosing his ministers, and their majority fell to 21, while a debate on a parliamentary reform petition from York gave Pitt the opportunity to remind everyone of his reforming beliefs and to contrast this with Opposition accusations of secret influence. On the same day, too, the City of London voted to address the King congratulating him on dismissing the Coalition Ministry.

Renewed hope was however dashed on 23 January when the Coalition defeated the second reading of his India Bill. It was a near miss in that he lost by only eight votes, but defeat destroyed his best chance for a majority. For the next two hours he sat in silence amidst a barrage of demands for an assurance that there would be no dissolution, upsetting even the independents. When the debate resumed next day he only undertook that there would be no dissolution before the House next met on Monday the 26th. He probably did not know himself what to do, and the weekend was spent in frantic consultation. The King urged a dissolution and at a five-hour Cabinet on the Sunday morning, and six hours more in the evening, argument swayed for and against. Pitt, mindful of his reputation for integrity, felt he was committed not to dissolve by his undertaking of 22 December, but more influential ultimately was the feeling that there was no time to hold a general election and meet a new Parliament before 25 March when the Mutiny Bill, considered essential for the discipline of the armed forces, expired. The King saw this as defeatism and summoned the entire Cabinet to him next morning to exhort action and threatened that, rather than surrender to Fox, he 'would quit the Kingdom for ever!'[41]

It became again a game of buying time until new expedients could be found to build a majority. The chance was available in pressure from a lobby of independent MPs, who met at the St. Alban's Tavern, to resolve the crisis by a union of the opposing parties. Pitt indicated a willingness to negotiate but resisted calls for his resignation while these took place, and this provided another two weeks' breathing space. In that time the wheels of patronage were again set in motion, with three more peerages announced on 31 January. The Lords were brought into play on 4 February with a motion attacking the Commons' actions as unconstitutional. Great publicity was given to Pitt's disinterested conduct in refusing to acquire for himself the £3,000-a-year sinecure Clerkship of the Pells, which became vacant on 11 January, but which he gave instead to an old Shelburnite, Colonel Barré, in lieu of his existing pension. And efforts were redoubled to encourage provincial corporations to imitate the City of London in addressing the King in favour of his Ministers.

It was this appeal to the public, which produced an unexpectedly massive response, that furnished the vital new source of strength for Pitt in the remaining stages of the crisis. A trickle of addresses from mid-January, supportive of the King and his Ministers, became a stream in February and a flood by March until over two hundred had been presented – five times as many as in any other petitioning movement in the previous thirty years. Fox fought back with a meeting of electors in his own Westminster constituency on 5 February, but a follow-up on the 14th was hijacked by ministerial supporters and Westminster ultimately presented two loyal addresses carrying 8,000 signatures.

Such outside support was crucial to Pitt as the temporary armistice in the Commons ended in mid-February. Negotiations for a union came to an abrupt halt over the Coalition's demand that Pitt must resign and the Duke of Portland be granted an audience by the King before any united Ministry could be formed on a fair and equal footing. On 14 January Fox had called for a Ministry which had the confidence of the Commons and the people. Now Pitt could show that the two were not the same, and on 20 February he portrayed Fox as 'the champion of the majority of this House against the voice of the people'.[42]

Pitt's most vulnerable point was still his need to get the supplies and the Mutiny Bill through a hostile House. This had worried him as early as 23 December, when he asked a dinner party of his closest supporters what to do if the Coalition stopped the supplies. Lord Mahon's prediction on that occasion that they would not venture that far seemed fanciful, but mounting public support for the King and his Ministers now encouraged Pitt to gamble on trying to turn his weakness into a strength.

On 10 February and again on the 18th the Coalition deferred approval of the Ordnance estimates until a response was received from the King to the Commons' address to remove his Ministers. Pitt at once accused them of stopping the supplies and (on the 19th) 'warned the House to beware of the confusion into which the nation would be plunged if the supplies should be withheld'.[43] When Fox compromised to appease anxious independents, by allowing discussion of the estimates without a vote, Pitt at last began to sniff the possibility of victory. He was still suffering defeats on constitutional issues (there was a majority of 31 against him on 16 February) and continuing independent pressure for a union forced him into further desultory parleys with the Coalition on 15 and 26 February. But as early as the 17th he thought that 'the enemy rather flinches' at postponing the supplies, while 'The *Independents* are still indefatigable for coalition, but as ineffectual as ever'.[44] Fox's majority fell to 12 on a motion to postpone hearing the estimates to the 20th, and though it rose to 20 and 21 on constitutional matters two days later, he then allowed through the Ordnance estimates to evade Pitt's charges of stopping supplies.

Fox still had the threat to the remaining estimates and the Mutiny Bill in reserve, but he was now running into difficulty himself. In the previous March, and again in December 1783, the postponement of the supplies had been sufficient to win major victories, but with the King and Pitt now firmly resolved to resist, and with his own efforts to rally outside support floundering, Fox had to work hard to maintain the determination of his own supporters. When on 26 February he warned them that they might ultimately have to refuse the supplies and pass a Mutiny Bill of limited duration, one of those present sensed 'a sort of boggle' at going to such extremities.[45] Next day a motion for their further postponement passed by only seven.

Matters moved rapidly to a climax. In later years Wilberforce could 'well remember how anxiously we watched the events of each succeeding day, counting every vote, in the earnest hope that Pitt might make a successful stand against the Coalition'.[46] On 1 March even Fox's formerly secure majority on constitutional matters fell to 12, for he was now being driven to extremities on this too, asserting that the Commons had a right to advise the King on the use of his prerogative when addressing him to dismiss his ministers. The royal reply on the 4th was adamant: the King knew of no further step he could take to meet the wishes of the House. Fox's response next day, to postpone consideration of the Mutiny Bill, passed by nine votes, and then suddenly opposition collapsed. A Foxite public rally in Westminster on the 7th was outmatched by a counter-rally by Pitt's supporters. On 8 March Fox's proposal that the

Commons should issue a remonstrance against the King's last message passed by only a single vote. A Coalition meeting on the 9th decided they could not carry a short Mutiny Bill and they allowed the full bill through its committee stage unopposed, indicating also that they would not oppose the further passage of the supplies. 'I write now in great haste, and tired to death, even with victory, for I think our present state is entitled to that name,' Pitt told his friend Rutland next day.[47] Once the supplies and Mutiny Bill were passed and the government's election preparations fairly complete, the King dissolved Parliament on 25 March, with some confidence that he could now secure decisive backing for his young Minister.

The white-hot furnace of the Commons debates from 12 January 1784, in which Pitt faced up to a hostile majority of over 50 and in the next two months overturned it, forged his title to head the king's government irrespective of his age. Although he was manfully seconded by Dundas and by his own close circle of friends, the responsibility of leadership fell squarely on his shoulders, day in, day out, since there was no other Cabinet member in the Commons to share the load. He had to withstand not only a constant verbal onslaught from across the floor of the House, but also physical attack, when his coach was wrecked by a Foxite mob as he returned from receiving the Freedom of the City of London on 28 February. In the process he grew enormously in stature. John Acland, the Bridgwater MP who abused him as a 'stripling' in November, became a steady supporter within weeks.[48] Mindful of the 'Angry Boy' rebuff, Pitt worked hard to cultivate an impression of measured authority, telling the Commons on 2 February that 'He had himself, during the whole series of extraordinary debates that had lately taken place, endeavoured to avoid being caught by the violence of their proceedings, and had preserved as calm and governed a temper as the nature of the case would admit'.[49]

Undoubtedly at this time of national humiliation and crisis, the Chatham name was a tower of strength to him and was exploited ceaselessly in cartoons and ballads, but equally his own fastidious concern for character and reputation ever since he entered Parliament now paid abundant dividends. In his *Journals* Horace Walpole noted, under July 1783, that Pitt's

> application was not a moment relaxed, and he was not less abstemious and temperate – even attention to his health was unremitted . . . No juvenile avocation diverted from his studies, nor left reproaches from the grave on his character. Fox seemed to leave pleasure with regret, and to bestow only spare moments on the government of a nation; Pitt to make industry and virtue the ladders of his ambition.[50]

Industry and virtue now paid off, especially in enabling him to condemn the nature of the Fox–North Coalition and to defend himself against counter-accusations: 'Little did I think ever to be charged in this House with being the tool and abettor of secret influence,' he could assert on 12 January. 'The novelty of the imputation only renders it so contemptible.'[51]

All his reputation and that of his father, his courage and his ambition, would however have availed him little without two essential allies: the King and the public. For George III the issue had become a fight to the death, or rather to abdication, 'in preventing a desperate faction from completing the ruin of the most perfect of all human formations – the British Constitution'.[52] Whereas Fox claimed for the Commons a right to determine his choice of Ministers, the King defended his royal prerogatives. He entered fully into the fray, lobbying for support and impressing his own resolution on his Ministers. Nevertheless, the King's support had failed to save Shelburne, and it needed to be complemented by public opinion which expressed itself with a strength and partiality that took everyone by surprise.

Indications of a loss of public respect for the Commons had appeared during the American War in the growing demand for parliamentary reform. A similar concern at the growing power of the Crown had been to some extent assuaged by the economic reform, anti-corruption measures of the Rockingham Ministry. The public, looking for a restoration of political stability as a basis for recovery from the disastrous American War, was in no mood for a constitutional crisis in which the Commons increased its pretensions against the powers of the King. Propaganda against the Coalition's India Bill was extremely successful. At Ludlow John Scott heard the Coalition's seven Commissioners described as 'the seven kings'; in Westminster Fox was greeted with cries of 'No Grand Mogul! No India Tyrant! No Usurper! No Turncoat!'[53] How far confidence in the incorruptibility of the new Minister encouraged this popular rallying in defence of the Crown's powers is uncertain. Undoubtedly it was a factor in leading Wyvill and the Yorkshire Association to align against the Coalition, and certainly there had been no similar response when Shelburne was the King's champion. But also the Coalition was now pressing far higher claims than it had a year earlier and accusations now abounded that Fox was playing the role of Cromwell. At all events the Loyal Addresses that poured in from all parts of the country enabled Pitt to adopt the role to which he always aspired: that of the Patriot statesman, backed by the vocal support of the nation, upholding the mixed and balanced constitution against the assaults of faction: 'the situation of the times requires of me,' he told the Commons defiantly on 20 February 1784, 'and I will add, the country calls aloud to me, that I should defend this castle; and I am determined, therefore, I will yet defend it.'[54]

The final reward of this patriotic popular mobilisation came in the ensuing general election, when the extent and nature of the government's victory surpassed expectations. In making his calculations to obtain a majority by traditional government means, in December, John Robinson added, 'But it will cost, I am sorry to say, much money.'[55] In the event the Treasury spent £32,000 on the election, compared with the £62,000 Robinson had spent in 1780 and £50,000 in 1774. Robinson's original calculations relied on defections from the Coalition and bargains with patrons of close boroughs, but the spirit of party around a major political issue made this a battle unlike normal elections, and he was disappointed of many of his hopes in these areas and seems to have reduced his expectations on the eve of the dissolution to a majority of 70. In fact the first divisions in the new House gave majorities of 147 and 168 for Pitt. Much of his success was thanks to the popular revolt against the Coalition in the more open constituencies. Counties and the boroughs with over a thousand voters returned 90 Pittites against the Coalition's 53, with three others doubtful. Robinson had originally expected the prestigious county seats to split 40–40, whereas they returned 48 Pittites against 29 for the Coalition and three doubtful. The London metropolis, which in 1780 had returned only one member for government and eleven for opposition, returned nine for government in 1784.

This popular reaction was the last of a whole series of extraordinary and unpredictable events which combined to place Pitt in power before his twenty-fifth birthday. Each time his rising career came to a standstill, it was accelerated again by some new development: Yorktown; Rockingham's death; the India Bill; the arousal of loyalist public opinion. With amazing rapidity the old political leaders fell away – Rockingham died, North and then Shelburne were discredited – while, of their potential successors, Fox became enmeshed in a personal battle with the King, and others such as Townshend, Thomas Pitt and the Grenvilles lost their nerve in the escalating political crisis. Amidst this ever-changing situation, it was Pitt who kept his head and showed the courage and ability to exploit his luck. In later years Wilberforce remarked on his 'sanguine temper leading him . . . to expect that doubtful contingencies would have a more favourable issue than others might venture to anticipate', and Lord Auckland referred to 'Pitt's opinion, that everything comes right in time'.[56] In the light of the dramatic switches in his fortunes during these early traumatic years in politics it is easy to see just how he developed such an optimistic disposition.

. . .

NOTES AND REFERENCES

1 S. Rogers, *Recollections*, 2nd edn (1859), p. 187.
2 To Westmorland, 26 July 1779, quoted in J. Ehrman, *The Younger Pitt* (1969), vol. 1, p. 58.
3 Add. MSS, 35,192, Lady Chatham to Alexander Hood, 14 June 1776; G. Pretyman Tomline, *Memoirs of the Life of the Rt Hon. William Pitt* (1821), vol. 1, pp. 7–8.
4 Earl Stanhope, *Life of Pitt* (1861), vol. 1, p. 31.
5 *Ibid.*, p. 47.
6 *Ibid.*, p. 58; HMC, *Mss of the Earl of Carlisle* (1897), pp. 465, 497; *Speeches*, vol. 1, p. 18.
7 HMC, *Carlisle*, pp. 538, 561–2; A.F. Steuart (ed.), *The Last Journals of Horace Walpole* (1910), vol. 2, pp. 389–90.
8 HMC, *Carlisle*, p. 593; HMC, *Mss of the Marquis of Abergavenny* (1887), p. 50.
9 Steuart (ed.), *Last Journals*, vol. 2, p. 416.
10 HMC, *Mss of J.B. Fortescue* (1892), vol. 1, p. 162.
11 J. Norris, *Shelburne and Reform* (1963), p. 242; L.V. Harcourt (ed.), *The Diaries and Correspondence of the Rt. Hon. George Rose* (1860), vol. 1, p. 31.
12 Lord E. Fitzmaurice, *Life of William, Earl of Shelburne* (1876), vol. 3, p. 422.
13 J. Fortescue, *The Correspondence of King George the Third* (1928), vol. 6, p. 175.
14 *Speeches*, vol. 1, pp. 47–50n.
15 General Fitzpatrick, quoted in Lord J. Russell (ed.), *Memorials and Correspondence of Charles James Fox* (1853), vol. 2, p. 19.
16 *Speeches*, vol. 1, pp. 50–64.
17 *Ibid.*, p. 63.
18 Quoted in J. Cannon, *The Fox–North Coalition* (Cambridge, 1969), p. 57.
19 J.H. Rose, *William Pitt and the National Revival* (1912), p. 125.
20 Stanhope, *Pitt*, vol. 1, p. 107.
21 For the Grenvilles see *C.C.GIII*, vol. 1, p. 214. For Thomas Pitt, see Fortescue (ed.), *Corresp. GIII*, vol. 6, p. 268.
22 O. Browning (ed.), *The Political Memoranda of Francis, Fifth Duke of Leeds* (1884), p. 86; Steuart (ed.), *Last Journals*, vol. 2, p. 489. Similar sentiments to Walpole's were expressed by the Duke of Grafton, see Stanhope, *Pitt*, vol. 1, pp. 109–10.
23 F. Salomon, *William Pitt der Jüngere* (Leipzig, 1906), vol. 1, p. 132, n. 2; Add. MSS, 69,143, f. 39.
24 HMC, *Fortescue*, vol. 1, p. 216.
25 PRO, PRO30/29/1/15 f. 769.
26 *Pitt/Rutland Corresp.* (1890), p. 4, Pitt to Rutland, 22 Nov. 1783.
27 BL Loan, 72/29, Robinson to Jenkinson, 1 Dec. 1783; *C.C.GIII*, vol. 1, pp. 288–9.

28 Stanhope, *Pitt*, vol. 1, p. 155; Rose, *National Revival*, pp. 152–3; Cannon, *Fox–North Coalition*, pp. 128–31; P. Kelly, 'The Pitt–Temple Administration 19–22 December 1783', *HJ*, vol. 17 (1974), pp. 157–61.

29 BL Loan, 72/29: to Jenkinson, 8 March 1783.

30 *Pitt/Rutland Corresp.*, pp. 5–6.

31 Cannon, *Fox–North Coalition*, pp. 130–3; *C.C.GIII*, vol. 1, p. 285.

32 Sir W.R. Anson (ed.), *Autobiography and Political Correspondence of Augustus Henry, Third Duke of Grafton* (1898), pp. 383–7, 393.

33 P. Kelly, 'British Politics, 1783–4: the Emergence and Triumph of the Younger Pitt's Administration', *Bulletin of the Institute of Historical Research*, vol. 54 (1981), pp. 67–8.

34 Tomline, *Life of Pitt*, vol. 1, p. 233; BL Loan, 72/29 ff. 163–5; *L.C.GIII*, vol. 1, p. 6, n. 2.

35 R.I. Wilberforce and S. Wilberforce, *The Life of William Wilberforce* (1839), vol. 1, p. 48.

36 Add. MSS, 45,728, f. 12; Add. MSS, 35,641, f. 70.

37 *L.C.GIII*, vol. 1, pp. xxvi–vii; Ehrman, *Pitt*, vol. 1, p. 133; BL Loan, 72/79, f. 164v, Robinson to Jenkinson, 22 Dec. 1783; Fitzmaurice, *Shelburne*, vol. 3, pp. 414–15.

38 *Speeches*, vol. 1, p. 105.

39 *Ibid.*

40 Browning (ed.), *Leeds Memoranda*, p. 95.

41 *Ibid.*, pp. 95–7.

42 *Speeches*, vol. 1, p. 147.

43 *Parl. Hist.*, vol. 24, col. 620. See also cols. 582, 609–10, 617.

44 *Pitt/Rutland Corresp.*, p. 7.

45 Malmesbury (ed.), *Diaries*, vol. 2, p. 61.

46 R.I. and S. Wilberforce, *Life*, vol. 1, p. 50.

47 *Pitt/Rutland Corresp.*, p. 9.

48 Cannon, *Fox–North Coalition*, p. 115, n. 2; Sir L. Namier and J. Brooke, *The House of Commons 1754–1790* (1964), vol. 2, p. 4.

49 *Speeches*, vol. 1, p. 140.

50 Steuart (ed.), *Last Journals*, vol. 2, p. 459.

51 *Speeches*, vol. 1, p. 105.

52 Stanhope, *Pitt*, vol. 1, appendix p. vi.

53 H. Twiss, *The Public and Private Life of Lord Chancellor Eldon* (1844), vol. 1, p. 163; Cannon, *Fox–North Coalition*, p. 190.

54 *Speeches*, vol. 1, p. 154.

55 BL Loan, 72/29: to Jenkinson, 10 Dec. 1783.

56 A.M. Wilberforce, *The Private Papers of William Wilberforce* (1897), p. 62; F. Bickley (ed.), *The Diaries of Sylvester Douglas, Lord Glenbervie* (1928), vol. 1, p. 107.

Chapter 2

'AWKWARD I *AM CERTAIN* IN A *CERTAIN QUARTER*':

PITT AND THE KING

Pitt's first Ministry lasted for seventeen years and three months (from 19 December 1783 until 14 March 1801) to become the second longest of the eighteenth century, surpassed only by that of Sir Robert Walpole (1721–42). Few contemporaries could have expected such longevity despite the magnitude of the 1784 election victory. Pitt was the ninth First Lord of the Treasury the King had appointed in the first twenty-three years of his reign.[1] Pitt's father, made Prime Minister as Lord Privy Seal in 1766, lasted just two years, and while Pitt's Chathamite inheritance made him popular in the country, it hindered his relations with the King, who still carried the scars of his father's imperious behaviour. The hastily improvised Cabinet hardly provided a solid basis for a lasting administration, and, apart from his brief subordinate term as Chancellor of the Exchequer, Pitt himself had no experience of governing – the kingdom had been 'trusted to a school-boy's care' claimed the popular opposition satire *The Rolliad* in 1785.

. . .

THE ALLIANCE OF OPPOSITES

To survive, Pitt needed to establish a secure working relationship with George III. As his own recent victory had shown, the life of an eighteenth-century Ministry generally depended more on the monarch's choice of his servants than on the preferences of the House of Commons. The King was enduringly grateful to Pitt for rescuing him from the hands of the hated Fox, and Pitt was enduringly ambitious to govern the country, but there were obstacles to their good harmony. Pitt had grown up resentful of the Court and its power which Chathamite tradition held to have wrecked his father's glorious career. As chief mourner at his father's public funeral he felt the insult when 'The Court did not honour us with their countenance, nor did they suffer the procession to be as magnificent as it ought'. Shortly before taking power he refused to be part of any government founded 'on the old politics of the Court', and he predicted that 'The part of our constitution which will first perish, is the prerogative of the King'. The King's Friend, John Robinson, found that Pitt and Temple, on entering office, were 'awkward I *am certain* in a *certain quarter*, they are not explicit; they do not . . . address themselves to the conviction of good sense, or the feeling of a *generous mind, harassed* and *oppressed*, but abruptly propose, what *cannot* be easily obtained, without offering or suggesting something expedient'.[2] Pitt excluded the most notorious of the King's Friends in the Commons from his initial appointments, instead seeking a Ministry with a clear 'Whig complexion'. Even as late as 1790, 'he hesitated not to say, if any distrust were to be entertained of either of the three branches of the constitution, it ought to be of the executive power'.[3] We have the paradox that the man who saved the power of the Crown from a factious political combination in 1783–4 was himself suspicious of the Crown's exercise of its powers.

Such prejudices inevitably engendered coolness and caution in Pitt's relations with George III. When he made Pitt his Minister, George had twenty-three years' experience of government behind him, having been King for all but a year of the Younger Pitt's life, and he was backed by a sizeable and experienced group of King's Friends both in the Ministry and in Parliament. The King and his supporters were undoubtedly concerned at the political baggage Pitt brought with him: Thurlow anxiously sounded him about his commitment to parliamentary reform during their July 1783 meeting, while, in December, Robinson queried 'Whether when things are settled and he finds himself firm, the father's spirit may not arise'. The King had been 'much hurt' when Pitt refused to save him in March 1783, and never forgot how this compelled his humiliating submission to the Coalition. In the delirium of illness in early 1789, 'The King abused Mr Pitt very much . . . and called him a Boy; said that He had wanted him to step forward at the close of . . . [Shelburne's] . . . Administration, but that He was afraid.'[4] They had policy differences – on parliamentary reform, on the impeachment of Warren Hastings, on the abolition of the slave trade, on foreign affairs – but the fundamental difference was in temperament, between the dogmatic Monarch and his pragmatic Minister. The King prided himself that 'My opinion is formed on principle, not on events, and therefore is not open to change', whereas his Minister came to believe that 'there was no wisdom in establishing general rules or principles in government or policy'.[5]

Fortunately for this essential relationship, Pitt found self-restraint an easier discipline than either his father or his rival Fox. He had not thrown himself into a personal vendetta against the King as did his father with George II or Fox with George III. According to Nathaniel Wraxall, friends warned him against an early tendency in this direction and he took the hint.[6] Fox's intemperance proved one of the mainstays of George's continued support for Pitt, given renewed force when Fox so unreservedly championed the French Revolutionary cause in 1792–3. A *modus vivendi* therefore emerged between Monarch and Minister in which both learned to exercise restraint. The King did not repeat his harangue to the entire Cabinet in January 1784, which echoed similar occasions in North's Ministry in 1779 and 1781 when he felt his ministers needed energising. Pitt's success in seeing off the crisis in his own way cleared the King's mind of lingering doubts about his resolution. As the Coalition attacks crumbled in March 1784, he told his Minister that 'I shall ever with pleasure consider that by the prudence as well as rectitude of one person in the House of Commons this great change has been effected, and that he will be ever able to reflect with satisfaction that in having supported me he has saved the Constitution, the most perfect of human formations.'[7]

The King thereafter was prepared to allow Pitt his head on reforming issues on which they disagreed, so long as he espoused such causes as a private member and did not seek to back them with the force of government. This compromise was offered by Pitt himself when he admitted to the Commons in January 1784 the improbability of parliamentary reform becoming a Cabinet measure, but declared that he would continue to support it individually. This had advantages for the King because the business would remain with cooler heads than the London radicals. Nevertheless he was alarmed and hurt when, in January 1785, the campaigner Christopher Wyvill announced Pitt's determination to bring forward reform in the next session 'as a man and as a Minister'.[8] Pitt in fact sought to overcome the King's opposition with the spectre that defeat of his efforts as a man would inevitably damage his ability to act as a Minister. When informing the King of his proposals, he stressed their moderation and warned that if the King's supporters voted against the measure it might 'weaken and dissolve the public confidence, and in doing so would render every future effort in your Majesty's service but too probably fruitless and futile'.

The King however was too experienced a politician to be caught by this and after consulting a Cabinet opponent of parliamentary reform, Lord Sydney, on Pitt's likely reaction, he urged that the measure should be left a completely open issue. Since Pitt was convinced of its propriety he should lay his thoughts before the House and, 'out of personal regard to him', George would stay silent. But he warned Pitt against using his position to pressure anyone into voting for the measure since, 'on a question of such magnitude I should think very ill of anyone who took part on either side without the maturest consideration, and who would suffer his civility to any one to make him vote contrary to his own opinion'. In fact the King's antipathy to parliamentary reform was far too well known for his silence to make any difference. Although Pitt made other attempts to muzzle the courtiers, in the end they voted with the majority against him. The King consoled his Minister by reporting commendation of his 'masterly performance'.[9]

Pitt's acceptance of defeat increased the King's confidence that the constitution was safe in his hands. His satisfaction mounted when Pitt opposed repeal of the Test and Corporation Acts in 1787, 1789 and 1790, and, when he also opposed parliamentary reform in the 1790s, George purred that Pitt would endear himself to 'all lovers of good order and our excellent constitution'. He accepted Pitt's support for greater civic rights for Catholics in England in 1791 and in Ireland in 1792, and less happily deferred to his Ministers on the enfranchisement of appropriately qualified Irish Catholics in 1793. But he drew the line when the new Lord Lieutenant, Earl Fitzwilliam, proposed to repeal the Test Acts in Ireland in 1795, expressing his total opposition in a long memorandum to his Premier. However Pitt too thought that proposal dangerous, or rather untimely, so that broad agreement was maintained until the proposal re-emerged with fatal consequences in 1801. Pitt's Ministry was unusual in that it both rose and fell on constitutional issues, hence it was important for his tenure of office that they were contained for so long.[10]

With his constitutional concerns appeased, the King wholeheartedly applied himself to providing advice, support and encouragement to his Minister in the Commons, being quick to console and reassure him over early reverses.[11] The two were in complete agreement on the general restorative policies needed after the American War: peace; consolidation of the national finances; and commercial expansion. George expressed his 'infinite satisfaction' at Pitt's vigorous efforts to increase taxes in 1784 and 1785, at the Sinking Fund and the commercial treaty with France in 1786, and at his excursions into revenue reform – the transfer of wine duties from customs to excise in 1786, and in 1787 the consolidation of the duties into a single fund from which state expenditure would be paid according to a prioritised schedule. The King declared this last to be 'so material a measure' that he went to Parliament to give the Royal Assent in person.[12]

The national finances were not matters in which the Monarch was sufficiently involved (Pitt did not tax him until 1800!), nor did he understand them sufficiently for them to create conflict between him and his Minister. Foreign policy, state patronage and the affairs of the Royal Family, however, personally involved the King, and it was on the avoidance of clashes there that harmonious relations between the King and his Minister were likely to depend.

. . .

MANAGEMENT OF FOREIGN POLICY

Foreign policy was particularly problematic since George III was also Elector of Hanover and hence was in a position to pursue his own separate German policy. Pitt soon discovered this when, in 1785, George independently joined Hanover as a founder member in a Prussian-led league of German princes to oppose an Austrian plan for exchanging its Netherlands provinces for Bavaria – notwithstanding the effect of this on British attempts to create an alliance with Austria and its ally Russia.[13] The King was in any case adamant that Britain should avoid European entanglements until it recovered from the American War and in consequence it was an immense task for Pitt and his Foreign Secretary, Carmarthen, to coax him into seizing the opportunity to contest France's hold over Holland in 1786–7.

Since Pitt had earlier shared the King's passive opinions, George was more responsive to his views than those of the lightweight Foreign Secretary, too influenced by his intriguing envoy in Holland (and former Coalition supporter), Sir James Harris. It needed Pitt's reassurance on the finances to overcome royal opposition to Carmarthen's Cabinet minute, for a £70,000 loan to the supporters of the Anglophile Prince of Orange, in May 1787. When the crisis finally broke in September (see Chapter 7 below), it was Pitt's coaxing that finally led the King to agree to British mobilisation in support of Prussian intervention to restore the Orangeists to power. Pitt sent his own emissary, Grenville, to Holland and fed his reports to the King to overcome his distrust of Harris. With masterly tact he drew along the King by degrees with assurances such as his 'entire conviction that the line your Majesty is pleased to point out is the only one which can be adopted with propriety'.[14] Success in the Dutch crisis made the King more willing to listen to his Ministers' proposals on foreign policy but though the initiative now passed from him to them, his consent could never be taken for granted as they found when he obstructed a more active Baltic policy in 1788.[15]

Problems of an opposite kind emerged when the King enthusiastically espoused war with Revolutionary France in 1793. This became the most frequent source of disagreements between the King and his Ministers thereafter, encompassing both military affairs and foreign policy. The King's support for the campaigns of his favourite son, the Duke of York, in Flanders were an embarrassment to Ministers looking to deploy resources elsewhere. Attempts to subordinate York to other commanders were justified by Pitt in lengthy letters to the Monarch. Finally (after settlement of differences with his new Portland Whig allies secured his parliamentary position in November 1794) he firmly but tactfully insisted on the Duke's recall. The King was 'very much hurt' but reluctantly consented, and Pitt hastened to soothe royal feelings by making the Duke Commander in Chief of the army three months later. Ministers indeed struck up a good relationship with York, who proved an efficient administrator, but neither he nor they could persuade the King to allow them to use his Foot Guards to bring the important West Indian expedition of 1795 up to strength.[16]

When in 1795 Holland was overrun by the French, and Prussia made a separate peace, the clash between ministerial policy and the King's Electoral interests also revived. Hanover was amongst those calling for a general German peace, and in the autumn the Electorate declared its neutrality. Pitt and his Foreign Secretary, Grenville, meanwhile endeavoured to retain public support and wavering foreign allies by holding out the prospect of general peace negotiations with France, and by seeking to reinvigorate the war effort of the two German military powers. Prussia would be lured back into the war with an offer of territorial gains at the expense of the smaller German states, while allowing Austria to exchange the Netherlands for Bavaria. George III vigorously resisted these proposals. In January 1796 he circulated a memorandum among leading Ministers opposing peace overtures. The need to secure public support was dismissed with the retort: 'My mind is not of a nature to be guided by the obtaining a little applause or staving off some abuse: rectitude of conduct is my sole aim'; and, as in 1785, he resisted the spoliation of his fellow smaller German princes, dismissing Grenville's explanations with the tart comment: 'I always choose to act on simple principles. Italian politics are too complicated paths for my understanding.'[17]

Yet the King was eventually forced to give way, and perhaps this was why his retorts were so stinging. His surrenders in 1796 were his biggest foreign policy defeats at the hands of Ministers in his whole reign. How did Pitt get his way? In part, age and the vast increase in reported information loosened the King's grip on foreign affairs. He confessed to Grenville, in April, that 'when the load is too great I find that I cannot retain in my mind any part of the contents . . . indeed the whole mode of carrying on the public correspondence is so much more diffuse and undigested than thirty years ago'. He was consequently weakly armed to resist a Foreign Secretary renowned for being both well informed and obstinate in his opinions, and who worked so closely with Pitt. The King found himself bombarded by the two cousins, pressing a common line of argument when key decisions had to be made, usually by letter but also in person when he summoned them to an unprecedented joint audience at Windsor in late July.[18]

Besides Grenville's knowledge and persistence, Pitt's main weapons were his own pertinacity, the loyalty of his colleagues and an astute use of his accumulated experience of how to handle the King's prejudices. The removal of the King's most loyal supporter in Cabinet, Lord Chancellor Thurlow, in 1792, and the incorporation of the Portland Whigs in a restructured Coalition Cabinet in 1794 (which at last gave it the clear 'Whig complexion' that Pitt had long desired), strengthened Pitt's position by enabling him to confront the King with the backing of Cabinet unity to which the King would reluctantly defer.[19] Repeatedly in this conflict of views in 1795–7 the King was told that the Cabinet was unanimous in its recommendations. In January 1796 the King tried to work on Dundas's pro-war sentiments without avail. The Minister most hostile to peace overtures, Windham, preferred to be recorded absent rather than have his dissent officially stated in Cabinet minutes. Even when, in June 1797, Grenville divided from Pitt over continuing the policy, the King's hopes were dashed when the Foreign Secretary nevertheless loyally supervised the negotiations directed by his cousin.[20]

So long as Ministers remained united and determined, and there was no obvious alternative government in sight, then the King was powerless to resist. This was not a weapon that Pitt or any other Premier could afford to use frequently or lightly, for harmonious relations with the King were necessary to the smooth passage of government business. Nevertheless since public loss of confidence in an unsuccessful war had brought down Pitt's most powerful predecessors, Walpole and North, he was obliged to confront the King for his own self-preservation. However, he did so conscious of the need to cause minimum aggravation, by avoiding the appearance of issuing an ultimatum. His tone was polite, dutiful but firm. Whenever the King disagreed with Cabinet minutes he was asked if he wished the matter discussed again in the light of his objections. Personal interviews were handled carefully. When the British negotiator, Lord Malmesbury, took his leave of the King before going to France in October 1796, he was seen beforehand in close conversation with Pitt who was then overheard telling his brother, as Malmesbury entered the royal closet, that 'I have been giving him his lesson before he goes in'![21]

Pitt had early concluded that personal interviews were not the way to manage the King. Business between Monarch and Minister was transacted standing in the royal closet, and Pitt's inherent shyness with those with whom he found difficulty in establishing rapport, particularly when that person was also King, inclined him to take refuge in extreme formality. This was not the way to be persuasive in the closet, where he was required to wait on gaps in the King's conversation to make his points and where, when disturbed, the King took defence in an 'eager and uninterrupted speech, admitting neither of pause nor answer, and shifting perpetually in unconnected digressions thro' every subject of His thoughts'. The best solution Pitt found to overcome this obstacle was the carefully composed letter in which, as Grenville once explained to his brother, 'All the points may be more forcibly urged by being collected and stated in reference to each other in a manner which the King's desultory way of speaking makes impossible.' In this way too might Pitt subtly turn the King's prejudices to advantage. Persuading him to stick with the peace policy against Grenville's change of heart in 1797, Pitt disarmingly invoked the King's devotion to consistency in public conduct: 'he knows that Your Majesty will feel that, the line of negotiation having once been taken, ought not to be hastily departed from'.[22] It was only the ultimate failure of these negotiations, however, that renewed accord on foreign policy between the Monarch and his Minister, but the continuation of the war gave occasion for further divergences on its conduct.

. . .

PATRONAGE AND POLITICS

Patronage was the essential lubricant of the eighteenth-century political system, and another area in which the King took a close interest. The brusque treatment of the King on patronage issues by one of his early Premiers, George Grenville (Pitt's uncle and Grenville's father), was instrumental in his fall. Pitt may have declared that 'arrangements' made him 'bilious', but he was keenly aware of their importance to any Ministry. When the King became incapacitated in late 1788, Pitt's major defence to stop the Opposition entrenching themselves in power, if they took office under a Regency, was to deprive them of patronage. His Regency Bill was loaded with restrictions, and perhaps he opted for a single Prince Regent, rather than the Regency Council proposed by Lord Chancellor Thurlow, precisely because it better enabled him to justify such restrictions. The Queen (on whom he could rely) would retain care of the sick King and management of his household, including appointments. The Prince Regent could make no grants of Crown property, nor reversions to offices, nor grant peerages except to his brothers as they came of age, and he could only grant offices during royal pleasure (i.e. which could be subsequently revoked) except for those where the law required greater permanence.[23]

Patronage was power, and, to govern effectively, a Minister had to be seen to exercise that power. Pitt protested in 1805, when the King rejected his nomination for Archbishop of Canterbury, that it could not be understood by either himself or the public 'in any other light than as a decisive mark of your Majesty's not honouring him with that degree of weight and confidence which his predecessors have enjoyed', and without which it was impossible for him to conduct the King's affairs with advantage. He conspicuously refrained from requests for himself. The King, grateful for his salvation in 1784, was anxious to make financial provision for his Minister against his own demise, and twice he expressed regret when Pitt requested reversions to lucrative sinecure Tellerships of the Exchequer for others rather than himself. In 1790 he was again unsuccessful in his wish to reward his Minister with the Garter after the Nootka Crisis triumph. (Was it a desire to have the King atone for slights to his father that led Pitt to ask for it to be conferred on the head of the family, his brother the Earl of Chatham, instead?) Finally in 1792 the King insisted that he should take the Lord Wardenship of the Cinque Ports and Pitt, both financially pressed and needing a public signal of royal favour in a difficult year, at last accepted. Usually Pitt preferred to look for his gratification and for public marks of royal favour in rewards for his friends and relations. He flagged up to the King where he had a personal interest: 'it will be to Mr Pitt the greatest personal gratification', he wrote in proposing Tom Steele for the sinecure office of Remembrancer of the Exchequer; and: 'Mr Pitt feels this personally as a most gratifying additional mark of your Majesty's favour and indulgence which he has so abundantly experienced', when the King approved an English peerage for his friend Mornington – both welcomed in 1797 at a time when Pitt's popularity was at a low ebb.[24]

Generally the King obliged, though he set upper limits to what Pitt could ask as personal favours. In 1784 and 1789 he refused Pitt's pressure for a dukedom for his demanding cousin Earl Temple, who had to settle for the marquisate of Buckingham instead. While George readily agreed to Pitt's request for a rich Suffolk living for his private secretary and former tutor, Dr George Pretyman, in 1785, he was less complaisant in 1787 when Pitt, declaring that 'he can request nothing from your

Majesty's goodness which he has more anxiously or personally at heart', nominated Pretyman to succeed Thurlow's brother (promoted to Durham) as Bishop of Lincoln and Dean of St Paul's. The King was willing to grant the former (worth £1,500 p.a.) but felt that adding the latter (£1,800 p.a.) was too much. Pitt felt beholden to Pretyman and, needing to demonstrate as much royal favour as his rival, Thurlow, he pressed his suit until the King reluctantly conceded, telling him that 'I cannot let my reason guide me against my inclination to oblige you . . . though I am confident it will be, by all but those concerned, thought very unreasonable.' However, Pitt stretched the benevolence of a less grateful monarch too far when he tried to make Pretyman Archbishop of Canterbury in 1805. The King's determined refusal to his request occasioned the protest cited above. Similarly, while the King was willing to sanction the advancement of Pitt's pet lawyer, Pepper Arden, to Attorney-General and to Master of the Rolls, in 1799 he backed the appointment of Sir John Scott rather than Arden as Lord Chief Justice of Common Pleas.[25]

Pitt's fear on entering office was that the Crown would be regarded as the real disposer of offices and honours. He had to accept the King's favourites, Lords Thurlow and Howe, into the Cabinet, but he excluded the Monarch's former advisers, Jenkinson and Robinson, until 1786 and 1787 respectively, when it could be seen that they gained their offices on his terms. In June 1784 Thomas Orde 'perceived some symptoms of jealousy in Pitt, when any mention was made of persons having claims on government because of attachment to the Crown, and a word about royal recommendation seemed to call up more blood than usual in his cheeks'.[26] However he could not exclude the Monarch's keen interest in patronage matters. Grenville explained in 1788, during one of his brother Buckingham's frequent clashes with the King on Irish patronage while Lord Lieutenant, that:

> I believe that it never happened to the most absolute Minister that ever governed this country to feel it in his power to exclude all personal interference from the Crown in the nomination of offices. I am sure it is not a matter of policy to any Minister to wish it; and . . . such at least is not the system of the present Government, . . . the limits [are] easily seen, where the King's recommendations cease to be the casual exertions of private favour, and begin to be systematic interference with the power entrusted to his servants.[27]

The King never went so far as systematic interference during Pitt's first Ministry. Where political considerations were involved, he usually deferred to his Minister,[28] except where he had developed a rooted dislike of the nominee, such as Buckingham, who he felt had run away in December 1783, and especially Fox. In 1784 he accepted Earl Gower's son-in-law as Solicitor-General in order to gratify the Gower connection, though he thought Thurlow's protégé Scott fitter. However, in 1799, in making Scott Chief Justice, the King extracted from him a promise not to refuse the Lord Chancellorship when called upon. While the King had conceded to Pitt's desire to lure Loughborough from Opposition ranks in 1792, the post of Lord Chancellor in particular was widely accepted to lie within the King's personal choice. George had begun to open the peerage to strengthen Lord North in the American War, and he extended it to further strengthen Pitt, contenting himself with adding a few of his own nominees – Carleton in 1786, Sir Joseph Yorke in 1789, Mt Edgcumbe in 1790 and Sir John Rushout, victim of a forgotten promise by Pitt, noticed by the King in 1797. He reluctantly accepted his Minister's unprecedentedly large lists of nominations despite his fear in 1790 that the House of Lords was becoming too numerous and that this would be found inconvenient (it threatened to swamp the former Crown Household domination of the Lords), only drawing the line at creating any new dukedoms except for royal princes.[29]

It was in the Church, the higher reaches of the law and his armed forces that the King was most sensitive to signs of political jobbery. George was uneasy when Pitt switched to Cambridge University as his parliamentary seat in 1784, realising the pressure his Minister would be put under from his clerical electorate for livings and sees, and Pitt was soon despairing that 'ecclesiastical preferment is the greatest plague I have'. To Pitt (like his predecessors) such preferment satisfied requests from supporters and facilitated electoral needs, and it was often the names of the patrons rather than the virtues of their protégés that he reported to the King, whereas the latter told him in 1797 that 'I think the nomination of Bishops and Judges a trust in the crown that ought to be administer[ed] with the greatest attention to the advancement of the former in religion and in the latter of the due administration of justice'. The King turned down Pitt's Church nominations when he had made prior engagements, demanded that he check with the Archbishop of Canterbury on the character and learning of Richmond's candidate for the Bishopric of Chichester, and at times gave directions to Pitt as to whom to look for – a Master of a Cambridge college for Bishop of Hereford, 'a respectable man' whose 'name should be of note' as Dean of Windsor (he suggested, and Pitt accepted, the Bishop of Carlisle). Pitt wished to provide a bishopric for William Paley, whose writings he greatly admired, but the King thought Paley's *Moral Philosophy* too liberal and refused.[30] On military patronage the King was firmer still, and Pitt kept well clear, unless forced to intervene to fend off political fallout when the King upset political subordinates, as when he promoted his equerry against Buckingham's nephew in 1788–9 (Pitt's persistence eventually secured the nephew another opening, but Buckingham shortly resigned his Lord Lieutenancy of Ireland), or when Dundas overzealously short-circuited forms by creating a new battalion of the 52nd Foot out of the Staffordshire militia in 1799 and the King insisted on its disbandment, resulting in the resignation of its commander's brother, Earl Gower, from the county Lord Lieutenancy, and the attempted resignation of Dundas himself.[31]

Generally, to avoid clashes, Pitt deferred to the King on military posts, while a rapid reaction game was often played out between Monarch and Minister over sinecures, honours and ecclesiastical posts. As soon as news was received of a vacancy each hastened to get a name forward, where they had one in mind, to pre-empt the other making any promises, and to forestall a flood of applicants who would have to be disappointed.[32] While Pitt's family loyalty to the pretensions of his cousin Buckingham strained the royal patience, the nearest he came to the indiscretions by which his uncle had offended the King was in 1794 when, after George had personally and with Pitt's knowledge promised the vacant Garter to his favourite admiral, Earl Howe, for his 'Glorious First of June' naval victory, Pitt decided that it was needed for the Duke of Portland in order to complete the newly concluded union with the moderate part of the Opposition. The King protested his prior promise and complained that he could not 'see why on the Duke of Portland's head favours are to be heaped without measure', but Pitt pressed that Howe might accept a step in the peerage instead, and circumvented the King's resistance by inducing the Admiral to renounce the Garter in Portland's favour. (Howe rejected the proffered marquisate as soon as Portland was installed.)[33] Even on this occasion Pitt provided a way to save the King from losing face, and Howe eventually got his Garter in 1797. He realised he could not afford to humiliate the Monarch publicly, and generally he knew when to press his case or defer in order to maintain amicable relations.

. . .

THE PERSONAL AFFAIRS OF THE ROYAL FAMILY

Lastly, and most delicately of all, Pitt had to handle the personal affairs of the Royal Family itself. At a time when the costs of civil government and the increasing size of the Royal Family were repeatedly bringing the Civil List (which paid for both) into debt, Pitt had to satisfy both the

King, who needed his debts paid, and the independents in Parliament, who were quick to cry out at the slightest hint of royal extravagance. Moreover, the most incorrigibly extravagant member of the Royal Family was the Prince of Wales, who had estranged himself from the King by siding with Fox. Pitt needed to win over the Prince, whose household posts and promises of patronage when he became King were a useful support and recruitment tool for Opposition and an increasingly corrosive agent on the power of the Minister of a King born in 1738.

Pitt's first task was to re-establish the Crown's finances by paying off the arrears on the Civil List. This he achieved by securing parliamentary grants of £60,000 in 1784 and £210,000 in 1786, though the King resented his insistence on a statement of future royal expenditure in order to get the latter through the Commons. The Prince of Wales, however, rejected hints in 1785 that his debts might be more easily paid if he abandoned the Opposition, and since the King refused assistance without both a full statement of how all the debts were incurred (which he refused to give) and a positive commitment to pay them off and incur no more, the Prince's debts continued to mount, reaching £370,000 by 1787. They had to be tackled to avoid discrediting the Monarchy. Using his 'dirty jobs man', Henry Dundas, to initiate negotiations with the Prince (both were freemasons), Pitt arranged a compromise settlement: a one-off sum to complete the Prince's new palace at Carlton House and an additional £10,000 a year from the Civil List in return for the Prince establishing a sinking fund from his income for the long-term repayment of his debts. It was a political nightmare for Pitt, since he had to secure the agreement both of the quarrelling father and son and also of a hostile House of Commons, for which he needed all his self-restraint and procedural skills to prevent discussion of the Prince's rumoured secret marriage to a Catholic widow, Mrs Fitzherbert, in defiance of the Act of Settlement and the Royal Marriages Act. Pitt's success in negotiating all these hurdles and apparently putting a curb on his son's extravagance drew the King's delighted praise that 'Mr Pitt's conduct never gives me any other impression but that of approbation'.[34]

The Prince was not however won over, and the extent of Pitt's vulnerability became apparent in the autumn of 1788 when the King succumbed to an attack of the hereditary blood disease porphyria. Its most public symptom was compulsive talking, verging on delirium, which contemporary medical opinion mistook for madness. A Regency loomed, and it became clear that if the Prince of Wales became Regent he would dismiss Pitt in favour of his Opposition friends. Pitt's dependence on the King could not have been more strikingly demonstrated. In battling for his political life, Pitt was saved by four things: Parliament's dislike of the Prince's extravagant, unseemly reputation, which made it prepared to debate the terms for his Regency at length; Pitt's fortunate discovery of a doctor, Willis, credible and confident enough to declare that the King could be cured; his own parliamentary skills in exploiting these factors to spin out time and establish restrictions on a Regency; and the King's physical constitution which was strong enough to survive the wrong treatment for the wrong disease and enabled him to recover with Pitt still clinging to office in February 1789.

Successful survival of the Regency Crisis, however, still left him facing the basic problems of royal finances: that the Civil List was inadequate for the rising costs of government and the Prince was incapable of restraining his profligacy. To these were now added the further complications, first, that Parliament having already given extra money would not be easily persuaded to give more, and second that the 1790s were a time of revolution abroad and high war taxation and radical reform demands at home. To request more money for the Royal Family was likely to play into radical hands, stimulating demands for more parliamentary control of royal expenditure, if not worse. Pitt's dilemma was starkly revealed in 1794 when the Prince of Wales's mounting debts at last forced him into a reconciliation with the King by agreeing to marry in order to continue the direct royal line. Politically it was an ostensible victory for Pitt, but he was then left to extract the necessary financial settlement from Parliament and he complained privately of having to jeopardise both his parliamentary power base, where 'the unpopularity necessarily attached to it will fall upon him as fully as if the debts had been contracted with his approbation', and his royal power base, where 'the Prince, on the other hand, will be no less angry with him for expressing his disapprobation of them and for not proposing to pay them at once'. When he approached the Commons in spring 1795, he was confronted with rebellion and imminent defeat and forced to settle for a smaller sum hedged with restrictions – provoking angry complaints from the King at breaking the promises the Monarch had made to his son. Within a year the King was further complaining that slack parliamentary drafting meant that the Prince had not got the protection from his creditors that he expected, while the disillusioned Prince separated from his wife and drifted away from the King and his Ministers again.[35]

To escape further trouble Pitt avoided bringing Civil List debts forward for payment, so that at his resignation it was a full year in arrears. In 1798 he had to submit the previous three years' Civil List accounts to keep the Commons Committee on Finance at bay, and this may also have influenced the pressure he put on the King to contribute a third of his Privy Purse to the voluntary subscription for the war. Equally, to avoid adding new charges to the Civil List, he adopted the expedient of miscellaneous supply grants by Parliament to pay the extra administrative costs of war and civil disturbance, and by 1799 these provided for more of the costs of civil government than the King's Civil List itself. In the same way he also provided for the establishments of the royal children as they came of age, so that by 1802 four-fifths of their allowances (£78,000) were by direct parliamentary grant. Whether intentional or not, this diminished the prerogatives of the Crown by eroding the Civil List system, whereby the Crown had financial independence to administer civil government without the intervention of Parliament, and enabled Parliament to gain control both of a significant part of government finances and also of Royal Family finances, formerly independently administered by the King. In 1800 the King sought a private means to provide for his family, through recognition of his possession of personal property distinct from that of the Crown. Pitt complied in the Crown Private Estates Act, but he exacted the price that resultant private income would be subject to taxation like that of his subjects. Pitt was the first Minister to dare to tax the Monarchy! Perhaps his earlier Chathamite suspicions made him less careful of preserving monarchical privileges and powers, and he certainly believed it important that the Crown should provide the example of patriotic sacrifice in the war. Pitt's treatment of the Monarchy in the 1790s contributed towards the perishing of its prerogatives that he had predicted.[36] Yet what Pitt's political management also achieved was to raise the King's prestige and popularity and re-establish the moral power of the Crown to an extent that the Premier may have regretted after 1801.

Minister and King did establish a working relationship strong enough to last seventeen years, but it was never close. They never succeeded in breaking through each other's guard, so that their relationship remained formal and distant. Although in 1798 the King urged his ailing Premier to attend to his health 'from the very great consequence of the subject, and that real affection I bear Mr Pitt', the only time that he addressed him as 'My Dear Pitt' was in the letter replying to his resignation in 1801. Pitt, like his father when in power, tended to treat the Monarch more as an institution than as a person. The royal equerry Robert Greville was surprised how, during the Regency Crisis, Pitt confined his enquiries about the King's condition to the official channels of the doctors and the Queen, and ignored those like himself who were in constant attendance on the sick Monarch. As has been seen, Pitt preferred to deal with awkward matters with the King by letter, and the King too found it better to put his most strongly held opinions into memoranda for his Minister. It cannot be said that any real affection developed between them. Lord Westmorland, a long-time friend of Pitt and from 1794 to 1798 an official of the Royal Household, declared in 1797 that he did not believe Pitt had ever seen the King in private ten times. Pitt lacked the King's interest in the arts and in agriculture. Remaining a bachelor, he lacked a family in which the King might interest himself, as he did with those of Lord North and Pitt's successor Addington. Nor would Pitt make the frank confidences of personal feelings and anxieties which earned them the King's avowed friendship and private company.[37] In a scarcely veiled comparison of the difference between Addington and Pitt in 1804, the King told the former that 'he only values those who view him as a man, and not who reflect alone on the King, consequently are led by interest, not sentiments of friendship'.[38] When the working relationship began to break down in 1800 and early 1801 there was respect, but no fund of mutual affection to fall back upon.

. . .

NOTES AND REFERENCES

1 Including Rockingham twice, in 1765 and 1782.

2 Stanhope, *Pitt*, vol. 1, p. 22; HMC, *Fortescue*, vol. 1, p. 216; R.I. and S. Wilberforce, *Life*, vol. 1, p. 38; BL Loan, 72/79, f. 164v.

3 Anson (ed.), *Grafton*, p. 393; *Speeches*, vol. 1, p. 429.

4 HMC, *Fortescue*, vol. 1, p. 216; BL Loan, 72/79, f. 165; Stanhope, *Pitt*, vol. 1, p. iv; F. McK. Bladon (ed.), *The Diaries of Colonel the Rt Hon. Robert Fulke Greville* (1930), p. 187.

5 Stanhope, *Pitt*, vol. 3, p. xxi; Bickley (ed.), *Glenbervie Diaries*, vol. 1, p. 152.

6 H.B. Wheatley (ed.), *Historical and Posthumous Memoirs of Sir Nathaniel William Wraxall* (1884), vol. 3, p. 230.

7 Stanhope, *Pitt*, vol. 1, p. x.

8 *Parl. Hist.*, vol. 24, col. 351; *L.C.GIII*, vol. 1, pp. 68, 119.

9 *L.C.GIII*, vol. 1, pp. 138–42; Stanhope, *Pitt*, vol. 1, pp. xv–xvii; A. Aspinall and E.A. Smith (eds.), *English Historical Documents*, vol. 11 (1959), pp. 287, 312.

10 *L.C.GIII*, vol. 1, pp. 464, 591; Stanhope, *Pitt*, vol. 2, pp. xxii–xxv, vol. 3, pp. xv–xvi; Bickley (ed.), *Glenbervie Diaries*, vol. 1, p. 147.

11 *L.C.GIII*, vol. 1, p. 174; Stanhope, *Pitt*, vol. 1, pp. xii, xv, xvii–xix.

12 Stanhope, *Pitt*, vol. 1, pp. xii–xiii, xix; J.H. Rose, *Pitt and Napoleon. Essays and letters* (1912), pp. 212, 215; *L.C.GIII*, vol. 1, pp. 208, 215, 279.

13 *L.C.GIII*, vol. 1, pp. 177–8; T.C.W. Blanning, '"That horrid Electorate" or "Ma patrie germanique"?: George III, Hanover and the Fürstenbund of 1785', *HJ*, vol. 20 (1977), pp. 311–44.

14 *L.C.GIII*, vol. 1, pp. 295–7, 321, 324–5; Stanhope, *Pitt*, vol. 1, p. xxi; Rose, *Pitt and Napoleon*, pp. 214–15, 217–19.

15 Stanhope, *Pitt*, vol. 2, pp. iii–iv; J. Black, *British Foreign Policy in an Age of Revolutions 1783–1793* (Cambridge, 1994), pp. 179–84.

16 Rose, *Pitt and Napoleon*, pp. 225–8, 230–3; *L.C.GIII*, vol. 2, pp. 105, 254, 271–4, 298, 381, 384; Stanhope, *Pitt*, vol. 2, pp. xxi–xxii.

17 *L.C.GIII*, vol. 2, p. 455; Rose, *Pitt and Napoleon*, pp. 238–9; Stanhope, *Pitt*, vol. 2, pp. xxxi–xxxii; HMC, *Fortescue*, vol. 3, pp. 143, 173–4.

18 HMC, *Fortescue*, vol. 3, pp. 169–70, 173–4, 186, 227–30, 239–42, 256, 310; Stanhope, *Pitt*, vol. 2, pp. xxx–xxxi, vol. 3, pp. iv–vi; *L.C.GIII*, vol. 2, pp. 498, 506–7, 559–60.

19 E.g. HMC, *Fortescue*, vol. 3, p. 284; Stanhope, *Pitt*, vol. 3, p. vi.

20 *L.C.GIII*, vol. 2, p. 458, n. 1; HMC, *Fortescue*, vol. 3, pp. 330–1, vol. 5, p. 306.

21 HMC, *Fortescue*, vol. 3, pp. 173–4; Bickley (ed.), *Glenbervie Diaries*, vol. 1, p. 83.

22 Add. MSS, 69,133, p. 57; *C.C.GIII*, vol. 2, pp. 169–70; Rose, *Pitt and Napoleon*, p. 242.

23 Browning (ed.), *Leeds Memoranda*, p. 130; *L.C.GIII*, vol. 1, p. 429.

24 *L.C.GIII*, vol. 1, pp. 237–8, vol. 2, pp. 623, 627, vol. 4, p. 283; Stanhope, *Pitt*, vol. 2, pp. xi–xii, xv–xvi.

25 *L.C.GIII*, vol. 1, pp. 187, 448–9; Stanhope, *Pitt*, vol. 1, pp. xx–xxi; Fortescue, *Corresp. GIII*, pp. 73–9; Twiss, *Eldon*, vol. 1, pp. 330–1.

26 To Shelburne, 17 June 1784, quoted in L.G. Mitchell, *Charles James Fox and the Disintegration of the Whig Party 1782–1794* (Oxford, 1971), p. 99.

27 *C.C.GIII*, vol. 1, p. 407.

28 E.g. *L.C.GIII*, vol. 1, pp. 515–17.

29 *L.C.GIII*, vol. 1, p. 11, n. 1, 46, vol. 2, p. 603; Stanhope, *Pitt*, vol. 2, pp. i, x, xiii; Twiss, *Eldon*, vol. 1, p. 301.

30 J. Black, 'Eighteenth-century papers', *British Library Journal*, vol. 20 (1994) pp. 211–12; *Pitt/Rutland Corresp.*, p. 13; *L.C.GIII*, vol. 1, pp. 186, 225–6, 360, 369–70, 394–5, vol. 2, pp. 622–3, vol. 3, pp. 163, 197; Stanhope, *Pitt*, vol. 1, p. 250, vol. 4, p. 408.

31 *L.C.GIII*, vol. 1, pp. 146, 408–10, vol. 3, pp. 286–95; Stanhope, *Pitt*, vol. 1, pp. vii–ix.

32 *L.C.GIII*, vol. 1, pp. 151, 182, n. 1, 349; *C.C.GIII*, vol. 2, pp. 197–8.

33 *L.C.GIII*, vol. 2, p. 224; Stanhope, *Pitt*, vol. 2, p. xx; National Maritime Museum AGC/VI, Howe to Pitt, 14, 16 July 1794.

34 *L.C.GIII*, vol. 1, pp. 233, 295. Pitt's relations with the Prince of Wales can be followed in A. Aspinall (ed.), *The Correspondence of George, Prince of Wales* (1963), vols. 1 and 3 *passim*.

35 P. Jupp (ed.), *The Letter-Journal of George Canning 1793–1795* (1991), pp. 247–8; *L.C.GIII*, vol. 2, pp. 345–6, 349–52, 460.

36 E.A. Reitan, 'The Civil List and the changing role of the Monarchy in Britain 1782–1804', *Proceedings of the Consortium on Revolutionary Europe* (1981), pp. 132–40; P. Hall, *Royal Fortune. Tax, Money and the Monarchy* (1992), pp. 6–9. In 1799 the Civil List accounted for only £1,045,000 of the

£2,180,000 spent on civil government (B.R. Mitchell and P. Deane, *Abstract of British Historical Statistics* [Cambridge, 1971], p. 391).

37 Stanhope, *Pitt*, vol. 3, pp. xvi, xxxii; Bladon (ed.), *Greville Diaries*, p. 260; Bickley (ed.), *Glenbervie Diaries*, p. 124; Fortescue, *Corresp. GIII*, vol. 4, pp. 163, 253, 327, vol. 5, p. 161; G. Pellew, *The Life and Correspondence of the Rt Hon. Henry Addington, First Viscount Sidmouth* (1847), vol. 1, pp. 407–10, vol. 2, pp. 288, 292.

38 Pellew, *Sidmouth*, vol. 2, p. 294.

Chapter 3

'REALLY MASTER NOW':
PITT AS PRIME MINISTER

. . .

LEADING MINISTER IN A COALITION CABINET

In 1803, in a statement 'often taken as the first real definition of the office of Prime Minister', Pitt asserted:

> the absolute necessity there is, in the conduct of the affairs of this coun-
> try, that there should be an avowed and real minister possessing the chief
> weight in council and the principal place in the confidence of the King. In
> that respect there can be no rivality or division of power. That power
> must rest in the person generally called the First Minister; and that min-
> ister ought, he thinks, to be the person at the head of the finances . . . if it
> should come unfortunately to such a radical difference of opinion that no
> spirit of conciliation or concession can reconcile, the sentiments of the
> Minister must be allowed and understood to prevail, leaving the other
> members of the administration to act as they may conceive themselves
> conscientiously called upon to act under such circumstances.[1]

On four occasions, in February 1784, March 1791, August 1792 and March 1803 (the occasion of his statement above), he rejected sugges-tions to serve as an equal with a rival under a figurehead First Lord of the Treasury. 'I fear his ambition is such,' wrote the Duke of Richmond in 1804, 'as will never permit him fairly to join with and put himself on an equal footing with anyone. He will be *Caesar aut nullus* [emperor or nothing].' He had to earn this position of pre-eminence, for it was not accepted readily. Many considered the 1783–1801 Ministry initially as a joint one. The King had invited Richmond, Gower, Thurlow and Pitt to form it. The experienced Sardinian envoy believed that Pitt, Thurlow and Shelburne would direct the affairs of the nation (the latter because

Pitt had been his pupil and the two secretaries of state his followers). Shelburne was quickly sidelined and conciliated with a marquisate, but Pitt had more difficulty in asserting supremacy over those actually in the Cabinet. In at least two early instances his colleagues outvoted him on matters close to his heart: on parliamentary reform in March 1784 and on his Irish proposals in July 1785.[2]

While opponents of the Fox–North Coalition recognised that they could form no government without him,[3] there was no clear definition of the extent of the power over his colleagues that this indispensability gave him. In particular, while Thurlow remained Lord Chancellor Pitt remained the leading Minister rather than Prime Minister, for the Chancellor enjoyed a privileged place in the confidence of the King. The Duke of Richmond thought the King's partiality to Thurlow 'so great and so decided, that his Majesty's confidence could not be obtained by any Ministry of which the Chancellor was not a part', and Pitt's supporters feared that 'the King's predilection is to Lord Thurlow, and if he could do without Pitt perhaps he would not scruple to sacrifice him'.[4] Even Pitt's ally, Grenville, admitted that the Chancellor possessed 'a commanding mind, of deep research, keen penetration, and extensive knowledge set forth beyond their real value by a vigorous and imposing eloquence'. Wraxall and the Sardinian envoy testified to his dominance over the House of Lords, and the King in 1789 wished Thurlow and Pitt to agree for they were 'both necessary to him, one in the Lords, the other in the Commons'.[5]

Thurlow shared many of the King's prejudices against reform causes endorsed by Pitt. They were temperamentally opposite: Pitt was cautious and cold in the generality of his personal relations, but warm, eager and impatient to progress business that had engaged his enthusiasm, whereas Thurlow was open and quick to overheat personally, but slow and anguished in business. Pitt and his friends shared North's verdict on Thurlow that 'in the Cabinet he opposed everything, – proposed nothing – and decided nothing'.[6] Even the King responded to Pitt's complaints that 'the good Chancellor is rather famous for loving delay', but, instead of the tolerance urged by the King, Pitt was soon bypassing Thurlow wherever possible on business matters, leading the Chancellor to complain of lack of consultation.[7] There were faults on both sides. If Pitt was contemptuous of Thurlow's slowness and anti-reform opinions, the Chancellor was disdainful of the way the self-publicised 'virtuous' First Lord of the Treasury tolerated the jobbery of his advisers and even pushed the limits of legality himself in some of his patronage and pension awards. After a period of uneasy co-operation relations deteriorated into hostility from 1788.[8]

Pitt could expect little support from the rest of the Cabinet against the powerful and obstructive Chancellor. At the Admiralty Lord Howe regarded his position as purely professional and avoided giving political opinions. When he resigned in 1788, Grenville asserted that Howe's department had never been connected with the rest of the administration 'even in the smallest degree'. The Lord President, Earl Gower, was an old friend of Thurlow. The main executive officers of government, the two secretaries of state, Lords Sydney and Carmarthen, were contemptuously described by their successor Grenville as 'unequal to the most ordinary business of their own offices'. Although they were reluctant volunteers in December 1783, Pitt felt too indebted for their self-sacrifice to force them out thereafter. Sydney shared Thurlow's hostility to parliamentary reform and the abolition of the slave trade, but, as the father-in-law of Pitt's older brother, he had to be treated with consideration. Pitt's biggest disappointment was the Duke of Richmond, a capable administrator with considerable military and diplomatic experience. After Rutland went to Ireland in March 1784, he was the only Cabinet member who fully shared Pitt's reforming views. Pitt was closer to Richmond than to any other member of the Cabinet in the first five years of the Ministry, frequently turning to the Duke for advice. Unfortunately he proved unreliable. Grenville described his judgement as 'capricious and visionary, fluctuating much with temporary impressions', yet often eagerly pressed to extremes.[9]

Consequently Pitt was soon making efforts to produce a more efficient administration, more obviously Whig to combat the charge of excessive royal influence, and incorporating more old landed wealth, which was important to the public acceptability of an eighteenth-century Cabinet. He tried unsuccessfully to persuade Richmond to replace Sydney as Home Secretary, the latter moving to Lord Privy Seal (vacated by Rutland). He then sought to entice the Duke of Grafton into the Cabinet in Sydney's place, and, when Grafton objected to the Home Office, tried to open the Foreign Office for him, but found the prickly Carmarthen unwilling to move before his foreign policy initiatives were set on course. Pitt's only success was to bring in his father's Lord Chancellor, Lord Camden, as Lord President of the Council at the end of 1784, with Gower switching to Lord Privy Seal (the former being rewarded with an earldom, the latter with elevation to Marquis of Stafford in 1786). Camden was undeniably Whig and a loyal family friend, but age and ill-health confined his contribution to prestige rather than energetic support.[10]

Pitt thus remained harnessed to a weak and indecisive cabinet. Richmond in 1784 lamented 'a want of confidential communication in the Cabinet, and . . . dilatory proceedings in some of the Departments'.

From Ireland Rutland wrote sympathetically in 1785 that 'I sat long enough in your Cabinet to be acquainted with the cavil and pertinacity of some of your colleagues' – this after being told of a Cabinet meeting where 'there was so much cavil, and such endless distinction upon trifles, that the hour of attending the House came before anything was decided'.[11] One substantial account of a Cabinet meeting on foreign policy in May 1787 survives to show Pitt far from dominant; indeed Thurlow and Richmond were the main speakers.[12] In these early years the government was largely one of separate departments. Several times in the mid-1780s Pitt was left struggling in the Commons to defend measures of other Ministers over which he had no control. On the Home Office's controversial London Police Bill in 1785, 'He professed himself not perfectly master of the subject, and therefore incapable of forming a competent judgement how far the provision now proposed to be applied, might be expected to effect the purpose.' Richmond's contentious programme to fortify the naval bases in 1786, and Howe's naval promotions of 1787, were other instances. These also revealed another vice of government by departments: the Admiralty objected to the fortifications programme and Howe allowed its members and their connections to vote against Richmond's project; in retaliation Ordnance Board members voted against an Admiralty regulation shortly afterwards and also against Howe's promotions.[13]

A former Treasury Secretary lamented in October 1785 the growing impression that 'Mr Pitt wants aid and assistance, and that many of the essential offices of Government are not filled with men of business, attention or abilities equal to the executive direction of them.'[14] Moreover Pitt's diffident handling of those outside his close circle of friends hindered his chances of getting the best out of them. Carmarthen later remembered Pitt as:

> uncommonly ungracious in his manner, tho' wishing to express civility and attention, frequently succeeds by an awkwardness which seems to possess the quintessence of sincerity unadulterated by any compliment of manners, which apparently assures attachment yet the pressure of the squeeze must soon resume its former level at the surface and the smile scarce returns upon the memory any other impression than its awkward distortion may afford.[15]

Pitt's reforming endeavours added to the Cabinet's disharmony. When Thurlow and Sydney stopped a bill to reform county elections in the Lords in 1785, he brought pressure on Sydney to allow it through in the following year, while the Chancellor was absent sick, provoking discontent in one and fury in the other. In 1786 Pitt joined the Opposition in voting for the impeachment of the arbitrary but capable ex-Governor General of India, Warren Hastings, who had the support of Thurlow (and the King). When in 1788 Thurlow and Sydney obstructed Dolben's bill to ameliorate conditions in the slave trade, Pitt cut short a visit to Cambridge and hastened to London, determined that if the Lords rejected the bill he would send it up from the Commons again. He told Grenville that 'If it fails then, the opposers of it and myself cannot continue members of the same Government, and I mean to state this distinctly to the Cabinet before the House meets tomorrow.' His colleagues again rejected the bill's drafting but resentfully backed down when Pitt returned a revised bill from the Commons.[16]

· · ·

THE ESCAPE FROM CABINET CONSTRAINTS

Pitt's reaction to these fundamental problems within the Cabinet was to turn elsewhere, to a small group of intimates and experts, for advice and consultation. This undoubtedly strengthened his own position through the abilities, information and facility to progress business that they provided. However it also exacerbated his Cabinet difficulties as Ministers sensed and resented that they were outside 'the secret', and as Pitt and his advisers began to interpose into areas of their responsibility.

The earliest member of this inner circle was Henry Dundas. His political skills in the Commons were vital to Pitt, whom he seconded in debate. During parliamentary sessions this gave him unique daily access to Pitt who, until 1789, had no Cabinet colleague in the Commons. Dundas's business abilities and experience rapidly gained him Pitt's confidence. A fellow Scot, Sir John Sinclair, wrote of him that 'I never met with any individual who could go through more business in a shorter time, or on whose judgement more confidence might be placed in any critical emergency', while even Pitt's fastidious friend, Wilberforce, admitted that he was 'a most excellent man of business . . . His diligence shames me!'[17] Dundas's particular interest in India soon gave him a predominant influence in the new India Board of Control, whose nominal head, Sydney, willingly abandoned its management to him.[18] But it was not just in managing the Commons, or Scotland or India that Dundas was useful to Pitt. If there was any dirty or unpleasant job to be done, Dundas was not afraid to take it on: he was Pitt's political 'fixer'. Pitt seems to have been captivated with the energy of this worldly-wise workaholic. They were both hard drinkers, both enjoyed a love of the countryside and they frequently indulged each of these at Dundas's Wimbledon villa. It was not long before Ministers were showing resentment at his influence. Visiting London in November 1784 the Irish Secretary detected 'hints of jealousy respecting Dundas, who is said to take possession of the Minister and to conduct him as he pleases'. Even the loyal Camden complained in 1789 that Pitt was too much under Dundas's influence. Memories of the unpopular Scottish Minister, the Earl of Bute, made his elevation a sensitive issue, particularly when he used his influence to promote fellow Scots, and there was some feeling that Dundas lacked the social status for Cabinet rank, all of which made the strength of their connection the more marked when Pitt made him Home Secretary in June 1791.[19] Fighting to keep him in charge of the management of the war in 1794, Pitt stressed 'the advantage of Dundas's turn for facilitating business, and of every act of his being as much *mine* as *his*'.[20]

Charles Jenkinson, the second of Pitt's 'men of business', was the one he would most have wished to avoid, for Jenkinson carried a reputation for intrigue as the arch-King's Friend, serving his royal master in almost every Ministry since 1762. Nevertheless the young First Lord of the Treasury soon found he needed Jenkinson's expertise in trade and finance. Appointed in 1784 to the Committee on Trade, Jenkinson soon dominated its proceedings, making vital contributions to Pitt's Irish Commercial Propositions and to commercial negotiations with France and other countries. In July 1786 he described himself as 'very much in Mr Pitt's confidence as he brings every question he can to the Committee of Council at which I preside and where I meet the Secretaries of State twice a week, sitting under me'. Pitt made him President of the Board of Trade in 1786, rewarding him with a peerage as Lord Hawkesbury and the lucrative sinecure Chancellorship of the Duchy of Lancaster. 'This, I think, will sound a little strange at a distance, and with reference to former ideas,' Pitt explained to his mother, 'but he has fairly earned it and attained it at my hands.'[21] Their relationship, however, remained a working one, for Hawkesbury, a cold bureaucrat, never became one of Pitt's intimate social circle. Although he no longer acted as political informant and adviser to the King, Pitt remained wary. In 1789 Hawkesbury complained that 'Mr Pitt goes on triumphantly and communicates with neither the Chancellor, the Duke of Leeds [Carmarthen] nor myself nor anyone with whom I have any connection with.'[22] It was not until 1791 that Pitt let him into the Cabinet, elevating him to Earl of Liverpool in 1796, but he took care to appoint members of his own close circle (Grenville, then Ryder) as Vice-Presidents at the Board of Trade. Liverpool's influence thus remained almost exclusively commercial, and *laissez-faire* enthusiasts such as Grenville saw his as a restraining hand on the Premier. He was responsible for the major re-codification of the Navigation Acts in 1786, reinforcing protections for British shipping, while, during the grain crisis of 1800, Grenville protested of Pitt's preference for a controlled market that 'We in truth formed our opinions on the subject together, and I was not more convinced than you were of the soundness of Adam Smith's principles of political oeconomy till Lord Liverpool lured you from our arms into all the mazes of the old system.'[23]

Robinson's description of Pitt's own entourage at the end of 1783 as 'Boys, Theoreticks and prejudiced persons' reveals his weakness on coming into power. Short of business experience himself, he lacked his own experienced confidential advisers to guide and support him. His cousin Temple and brother-in-law Mahon soon proved erratic and temperamental liabilities, so that Pitt was forced to turn to men such as Dundas and Jenkinson from North's Ministry until members of his own entourage gained experience and proved their business capacity. The first to do so, acquiring an influence only matched by Dundas, was Temple's brother, William Grenville. Family connections made him joint Paymaster of the Forces in 1784, but he was also appointed to the Indian Board of Control and the Committee of Trade. Pitt soon recognised his worth, recommending him to Rutland for Irish Secretary in 1785 because 'in temper and disposition he is much the reverse of his brother, and in good sense and habits of business very fit for such a situation'. Pitt quickly found, however, that he could utilise his cousin's talents himself, making him chair of the Commons committee examining the public finances in preparation for the Sinking Fund and working closely with him on the instructions for the commercial negotiations with France in 1785–6. Thereafter, when there was a difficult job to be done, Pitt looked to Grenville to do it, sending him as his personal emissary to Holland and France during the 1787 Dutch crisis, appointing him Speaker of the Commons when the incumbent died in the midst of the Regency Crisis, sending him to lead the Lords and manage Thurlow in 1790. Grenville's application to business, his grasp of detail and firmness in his opinions were great assets for Pitt, though the Premier found them double-edged at times. Sharing Pitt's love of the classics, his passion for landscape gardening and his eagerness to devour modern economic theory (they read Adam Smith together and were introduced to their *guru* by Dundas), they became the closest of friends and colleagues. Although differing over parliamentary reform and Hastings, Grenville strongly shared Pitt's antipathy to the slave trade. Only his brother Buckingham's dread of the cost of his re-election for the county, and Pitt's desire to ease out Sydney gently, stopped Pitt from making him Home Secretary until June 1789.[24] When he moved to the Foreign Office in 1791, an Under-Secretary described the cousins as 'two friends . . . so inseparably connected that there is but one sentiment between them', and the diplomat Lord Auckland considered that 'whatever is written to the one may be considered as written to the other'.[25]

Sustained in the late 1780s by these allies outside Cabinet, and employing Dundas and Grenville in particular as his 'hit men', Pitt extended his influence into areas of administration beyond the Treasury. India and Scottish patronage passed from Sydney to Dundas. The Home Secretary's control of Ireland too was bypassed by Pitt's direct correspondence with the Lord Lieutenant, his friend Rutland, after whose death in 1787 Grenville continued the correspondence with his successor, Buckingham. In 1786 Orde found Sydney 'little consulted or regarded in his department, and I have reason to believe him to be often rather indignant at the neglect with which he is treated'.[26] In that year both Sydney and Carmarthen contemplated resignation because of brusque treatment from an increasingly assertive Pitt, but the first Cabinet Minister to resign was Lord Howe, after Pitt established close co-operation with the reforming Comptroller of the Navy, Sir Charles Middleton. Pitt pressured Howe into leaving Middleton in his post, contrary to precedent, on being promoted to admiral in 1787. Howe simmered at his loss of face within the navy for nearly a year before going in July 1788. Pitt thereupon seized the opportunity to extend his control over the administration by recommending to the King the appointment of his brother the Earl of Chatham. 'I feel the arrangement is liable to some invidious objections,' he told Wilberforce, 'but I am satisfied they are more than counterbalanced by the solid advantage of establishing a compleat concert with so essential a department, and removing all appearance of a separate interest.'[27]

Pitt further extended his Cabinet influence when Grenville replaced Sydney in the following year, and Dundas was added two years later. This engrossment of power was resented by Ministers outside Pitt's inner circle. Richmond complained angrily at the lack of prior consultation when Grenville was given a peerage and leadership of the Lords in November 1790, warning that: 'this country will not be satisfied to see you two younger brothers take the lead of the two Houses of Parliament, and by yourselves govern the country'. It was not right 'that your colleagues of the Cabinet should never hear of what is doing in these respects till the things were done. Those with whom I have formerly been connected in politics and in friendship used to treat me with more attention.' He blamed Pitt for 'an idleness in your disposition that too often makes you neglect to cultivate the friendship of those who are most attached to you, and which makes you expose your judgement to be biased by the opinion of the narrow circle to whom you confine your intimacy'. Feeling his own influence with Pitt waning, Richmond increasingly absented himself from Cabinet meetings. Thurlow grumbled that the want of confidence between members of the same administration was 'not only unpleasant to individuals but injurious to the general interests of the Govt'. Similarly Carmarthen (since 1789 Duke of Leeds) felt this neglect at the same time as he experienced Pitt's growing intervention in his business. When this was followed by Pitt's withdrawal of his ultimatum to Russia, Leeds resigned in April 1791.[28]

. . .

SECURING THE PREMIERSHIP: PITT VERSUS THURLOW

Between 1788 and 1791 Pitt made a deliberate effort to gain control of the Cabinet, but, so long as Thurlow remained, his success was incomplete, and the Chancellor reacted belligerently. Backed by the King and the ablest lawyers of the day, particularly Sir Lloyd Kenyon (Master of the Rolls, 1784) and John Scott (Solicitor-General, 1788), he was regarded as untouchable. Indeed a major problem for Pitt was the lack of any alternative to the Chancellor except the Opposition's leading lawyer, Lord Loughborough.[29] Thurlow's dominance over the House of Lords, the weight of his legal opinion on bills and international treaties and the need for his Great Seal on patents of appointment gave him abundant opportunity to be obstructive. Pitt's main problem in domestic government until 1792 was not that the King actively sought to impose his own policies as Pitt had originally feared, but that, by maintaining Thurlow in the Ministry, the King effectively restricted Pitt's ability to implement his own policies.

From 1788 Thurlow and Pitt engaged in open conflict. The breach was occasioned by perceived provocation on both sides. Pitt was irritated by Thurlow's leadership of the Lords' opposition to Dolben's slave trade bill. Thurlow was irritated by two unilateral patronage decisions of Pitt which infringed his territory. When in July Kenyon became Lord Chief Justice, Pitt seized the opportunity to promote his lightweight friend, the Attorney-General, Pepper Arden, to the vacated Mastership of the Rolls. Thurlow had resented Arden's earlier advancement and now delayed sealing the patent. Pitt had anticipated trouble, truculently telling Arden that 'I may just as well quarrel on that as on any other subject with him'.[30] He forced his point in an interview which, 'though not fully satisfactory', at least removed the obstacle.[31] However, the real running sore was the succession of the Treasury Secretary, George Rose, to the House of Lords post of Clerk of the Parliaments. Rose wished to add it to his collection of sinecures performed by deputy and also to obtain its reversion for his son. Thurlow thought the post should be an active one, and though he lost out to Pitt's assertion of his Treasury assistant's right to the office, the Chancellor did stop the grant of its reversion.[32]

The consequences of this breach were soon experienced in Thurlow's independent conduct during the Regency Crisis. His position as Lord Chancellor allowed him direct access to the Prince of Wales, and the possibility existed that he would throw his considerable weight behind the Prince's claims to a powerful Regency in return for keeping his place. Pitt knew he was talking to the Opposition and, according to Wilberforce, right up to the moment when the Chancellor rose to speak in the Lords, Pitt did not know whether he would support or oppose him. The Opposition, however, opted for their own man Loughborough as Chancellor-elect, and Thurlow's famous declaration, 'When I forget my King, may my God forget me', both saved Pitt's bill and strengthened the Chancellor's public reputation.[33]

When the King recovered, he pleaded his need for cordiality between the two. But there was a new flare-up in 1789, when Pitt sacked the Counsel for the Treasury, Thurlow's friend Francis Hargrave, for his pamphlet challenging the law in the Regency Bill. Thurlow retaliated by questioning the legality of a pension which Pitt intended to confer on Lord Auckland. Again the King sought reconciliation by suggesting that Kenyon, whom both trusted, adjudicate the pension issue (he confirmed Thurlow's opinion). Relations were patched up, although Camden warned that it was merely a hollow truce, not a peace, for they had no confidence in each other. So it proved as Thurlow held up the passage of Pitt's Tobacco Excise Bill through the Lords with objections to its drafting. The Chancellor was reported as giving frequent dinners to the judges to woo them to his side, and, in October–November 1790, hostilities resumed when Dundas got the better of the Chancellor on a Scottish patronage matter. Thurlow threatened to suspend all co-operation in the Lords. It took more pressure from the King and a visit by Dundas to the Chancellor to clear the air, though Thurlow warned that, while the Rose issue remained, no real cordiality could take place.[34]

Strengthened by the general election result and his foreign policy triumph over Spain in 1790, Pitt consequently prepared to force matters to a decisive conclusion. Grenville was sent to take the leadership of the Lords and counter Thurlow's dominance. The Duke of Grafton was again invited to join the Cabinet as a prestigious Whig counterweight.[35] And Pitt worked to improve relations with the Opposition, defending the right of the new House of Commons to continue the impeachment of Hastings, which 'dulcified' their spokesman Burke. In March 1791 Grenville approached his Foxite brother Tom on the possibility of the Opposition Whigs joining government with three Cabinet posts (those of Leeds, Stafford and Camden) put on offer. The intention almost certainly was to secure the strongest possible position from which to force a final showdown with the Chancellor. However, this coup, if such it was, was frustrated by the Opposition's insistence that Pitt must surrender the headship of the Treasury, and overtaken by the outcry against Pitt's Russian Armament in which Grafton joined and in which the Opposition saw a chance to overthrow the ministry.[36]

The actual Cabinet reshuffle was consequently more limited. Pitt strengthened his position by bringing in two more of his advisers, Dundas and Hawkesbury (though the latter was also a friend of Thurlow). The Chancellor, rightly, was 'convinced Pitt meant to get rid of him as soon as he could make up his mind on a successor', and continued to complain of lack of consultation, accusing Pitt of summoning Cabinet meetings at times when the Court of Chancery was in session. He only heard of Grenville's transfer to Foreign Secretary through reading the foreign envoys' replies to a government circular. Grenville's efforts at conciliation catastrophically failed when Thurlow exploded on being summoned to seal the Duke of York's marriage contract with the Princess of Prussia without prior consultation (everyone assumed the King had told him). In the Lords he delayed bills approved by Pitt to ease restrictions on English Catholics and for juries rather than judges to decide libel suits, abusing Grenville for giving 'the silliest of reasons for going on with the silliest of Bills'. By the end of 1791 Grenville abandoned hope of managing him and left events to take their course.[37]

However Pitt and his cousin were not strongly placed to force the King's partialities. Pitt's battering over the Russian Armament left him hesitant to push delicate issues and Grenville was under criticism for taking a fat sinecure at this time (Thurlow also challenged the legality of Pitt granting it for life).[38] Pitt still lacked a satisfactory replacement for the Chancellor. Such considerations helped produce a renewal of the efforts to woo over the more moderate part of the Opposition, including their legal heavyweight Lord Loughborough, when they differed from Fox over the French Revolution and new demands for domestic reform. Pitt withheld highly damaging evidence of Opposition contacts with the Empress of Russia when debate resumed on the Russian crisis in April 1792, and on 1 May he authorised Auckland to approach his former

Grenville = Pitts cousin

colleague, Loughborough, for concerted action on the domestic unrest. These preparations were forestalled by Thurlow himself in May. Successfully obstructing in the Lords an anti-slave trade bill on which Pitt had just delivered one of his greatest speeches, he then assailed Pitt's cherished Sinking Fund provisions in the National Debt Bill and carried enough government supporters with him to bring the measure within six votes of defeat. But this time he overreached himself by directly attacking a measure in Pitt's own department. Pitt now had sufficient justification to force the issue with the King and, ignoring royal pleas for further reconciliation, he insisted that either he or Thurlow would have to go. Cornered, the King agonised but at last gave way: it was 'revolting to his feelings', nevertheless 'The Chancellor's own penetration must convince him that however strong my personal regard, nay affection, is for him, that I must feel the removal of Mr Pitt impossible with the good of my service.' Thurlow expressed surprise that the King let him go so easily but added that 'As to that other man, he has done to me just what I should have done to him, if I could.'[39]

Pitt's friend Rutland once warned that only three things could bring him down: the King's death, an unsuccessful war or a breach with Thurlow.[40] Pitt worked quickly to avert this fatal result. He saw Thurlow's key legal followers, Kenyon and Scott, individually to justify his ultimatum.[41] Thurlow, consoled by the King with the reversion of his peerage to his nephews, magnanimously urged his friends to continue in office, though neither would take the vacant Chancellorship which had to be put into commission until a candidate could be found. This was still Pitt's biggest weakness and Thurlow's greatest strength. Dundas pressed his fellow Scot and former colleague Loughborough in favour of union, offering four Cabinet places (Chancellor, Home Secretary, Lord President and Privy Seal), two or three privy councillors and the Lord Lieutenancy of Ireland, and ultimately throwing in the Governor-Generalship of India too.[42] Fox, however, was still able to invoke Opposition suspicions that Pitt would never admit him to Cabinet on the equal terms necessary to satisfy their honour and pride. He even raised the alternative possibility of forming a new administration with the ex-Chancellor from which Pitt might be excluded! In fact Pitt, in his anxiety to achieve his ends, had far exceeded the King's authorisation of 'Anything Complimentary to them, but no Power'. When he and Dundas met Loughborough in mid-June 1792, Pitt had to admit that the approach was not at the King's command, though he undertook to secure the approval of both the King and Queen. When pressed to include Fox also, Pitt confessed that he had thought the split within the Opposition was more complete. He denied any personal objections, but feared that the King's hostility to Fox's pro-French conduct would prevent him acquiring the Foreign Office immediately. Pitt must have known this was a post too far. When they met again, he excused himself by asserting that hostility within ministerial circles precluded Fox's inclusion. This effectively halted discussions, though in July Pitt tried to revive them with an offer of the Garter to the Opposition leader, the Duke of Portland.[43]

The Opposition outsmarted him, however, by making a direct approach to the King via the late Foreign Secretary, the Duke of Leeds, who might head a coalition government based on equality between Pitt (who should resign the Treasury and be a Secretary of State) and themselves. The King was unpleasantly surprised to learn what had been happening behind his back, and Pitt (who had just received the Wardenship of the Cinque Ports from the King) was acutely embarrassed and forced to deny that any 'new arrangement, either by change or coalition, had ever been in contemplation'.[44] The monarch vented his ire on Dundas in October by refusing to make him a governor of the Charterhouse – George alleged insufficient social status, but Dundas's part in pressing the negotiations was well known. This royal rebuff drew from Pitt an admission of the extent of his setback, confessing to his colleague 'how impossible it is, either for you or me *circumstanced as we are*, to indulge any sentiment of discontent'. It took an abject letter from Dundas to persuade the King to relent.[45] The uncertainty was only finally resolved when in November domestic and external crises, the latter with Revolutionary France, adventitiously came to Pitt's assistance to distract the King. It also provided Loughborough with the excuse to desert the Opposition and become Lord Chancellor, with the King's reluctant consent, in January 1793. Only then could Pitt be sure of his victory over Thurlow.

. . .

COALITION AND CONTAINMENT
OF THE PORTLAND WHIGS

The Prime Minister's Cabinet problems were still far from over, however, for the outbreak of war in February 1793 revealed further weaknesses. Pitt brought the veteran Lord Amherst into the Cabinet in the post of Commander in Chief of the army which he had held during the American War, but his experience was counteracted by age and failing eyesight and he proved barely up to his administrative duties. Military direction of the war remained in the hands of Dundas in consultation with Pitt, but Richmond fundamentally disagreed with their strategy. Richmond at the Ordnance and Chatham at the Admiralty were widely blamed for the failure of the attack on Dunkirk in September, and when Richmond then appeared to obstruct preparations for a West Indian expedition Pitt found it necessary to bring him into line with a sharp warning that, 'at a Time when cordiality and dispatch are so necessary in the intercourse between different departments of Government, the King's Service in what relates to the Ordnance can no longer be continued with advantage on its present Footing'.[46] Pitt was now dominant over the Ministry and less prepared to tolerate the problems of government by departments.

His Cabinet, however, was in need of major replenishment. Stafford and Camden had grown old, and the latter died in April 1794. Pitt's inner circle, which dominated the efficient Cabinet posts, lacked the social standing to sustain the Ministry by themselves. Richmond had questioned how long the country would tolerate a government of younger sons and considered that 'high rank and more fortune and dignity' were required to lead the Lords, while another government supporter, Lord Chesterfield, feared in 1792 that 'we cannot go on well unless we have some acres to add to our abilities'.[47] Only the frequently absent Richmond and the elderly Stafford had large acres. Carmarthen had acquired them as Duke of Leeds, but resigned in 1791. Camden and Chatham had small estates, and Hawkesbury still less. Pitt, Grenville and Dundas were all younger sons. Pitt scraped together enough money to purchase a country villa in Kent in 1785, but he remained plagued by financial difficulty which was only partly eased when he accepted the Wardenship of the Cinque Ports. Grenville's desperation to secure the means to sustain his new peerage and enable him to marry Lord Camelford's daughter had led him to risk major embarrassment to Pitt by seeking successive sinecures until he acquired the plum Auditorship of the Exchequer in 1794. The King himself questioned the social standing of Dundas over the governorship of the Charterhouse. There was a public expectation that the government of the country should be chiefly composed of those who owned large amounts of it.

These concerns, as well as a desire to create a government of patriotic unity to carry on the war, led Pitt to try to lure over individuals from the Opposition in 1793, and in 1794 to reopen negotiations for a coalition with Portland's conservative wing of the Opposition, which had now clearly broken with Fox. This time he discarded the use of intermediaries and negotiated directly with Portland himself. The meeting of these two reserved men in May 1794 was a success. They found common ground on the need to expel the spirit of Jacobinism, though to clinch the junction Pitt had to raise his offer from three Cabinet posts, the Irish Lord Lieutenancy and the promise of first call on future Cabinet vacancies, to five Cabinet seats immediately, one to move to Lord Lieutenant of

Ireland when that became available. He also sacrificed his desire to make Hawkesbury Lord President, and accepted in principle the Portland group's desire to make the restoration of the French Monarchy a war aim. However he ensured that he, Dundas and Grenville remained in control of most of the major active offices of state, and in particular of the management of the war. He had to offer one Secretaryship of State to Portland, but did so by separating the functions of the Home Office into a Home Secretary for domestic and Irish affairs and ultimately, to satisfy Portland, the colonies and their patronage, and a Secretary of State for War. Dundas initially refused to take this last diminished office, which he claimed was redundant since Pitt as Finance Minister was the real war minister, and Pitt had to muster every resource of persuasion to get him to agree, eventually turning to the King to ask him personally to accept the post and rushing the letter to Wimbledon himself, where, confronted with the King's wishes and the Premier's agitated state, Dundas at last agreed.[48]

On 11 July 1794 the junction was finally confirmed, with Portland as Home Secretary, Earl Fitzwilliam as Lord President, with the promise of the Irish Lord Lieutenancy, Earl Spencer as Privy Seal, William Windham as Secretary at War, and the Earl of Mansfield as Minister without Portfolio, together with a raft of lesser offices and honours for their followers. Pitt at last had the Ministry of 'so clear a Whig complexion' that he always desired. His supporters wondered if he had given away too much of his hold on power, and their hopes of office and honours, in order to obtain it. Including Loughborough, there were now six members of the former Opposition in the restructured thirteen-strong Cabinet. When Addington asked if Pitt was not afraid of being outvoted in own Cabinet he replied, characteristically, that 'he was under no anxiety on that count, since he placed much dependence on his new colleagues, and still more on himself'.[49]

Pitt's optimism was soon tested. The Portland Whigs had made the government of Ireland an essential condition of their coalition with Pitt. They planned key changes of officials to break the hold of the junto who ran Ireland for Pitt. Their intended Lord Lieutenant, Fitzwilliam, always suspicious that Pitt was double-dealing, became impatient when the end of the year approached with no sign of Pitt finding an alternative post for his Lord Lieutenant, Westmorland.[50] In October Pitt's new allies suddenly presented an ultimatum threatening their mass resignation if Fitzwilliam was not immediately appointed.[51]

Mindful of the events of July and 'the yielding nature of your temper when you are anxious upon a subject', Dundas pressed Pitt to be firm, but Pitt had already seen the necessity of rising to the challenge. While ready to fulfil his side of the bargain, he insisted that Fitzwilliam could not be appointed before a suitable alternative was found for Westmorland, that Irish business must remain subject to the approval of the whole Cabinet, and that there should be no new system in Ireland and no massacre of his Irish supporters.[52] Neither side in fact wanted a breach, so a compromise was arranged in discussions between Pitt and Fitzwilliam, on 11 November, culminating in a meeting on the 15th of Pitt and Grenville with Fitzwilliam, Portland, Spencer and Windham. A court post was found for Westmorland, enabling Fitzwilliam to take the Lord Lieutenancy. In return Fitzwilliam renounced his rumoured intention to remove the Irish Chancellor, and it was accepted that any change of personnel should be gradual. They also agreed that no further measures of Catholic relief should be proposed by government.[53]

This revived spirit of co-operation led Pitt to risk the sacrifice of three more of his own ministers in the interests of the better management of the war. His new allies made little secret of their discontent with Chatham's handling of the Admiralty and Richmond's absence from the Cabinet for whose decisions he was supposed to share responsibility. In December Pitt steeled himself to demand that his brother exchange posts with the Privy Seal, Earl Spencer, again asking the King to smooth the way by urging Chatham's acceptance. He evaded Richmond's offer to resume attendance and, once another military expert, Lord Cornwallis, was persuaded to replace him, he requested the Duke's resignation at the end of January 1795. Richmond's departure left Pitt the sole survivor from the 1784 cabinet. At the same time the flagging Lord Amherst was persuaded to resign, leaving the office of Commander in Chief to the Duke of York outside the Cabinet.[54]

Even as Pitt completed this reshuffle, however, crisis re-erupted over Ireland. Fitzwilliam quickly persuaded himself of the gravity of the Irish situation, and, convinced by his Irish allies that nothing could be done without major changes, he abruptly removed five leading officials including the influential head of the Customs, Beresford. He also appointed one of his allies directly to the premier law-officer post of Attorney-General in defiance of the 15 November agreement.

Preoccupied with his Cabinet changes, the sudden collapse of Holland to French attack and the opening of the new parliamentary session, Pitt was slow to react. It was Grenville who responded first, on 28 January, by reminding Fitzwilliam of his earlier promises. He also expressed his concern to Portland. Next day the King told Pitt of his concern at the change of system, and quickly became still more alarmed when the Lord Lieutenant recommended allowing the passage of a Private Member's Catholic relief bill through the Irish Parliament. A long royal memorandum, fraught with future significance for Pitt, declared that Catholic Emancipation was:

> beyond the decision of any Cabinet of Ministers – that, could they form an opinion in favour of such a measure, it would be highly dangerous, without previous concert with the leading men of every order in the State, to send any encouragement to the Lord Lieutenant on this subject.

Rather change the new Irish administration, urged the King, than see it ruin one, if not both, kingdoms. Pitt's reply showed how far immediate business had made him inattentive to what was happening in Ireland, begging leave to submit to the King 'what may present itself to his mind on the subject on more mature reflection than he has had the opportunity of giving it at this moment'.[55] It was not until 9 February that Pitt told Fitzwilliam that his changes of personnel were unacceptable since they far exceeded the original agreement. The touchy Fitzwilliam responded at once with a 'back me or sack me' letter. He claimed to have told Pitt privately of his intention to remove Beresford, also that Pitt himself had admitted that the government might be forced to accept Catholic relief by popular demand, and he declared the impossibility of stopping the measure going forward.[56]

Fortunately Pitt was saved from crisis with the King, or breach with his new allies, by the actions of their leader, the Duke of Portland, who himself decided that Fitzwilliam had gone too far too fast, and recommended to the Cabinet on 21 February that he be recalled. Quite unexpectedly the crisis welded the new allies into the Ministry. Rather than acting as a group in support of their colleague, as in October, those in the Cabinet backed Portland against Fitzwilliam, and the latter's furious response, attacking them for treachery and Pitt for deceit, drove them into Pitt's arms. Pitt sought to ease Portland's agony over the breach by allowing Fitzwilliam to resume his Cabinet seat on his return, but the humiliated Lord Lieutenant refused. He had been the most hostile to Pitt, and the most zealous for the former Opposition members to continue to act together as a party, so that his withdrawal greatly facilitated cordiality within the new coalition.

The Fitzwilliam episode demonstrates both weaknesses and strengths in Pitt's mode of leadership. That Fitzwilliam believed he was abiding by the November agreement reveals the dangers of the Premier's informal business methods. Fitzwilliam made brief notes of the 15 November meeting which he showed Pitt afterwards, and Grenville also appears to have made notes from which he hurriedly drew up an *aide-mémoire* for his colleagues in the following March, but Pitt failed to have official minutes taken and approved by all present. Fitzwilliam believed he had authorisation to go ahead, whereas those in London felt that stress had been put on the need for consultation. Pitt could recollect no mention of Beresford. His alleged words on Catholic relief ring true, though Pitt was certainly thinking long term since he agreed with Portland's wish to postpone consideration till after the end of the war. Pitt's other preoccupations meant that he failed to spot the crisis coming, either in October or in January, but he had a loyal supporter in Grenville, alert enough to act in his stead. Yet again he was remarkably lucky in the way that events unfolded, emerging so well because his new allies dissociated themselves from Fitzwilliam's actions.

Between 1788 and 1795 the composition of the Cabinet changed completely. With Thurlow's fall in 1792, Pitt had acquired an exclusive dominance, but not on a durable base. To secure durability he had been prepared to risk his dominance by coalition with the Portland Whigs. It was a gamble which came off when Fitzwilliam's impulsiveness broke their solidarity. Thereafter, except when they combined in the following July to persuade Pitt to prepare a massive follow-up to the initially successful French royalist landing at Quiberon (to the horror of the absent Dundas), Pitt's new allies failed to act as a united pressure group within the Cabinet. The disastrous collapse of the Quiberon operation left only Windham to persist in the fervently monarchist stance they had pressed upon Pitt during the 1794 coalition negotiations. The Premier was able to persuade the others of the need to negotiate with the French Republic. He was even able to reclaim the government of Ireland when none of them was willing to succeed Fitzwilliam, installing his old friend Pratt, now 2nd Earl Camden. When Mansfield died in 1796, Pitt used the opportunity to reconcile his aggrieved brother by promoting him to Lord President of the Council. He left the Privy Seal vacated by Chatham open for future needs, finally offering it to Westmorland in 1798, as the last instalment of his compensation for leaving Ireland in 1794. The final addition to his Cabinet was Camden, when Cornwallis replaced him as Lord Lieutenant of Ireland in June 1798. At that point the former Opposition members had shrunk to four (including Loughborough) in a twelve-man Cabinet.

· · ·

THE ZENITH OF PITT'S PRIME MINISTERIAL SYSTEM

The result was to leave Pitt, backed by Grenville and Dundas, firmly in control of the Cabinet and the direction of war policy. In these circumstances the informality which had bedevilled the Fitzwilliam episode was more to Pitt's advantage. The inner triumvirate met in advance of Cabinet meetings to co-ordinate a common line because, as Grenville declared, 'before we summon our numerous Cabinet, it is much better that those who are to execute should understand each other upon the subject'.[57] By settling their differences in advance and acting as a united front who knew what they wanted, they were able to exploit the looseness of Cabinet procedures. Windham complained unavailingly in 1799 that meetings were called without previous notice of questions to be discussed, no formal record was kept to which Ministers could refer, and too often matters were discussed in a piecemeal fashion out of which overall policy emerged without any formal decision being taken, so that he never knew at what point he was to express his opposition.[58] The real decisions were made by Pitt and his men of business outside the Cabinet, which then discussed their prearranged agenda and left them to interpret for themselves what the meeting had decided. When other Ministers roused their colleagues to question what was being done, as Chatham did on strategic policy in March 1800, the result was another meeting of the triumvirate for a discussion next day at 11 o'clock before the Cabinet met at mid-day, and no alteration until Dundas for other reasons resolved to change course ten days later. Only when differences emerged within the inner circle did the rest of the Cabinet play a significant part in resolving policy.[59]

Pitt's remaining major Cabinet problems consequently resulted from disagreements among the inner three, and particularly when he differed from his obstinate cousin over foreign policy. In February 1795 Grenville opposed Pitt's desire for a new subsidy treaty with Prussia to recover Holland because it would jeopardise their attempt to create a Triple Alliance of Britain, Austria and Russia. When a meeting of the triumvirate failed to agree, Pitt took his proposals to the Cabinet. Grenville offered to resign at a time of Pitt's choosing if the result took the shape 'which I will fairly say with your decided opinion on the subject I think it ought'. Pitt, 'miserable' at the prospect, spent an hour before the Cabinet on 1 March trying to change his mind. When the meeting decided 6–5 in Pitt's favour, the Premier held out the possibility of a subsequent meeting reversing the decision, of another Secretary of State signing the instructions, and at the very least urged Grenville to avoid an '*éclat*' at that delicate time and defer his departure till near the end of the parliamentary session. At the same time Pitt sought royal backing, by playing on the King's concern for Hanover, in order to clinch his Cabinet majority, and on the 8th he obtained advanced royal approval of the minute he intended to put to Cabinet. Uncertain news from the continent, however, delayed the decision for another month. Then, urged on by the now enthusiastic King, the whole Cabinet except Grenville agreed to Pitt's proposal. Grenville fought to the end and then had his dissent officially recorded on the Cabinet minute. Perhaps this unusual formula (apparently used here for the first time) was devised by Pitt to avoid his cousin resigning, since this was no longer mentioned, but in any case the Prussians made peace before the instructions, signed by Dundas, could be delivered.[60]

The two cousins' second clash, in the spring of 1797, was more serious and brought them close to breaking their friendship. Convinced of the need for peace, Pitt resolved on a direct approach to France, whereas Grenville believed that peace could only be had at the cost of national humiliation and concessions which would leave Britain without safety or honour. For three weeks in May he managed to keep Pitt from bringing their disagreement to Cabinet for resolution, but over two stormy meetings on 31 May/1 June Pitt got his colleagues to agree to an overture. The French reply, insisting on negotiations separate from Britain's allies, led Grenville to demand a high-toned response. A Cabinet on 14 June saw 'violent disputes', after which Pitt went behind his Foreign Secretary's back and consulted with the Under-Secretary, his own protégé Canning, about altering Grenville's draft. Next morning the Cabinet met again with 'more violence'. It was narrowly inclining to Pitt (with all the Portland Whigs backing Grenville), when the hesitant Liverpool finally backed Pitt and gave him a clearer 6–4 majority. Before discussion resumed in the evening, Pitt drew up his alternative reply. Grenville was faced with consenting to something he disapproved or jeopardising the Ministry by resigning at a dangerous moment. He realised which way the discussion would go, but in contrast with another opponent, Windham, who stayed away, Grenville fought all the way in a Cabinet which continued past midnight. 'Great violence. Ld. G. nearly going out,' noted Canning. But Pitt stood firm, and again a minute was sent to the King with Grenville's dissent recorded on it. Again Pitt depended on the King's approval to secure his victory, and by dint of a cleverly worded letter won the King's consent. When the next French answer was received, Grenville's proposed reply was again rejected by Pitt at a Cabinet on the 24th. 'Great violence,' recorded Canning again, adding that Grenville in fact stormed out of the meeting. Again Pitt held his ground, produced his own note and before the next day's Cabinet told Grenville that he must cease his opposition or resign. Grenville conceded, provided he had some certainty of a stand somewhere. Canning exulted that Pitt 'has exerted himself, and is really master now'.[61]

This mastery was severely tested in the negotiations that followed, but Pitt now knew that his will was stronger than that of his cousin: 'collateral difficulties', he told his envoy Malmesbury, 'may I think, always be overcome by a mixture of firmness and temper'.[62] He briefed Malmesbury privately before the negotiation and maintained a correspondence with him throughout. Canning was used to keep watch on what Grenville wrote, and to ensure that Pitt remained the best informed on all aspects of the negotiation, but it was all to no avail when a coup in Paris in September resulted in the French breaking off the talks and ordering Malmesbury home. The failure of the negotiations at least enabled Pitt and Grenville to resume their close relationship again.

For Pitt, the Cabinet was never an effective instrument of government. It was there as a showcase of the political support around him, and in its composition he sought to make a statement of the preponderant Whig values of his Ministry. He found its unanimity (when achievable) a useful weapon for influencing the King. Except at the very beginning, when he could not avoid taking in some of the King's following, and again when he accepted Portland's nominees in their junction in 1794, he ensured that his was the sole recommendation of ministerial appointments. Some changes he discussed with Grenville (the succession to Howe in 1788 and Sydney in 1789) or with Dundas (the replacement of Chatham by Spencer in 1794). Grenville was also involved in the negotiations with the Opposition in 1791 and Dundas in 1792, but he conducted the final successful negotiation in 1794 entirely alone. Usually the first time his Cabinet colleagues heard of a new member was when they received his letter announcing it. Even Dundas admitted having had no inkling of Westmorland's appointment in 1798.[63] The only person who had always to be consulted in advance was the King, and sometimes Pitt additionally sought his assistance to persuade reluctant Ministers to move, as with Dundas, Mansfield and Chatham in 1794, though reportedly the King refused to press Liverpool in 1796.[64] Besides considerations of social rank and political following, he looked to include someone of military experience (Richmond, Amherst, Cornwallis) as a professional adviser. He further used membership as an honorific retreat for faithful servants removed from high office elsewhere (Westmorland and Camden, both recompensed for their sacrifice in Ireland). However while the unreliability of his ministerial colleagues of the 1780s led him to insert his own men of business (Grenville, Dundas, Hawkesbury) into the effective offices of state, he still largely made policy with them outside the Cabinet, and he was also prepared to leave Cabinet seats unfilled, as with the Privy Seal (March to November 1784, September 1796 to February 1798), for use in future political arrangements. Where possible he sought to control the timing of Cabinet changes to points outside or towards the close of the parliamentary session. Only Howe and Leeds left against his choosing, and he managed to delay the former's departure until the parliamentary vacation to avoid *éclat*.

There remained limitations in his increasing dominance over the Cabinet. Where he lacked his own separate contacts within departments, he remained uninformed and powerless. Lady Elliot heard in 1796 that he knew nothing of what passed in the Duke of Portland's office.[65] On policy issues within departments, he, or his allies Dundas and Grenville, could suggest and occasionally cajole, but Pitt could not *order* a Cabinet Minister to do anything. Only a decision of the whole Cabinet could compel that. Pitt indeed was handicapped by his unwillingness to force out redundant Ministers. Sydney, Carmarthen and Richmond were allowed to continue far beyond their useful term of office, the latter even despite many years' non-attendance at Cabinet. Nor could he bring himself to drop Dundas or Grenville when the two fell apart in 1800. Ministers who refused to co-operate in his projected reshuffles were equally allowed to remain where they were: Carmarthen in 1784; Liverpool who in 1796 would not vacate the Duchy of Lancaster; Windham who rejected Master of the Mint in 1799 and Treasurer of the Navy in 1800.[66] That Pitt allowed them to remain reflects in part his dislike of unpleasant personal confrontations. He ignored repeated appeals from Richmond and procrastinated for six weeks in 1795, eventually informing him of his dismissal by letter. But to some extent this also indicates his low esteem of the role of the Cabinet. Its support was necessary to him, and he fought hard when threats emerged from within it, but he always looked to it to be reactive and not proactive, and he preferred to do his real business outside its meetings.

. . .

NOTES AND REFERENCES

1 Aspinall and Smith (eds), *Eng. Hist. Docs*, vol. 11, p. 125.
2 A.G. Olson, *The Radical Duke* (Oxford, 1961), p. 232; Stanhope, *Pitt*, vol. 1, p. iii; L.S. Olschki (ed.), *La Relation du Marquis de Cordon* (Florence, 1932), p. 34; Ehrman, *Pitt*, vol. 1, p. 133; Browning (ed.), *Leeds Memoranda*, p. 99; HMC, *Rutland*, vol. 3, p. 231.
3 BL Loan, 72/29, Robinson to Jenkinson, 8 March 1783; Add. MSS, 69,143, f. 39 (Minute by Thomas Pitt, 28 March 1783).
4 Russell (ed.), *Memorials of Fox*, vol. 2, p. 236; HMC, *Rutland*, vol. 3, pp. 143, 321.

5 Add. MSS, 69,139, pp. 4–5 (Grenville); R.I. and S. Wilberforce, *Life*, vol. 1, p. 233; Wheatley (ed.), *Wraxall*, vol. 3, p. 201; Olschki (ed.), *Relation du Cordon*, p. 34. See also G.M. Ditchfield, 'Lord Thurlow', in R.W. Davis (ed.), *Lords of Parliament* (Stanford, 1995), pp. 64–78.

6 K. Garlick and A. Macintyre (eds.), *The Diary of Joseph Farington* (16 vols, 1978–84: vols. 7–16 ed. by K. Cave), vol. 3, p. 712; Add. MSS, 69,139, p. 5.

7 Stanhope, *Pitt*, vol. 1, p. xvii; HMC, *Fortescue*, vol. 2, p. 12; HMC, *Abergavenny*, p. 63.

8 Add. MSS, 69,139, ff. 5–6; HMC, *Rutland*, vol. 6, p. 159 for Thurlow's views on Dundas.

9 Add. MSS, 69,139, ff. 3v–4; Olschki (ed.), *Relation du Cordon*, pp. 33–4; *C.C.GIII*, vol. 1, pp. 370, 385.

10 Browning (ed.), *Leeds Memoranda*, pp. 102, 104–5; Anson (ed.), *Grafton*, pp. 392–4.

11 Browning (ed.), *Leeds Memoranda*, p. 102; HMC, *Rutland*, vol. 3, pp. 195, 224.

12 Malmesbury (ed.), *Diaries*, vol. 2, pp. 303–6.

13 HMC, *Rutland*, vol. 3, p. 301.

14 BL Loan, 72/29, Robinson to Jenkinson, 27 Oct. 1785.

15 Add. MSS, 27,916, f. 62.

16 HMC, *Rutland*, vol. 3, p. 319; HMC, *Fortescue*, vol. 1, p. 342; Add. MSS, 38,223, f. 96.

17 Wheatley (ed.), *Wraxall*, vol. 4, p. 10; J. Sinclair, *The Correspondence of the Rt Hon. Sir John Sinclair* (1831), vol. 1, p. 100; R.I. and S. Wilberforce, *Life*, vol. 1, p. 326.

18 Stanhope, *Pitt*, vol. 1, p. 228.

19 HMC, *Rutland*, vol. 3, p. 152; R.I. and S. Wilberforce, *Life*, vol. 1, p. 233; *L.C.GIII*, vol. 1, p. 530, n. 1. Dundas initially held the Home Secretaryship as *locum tenens* until Lord Cornwallis returned from India, and stayed on when the latter declined it.

20 HMC, *Fortescue*, vol. 2, p. 595.

21 PRO, PRO30/29/1/15, Hawkesbury to Stafford, 30 July 1786; Stanhope, *Pitt*, vol. 1, p. 306.

22 To Dorset, 2 July 1789 (Sackville Family Papers), quoted in M.W. McCahill, *Order and Equipoise. The Peerage and the House of Lords 1783–1806* (1978), p. 134.

23 PRO, PRO30/58/3, Grenville to Pitt, 24 Oct. 1800.

24 Sydney was compensated with an earldom, the sinecure Chief Justiceship in Eyre (worth £2,550 p.a.) and a place on the Admiralty Board for his son.

25 J. Hutton (ed.), *Selections from the Letters and Correspondence of Sir James Bland Burges* (1885), p. 174; G. Hogge (ed.), *Journal and Correspondence of William Eden, 1st Baron Auckland* (1861–2), vol. 2, p. 414.

26 HMC, *Rutland*, vol. 3, p. 309.

27 A.M. Wilberforce (ed.), *Private Papers*, p. 22.

28 Stanhope, *Pitt*, vol. 2, pp. 77, 79; Browning (ed.), *Leeds Memoranda*, pp. 148–9, 156–7.

29 HMC, *Rutland*, vol. 3, p. 298.

30 Twiss, *Eldon*, vol. 1, p. 188.

31 *C.C.GIII*, vol. 1, pp. 398–9.

32 R. Gore-Browne, *Chancellor Thurlow* (1953), pp. 208–9, 246; *L.C.GIII*, vol. 2, p. 410. (Pitt finally secured the reversion for Rose's son from the more compliant Loughborough in 1795.)

33 R.I. and S. Wilberforce, *Life*, vol. 1, p. 385.

34 Gore-Brown, *Thurlow*, pp. 280, 282–3; R.I. and S. Wilberforce, *Life*, vol. 1, pp. 233–4; Stanhope, *Pitt*, vol. 1, pp. ix, xi–xiii; *L.C.GIII*, vol. 1, pp. 449–50, 501–2; Ditchfield, 'Lord Thurlow', pp. 74–5.

35 *L.C.GIII*, vol. 1, pp. 516, 518.

36 R.I. and S. Wilberforce, *Life*, vol. 1, p. 286; Buckinghamshire Record Office D 56/1/1b Project of Facilities 1791; P. Jupp, *Lord Grenville 1759–1834* (Oxford, 1985), pp. 123–4.

37 PRO, PRO30/8/183, Thurlow to Pitt, 1 June 1791; G.T. Kenyon, *The Life of Lloyd, First Lord Kenyon* (1873), pp. 245–6; PRO, PRO30/29/1/15, Dundas to Stafford, 20 Oct. 1791.

38 *C.C.GIII*, vol. 2, p. 197; Kenyon, *Life of Kenyon*, p. 244.

39 Twiss, *Eldon*, vol. 1, p. 213.

40 HMC, *Rutland*, vol. 3, p. 321.

41 HMC, *14th Report, Appendix Pt.4, Mss of Lord Kenyon* (1894), p. 535; Twiss, *Eldon*, vol. 1, pp. 212–13.

42 Malmesbury (ed.), *Diaries*, vol. 2, p. 458.

43 *Ibid.*, pp. 458–69; Countess of Minto (ed.), *Life and Letters of Sir Gilbert Elliot, First earl of Minto* (1874), vol. 2, pp. 40–56; Browning (ed.), *Leeds Memoranda*, p. 188; F. O'Gorman, *The Whig Party and the French Revolution* (1967), pp. 86–95, 102–3.

44 Browning (ed.), *Leeds Memoranda*, pp.175–97; O'Gorman, *Whig Party*, pp. 96–104.

45 Ann Arbor, William L Clements Library, Melville Papers, Pitt to Dundas, 1 Oct., Pitt Papers, 4 Oct. 1792 (author's italics); *L.C.GIII*, vol. 1, pp. 617–20.

46 BL Loan, 57/107, Pitt to Richmond, 24 Sept. 1793.

47 Stanhope, *Pitt*, vol. 2, p. 77; Browning (ed.), *Leeds Memoranda*, pp. 185, 199.

48 BL, Althorp Mss G15, T. Grenville to Spencer, 26 May; Sheffield Central Library, Wentworth Woodhouse Muniments F31 (b), Portland to Fitzwilliam, 25 May 1794; Ehrman, *Pitt*, vol. 2, pp. 409–14; O'Gorman, *Whig Party*, pp. 195–208.

49 R.I. and S. Wilberforce, *Life*, vol. 1, pp. 103–4; Pellew, *Sidmouth*, vol. 1, pp. 121–3.

50 [L. Melville (ed.),] *The Windham Papers* (1913), vol. 1, p. 260; *C.C.GIII*, vol. 2, p. 277; Rose, *Pitt and Napoleon*, p. 23.

51 For the Fitzwilliam episode see Rose, *Pitt and Napoleon*, pp. 20–36; E.A. Smith, *Whig Principles and Party Politics. Earl Fitzwilliam and the Whig Party* (Manchester, 1975), pp. 175–218; Ehrman, *Pitt*, vol. 2, pp. 420–38; D. Wilkinson, 'The Fitzwilliam episode, 1795: a reinterpretation of the role of the Duke of Portland', *Irish Historical Studies*, vol. 29 (1995), pp. 315–39.

52 *Windham Papers*, vol. 1, pp. 256–75; Stanhope, *Pitt*, vol. 2, pp. 281–92; John Rylands Library, English Ms 907, Dundas to Pitt, 13 Oct. 1794.

53 *L.C.GIII*, vol. 2, pp. 262–3; HMC, *Fortescue*, vol. 3, pp. 35–9; Stanhope, *Pitt*, p. 17.

54 Sheffield Central Library, Wentworth Woodhouse Muniments F31, Portland to Fitzwilliam, 2 Dec. 1794; *L.C.GIII*, vol. 2, pp. 278–80, 298.

55 HMC, *Fortescue*, vol. 3, pp. 13–15; Stanhope, *Pitt*, vol. 2, pp. xxii–xxv; *L.C.GIII*, vol. 2, p. 299.

56 Earl Stanhope, *Miscellanies* (1863), pp. 19–23; Smith, *Fitzwilliam*, pp. 193–6.

57 Rose, *Pitt and Napoleon*, p. 270. See also ibid., p. 260; HMC, *Fortescue*, vol. 5, p. 487, vol. 6, pp. 151, 170, 235.

58 HMC, *Fortescue*, vol. 5, pp. 306–7.

59 HMC, *Fortescue*, vol. 6, p. 170; P. Mackesy, *War without Victory. The downfall of Pitt* (Oxford, 1984), pp. 80–8.

60 HMC, *Fortescue*, vol. 3, pp. 25–31, 50; *L.C.GIII*, vol. 2, pp. 312, 330–1. For a fuller account see M. Duffy, 'Pitt, Grenville and the Control of British Foreign Policy in the 1790s', in J. Black (ed.), *Knights Errant and True Englishmen* (Edinburgh, 1989), pp. 159–62.

61 Leeds Central Library, George Canning Papers, Bundle 14, Canning to Leigh (30 June) 1797, Bundle 29d, Diary entries May–June 1797; R.I. and S. Wilberforce, *Life*, vol. 2, p. 223; Mrs H. Baring (ed.), *The Diary of the Rt Hon. William Windham, 1784–1810* (1866), pp. 365–8; Rose, *Pitt and Napoleon*, p. 242; Duffy, 'British Foreign Policy', pp. 164–8.

62 Malmesbury (ed.), *Diaries*, vol. 3, p. 554.

63 BL Loan, 72/38, ff. 78, 95, 101; Add. MSS, 38,192, Pitt to Hawkesbury, 7 July 1794; Rose, *Pitt and Napoleon*, pp. 283–4; *L.C.GIII*, vol. 3, p. 16, n. 3; BL, Althorp Mss, Dundas to Spencer, 10 Feb. 1798.

64 Bickley (ed.), *Glenbervie Diaries*, vol. 1, pp. 79, 105–6.

65 Minto (ed.), *Life and Letters*, vol. 2, p. 390.

66 Browning (ed.), *Leeds Memoranda*, pp. 104–5; Bickley (ed.), *Glenbervie Diaries*, vol. 1, pp. 79, 105–6; *L.C.GIII*, vol. 3, p. 196; Rose, *Pitt and Napoleon*, p. 290.

Chapter 4

'THE AMBITION OF MY LIFE':
PITT AND THE BUSINESS
OF GOVERNMENT

. . .

THE GOVERNING PASSION

When he resigned in 1801, Pitt regretted leaving 'a station which it would be the ambition of my life, and the passion of my heart to continue to fill'. Like his father, he saw it as his destiny to govern the country. His 'extraordinary adherence to power and place' was later noted by the Foreign Office Under-Secretary, Burges, who added that 'Ambition of glory and power [were] his leading principles.' The MP Wraxall spoke of 'His elevated, ambitious mind, which grasped at solid power'. Friends justified him. 'If he was anxious for glory,' insisted Pretyman, 'it was for the glory of having served his Country with zeal, fidelity, and disinterestedness; if he aspired to power, it was because Power would open a wider field for his diligence and exertions. Ambition is a virtue or a vice, a blessing or a curse, according to the motives from which it proceeds, the objects to which it is directed and the means which are employed to gratify it.' Wilberforce found it 'highly gratifying to converse familiarly with him on the plans he was forming for the public good; or to witness the pleasure he experienced from indulging speculations of the benefits which his country might derive from the realising of such or such a hope'.[1] This was the 'buzz' which drove him and which distinguished him from other leading politicians of his day. His rival Fox thought literature 'in every point of view a preferable occupation to politics' and confessed in 1804 that 'Power was now no material object to him', while Grenville was 'sure that the notion of indefinite and unlimited service in such a situation as mine, is not fitted to the frame of my mind'. In any clash of wills, Pitt's impelling desire to govern was always likely to prevail over opponents. Except during his despondency at his first reverses in January 1784, he never seriously entertained the idea of retirement until he suddenly went in February 1801. Thoughts provoked by the Ochakov humiliation in 1791 were quickly dismissed with the excuse of its likely effect on the King's mind, while a scheme in early June 1797 to hand over to Addington was only devised to lure the French into peace talks, with Pitt returning once peace was signed, and was quickly discarded when the French proved willing to negotiate with him as Premier.[2]

Entering power with less than nine months' administrative experience and chosen primarily for his ability to lead the Commons, he rapidly acquired a reputation for being a good 'man of business', and this was a major bonus for the King's government. John Ehrman sees his distinguishing feature as the systematic way in which he approached issues, taking care to seek the facts before he formed a plan: his use of systematic information and measurement as decision-making tools gave a modernising, professional tone to the process of government.[3] The style reflected his own aptitudes. He had a powerful capacity to digest information. '[H]is mind was so quick,' said Dundas, 'that he saw through everything' – his 'great' or 'extreme' quickness of apprehension was often remarked upon by those who did business with him. Lord Cholmondely, attending him on a matter of the Prince of Wales's accounts, found it 'impossible to do justice to the perspicuity and rapidity of his calculations. In the course of a few minutes he went through and settled every item, leaving me lost in admiration at his ability.' Douglas at the Treasury Board observed his 'peculiar talent of reducing formal proceedings as reports, clauses of statutes etc. into the best and most precise, short and elegant words'.[4] This capacity to assimilate detail was combined with an 'extraordinary memory', 'so tenacious that he never forgot anything he had once learned'. He undoubtedly exploited this to his advantage. Douglas thought his manner in hearing petitions 'awkward and not judicial, but his questions and observations were those so able a man might be expected to make. He seemed to have read the memorials with more attention than Rose [the Treasury Secretary], and not unwilling to show that he had.'[5] This capacity to master detail was deployed in lucid explanation of complex financial and administrative issues which created an immediate and immense impression of competence. In early 1785 Lady Gower described how 'sensible thinking people' were astonished at his display of 'so perfect a knowledge of the Commerce, Funds, and Government of the Country that one must imagine to hear him on these subjects, that he had the experience of fifty years'.[6]

Wilberforce thought that all professional men or heads of boards would acknowledge 'that he was ... the most easy and accommodable man with whom they ever did business'. His secretaries concurred about his amiable temper: 'an equanimity, a freedom from irritation, a self-command, which I never noticed in the same degree in any other person', thought Pretyman; while Dacres Adams confessed that, 'with all my shortcomings no harsh word or look ever escaped him, but all towards me was kindness and indulgence'. An official, John Fordyce, was struck by 'the undivided and unprejudiced attention which he gives', and Dudley Ryder described his 'peculiar talent of making persons with whom he conversed pleased with themselves by taking up their ideas – and enlarging upon them and improving them'.[7] Business was indeed to Pitt a social activity. He abhorred writing letters and much preferred to talk over issues directly with those concerned, seeking advice, information and sounding boards for his ideas. The Master of the Rolls was asked for a quarter-of-an-hour's talk on the Indian judicature in 1784. Puzzled by an item in the Dutch negotiations in 1788, he summoned Grenville since 'I do not like to trust my own opinion, which is nearly all I have to trust on this subject at present. I should be glad therefore, if possible, to talk it over with you as soon as you can make it convenient.' He preferred working as informally as possible. Dundas later recalled that, 'In transacting the business of the State, in forming our plans etc. we never retired to Office for that purpose. All these matters we discussed and settled either in our morning rides at Wimbledon, or in our evening walks at that place. We were accustomed to walk in the evening from 8 o'clock to sometimes 10 or Eleven in the Summer Season.'[8]

When Pitt was in his prime, his day in London began early with reading or writing. Breakfast was usually at 9 a.m., sometimes with acquaintances with whom he needed to talk business. Sometimes, according to his valet, he was so engrossed in business that he neglected breakfast entirely and went away perhaps at 12 o'clock without eating anything. About midday he would take a short ride in the park for exercise, and much of the rest of the time would be spent in interviews or committees until dinner at about 5 o'clock. This was the point in the day when he liked to unwind. He rarely dined alone, but would sit down with a few persons he loved and respected 'and laying aside all care enjoy their conversation till the Evening hour of business arrived'. A regular guest was Pepper Arden who took the role of court jester – to laugh and be laughed at – in which Pitt joined along with the rest. He responded to invitations to dine with friends and, before the pressures of war absorbed him, sometimes went on to evening social gatherings such as those held by the ministerialist hostess, the Duchess of Gordon. Otherwise business began again about 9 in the evening, when he 'retired to his room refreshed and invigorated, and frequently continued his labours to a late hour, being in general attended by the Secretaries or others who took an active part in the business of the different public offices'. A letter from Pitt and Grenville in Downing Street at 11 p.m. on a Saturday night in 1786 explained to Jenkinson that they were going through the drafts and instructions for the French commercial treaty and begged for his presence in town as early as possible on Sunday to discuss doubts that had emerged.[9]

For recreation or as a retreat at which he could concentrate on particular issues without distraction, Pitt initially rented a villa near Putney and later, if he could not get away too far, he resorted to Dundas's house on Wimbledon Common and sometimes to Eliot's at Battersea Rise. But in the autumn of 1785 he bought Holwood House, about fifteen miles from London and not far from the old Chatham family home at Hayes in Kent. 'To Holwood,' wrote Pretyman, 'he returned upon every opportunity, but rarely without a friend or two, and in general some person in office joined him there, that business and recreation might be mixed.' There it was that Wilberforce 'sallied forth' with Pitt and Grenville after breakfast one morning in April 1790, 'armed with bill-hooks, cutting new walks from one large tree to another, through the thickets of the Holwood copses'. The house was a small one in 200 acres, but Pitt gave vent to his enthusiasms for architecture and gardening by subsequently having the house enlarged to be able to accommodate four or five friends and doubling the land by purchase, turning the road and landscaping the grounds to his taste. Five miles away was Lord Auckland's seat at Beckenham, a proximity that made Auckland a usefully available financial adviser after his return from Holland in 1793 – invited to call at any time that suits or to 'take a business dinner' to discuss taxes in early 1796. The proximity of Auckland's family also nearly provided Pitt with a wife in 1797. Appointment as Warden of the Cinque Ports in 1792 gave Pitt another retreat at Walmer Castle, where he could also take the sea air and which he made freely available to his friends for the same purpose. It was at Walmer that Pitt spent nearly ten days of air and exercise with Dundas in September 1793, completely consuming all his mornings with 'the occupation of missing partridges', while across the water British gunners sought bigger game as they bombarded Dunkirk. To Walmer he went 'for a week or ten days' in October 1795, hoping to return with his budget prepared to be opened before Christmas.[10]

How Pitt gestated major financial legislation can be followed in the autumn of 1797, when he decided to make a fundamental change in his methods of financing the war – including what was effectively a switch towards an income tax through a graduated increase in the assessed taxes on property. In mid-September Pitt closeted himself at Holwood with the Treasury Secretary, George Rose, to begin planning. Although called to London by the collapse of the Lille peace negotiations, he had made sufficient progress before the end of the month to invite Auckland to dinner at Holwood to show and discuss the outline and to ask Speaker Addington to come for a few days to 'talk over all that is to be talked of'. On 11 October he was at Walmer with his projects worked up into two papers, which he sent to close friends like Addington and financial experts such as Liverpool for their views. On 25 October he sent out to colleagues such as Grenville his financial projections down to 1801, showing how his scheme could subsequently be applied to reduce the growing National Debt. By then he had also extended his soundings to his young acolyte, Canning, on whom he tried out his justifications, before submitting his proposals to the Commons on 24 November.[11] Pitt did not keep his plans to himself. He eagerly sought feedback. Nor did he confine himself to his expert men of business. What captivated his younger disciples was the way he was prepared to discuss his ideas and his doubts with them too.[12]

Wilberforce noted the 'peculiarity of his character that he was habitually apt to have almost his whole thoughts and attention and time occupied with a particular object or plan which he was then devising and wishing to introduce into practise'. 'I am half mad with a project which will give our supplies the effect almost of magic in the reduction of the debt,' he wrote as he developed his Sinking Fund scheme in September 1785. Not the least engaging of his characteristics was the way he would immerse himself in a subject, developing his ideas through discussions with experts and friends, and, once he had seen a way forward, work himself into an enthusiasm that could carry others along with him. Wilberforce remembered Pitt 'as usual full of his scheme and detailed it to his professional friend with the warmth and ability natural to him on such occasions'. His enthusiasm and irrepressible optimism – what Dundas called 'the eagerness or the sanguineness of your temper' – led him further into fields of administration, trade and manufacture than other premiers might have gone, into areas which Wilberforce with obvious distaste described as 'subjects of a low and vulgarising quality, such as the excise on tobacco, wine, etc.'. '[H]is talents, quickness, temper and application well qualified him to have been a Prime Minister in the real sense of the word,' wrote Burges.[13]

. . .

GUIDING THE NATIONAL RECOVERY

Inexperienced though he was when he came to power, Pitt needed little imagination to recognise the administrative problems that faced him.

He had immediately to produce his own alternative to the Fox–North India Bill. This he did by utilising proposals Dundas had put forward in the previous year tending to strengthen central direction by the Directors of the East India Company as against the Court of Proprietors and by the Governor-General and the Presidency Governors as against their Councils. Now Pitt also subjected the Company to a Crown-appointed Board of Control on matters of civil and military government and of the revenues of its East Indian territories. It was a conveniently quick expedient rather than the comprehensive solution that Pitt loved to seek at this stage of his career. While it was being enacted, he readily accepted amendments from the Company in January and the Opposition in July 1784. He amended the bill himself in 1786 to reinforce the powers of the Crown-appointed Governor-General, and pushed through a further Act in 1788 'clarifying' the right of the Board of Control to order payment by the Company of expenses incurred in ensuring the security of India. In practice Pitt's government, like its predecessor, encroached upon the rights of the East India Company. Indian issues still carried political sting – his Coalition Ministry was divided over the conduct of the former Governor-General, Warren Hastings, and Pitt's 1788 Declaratory Act had a rough ride in the Commons – but the compromise nature of the 1784 Act and the device of *ad hoc* amendment thereafter largely defused India as a central political issue. Pitt was little interested personally in India. Only in 1787–9 and 1791 did he attend more than half the meetings of the Board of Control, and he was content to leave its management to Dundas, whose authority was confirmed when he became the first, salaried, President of the Board of Control in 1793.[14]

Once his India Act was passed, Pitt saw the Irish situation as 'the most important and delicate we now have to attend to', and during the parliamentary recess he had the time to seek a systematic solution. Stressing the necessity of establishing fundamental principles of policy on Ireland as the basis of a permanent system, he told the Lord Lieutenant of his 'great wish' that 'all the several leading points may be enough digested to be considered in one view and as members of one general system, to be decided on by the Cabinet long before the Parliament of either country meets'. His Irish Commercial Propositions of 1785 attempted a comprehensive answer to how to reintegrate British and Irish interests now that the latter had won semi-autonomy during the American War. His master plan, however, failed when he made it too elaborate. 'Leaving nothing to future liberality or wisdom,' lamented Grenville, 'he endeavoured to obviate every doubt, to anticipate by previous stipulation every practical embarrassment which so extensive an arrangement might subsequently produce, and to reconcile things in their nature incompatible, the unity of commercial legislation and the division of supreme authority.' Everyone found something to object to in detailed provisions attempting to answer everyone's objections.[15]

His initial solution for India was only partly successful, and that for Ireland failed, but he ultimately secured his administrative reputation by his successful handling of the third major problem he inherited, that of restoring public confidence in the national finances. The Treasury was where he had his prior experience, but he was still sufficiently inexperienced to be prepared to tackle all its problems at once, and he attacked them with all the exuberant energy of a young man. Pretyman thought that firmness and energy of mind was the striking part of Pitt's character: 'While he was in full health and strength he was never depressed by any danger however threatening, or by any embarrassment however distressing, and by uniformly acting with a vigour and resolution best calculated to avert or to diminish the evil, he rose out of every difficulty with fresh honour and increased reputation.'[16]

The financial situation was ideally suited to his business aptitudes. Abundant ideas and information were at hand from a reform debate that had been running for at least a decade. Lord North, whom he so despised, had been an active head of the Treasury, taking steps to improve the efficiency of its personnel, initiating schemes to consolidate Customs, Excise and Stamp Duties, and in 1780 establishing a statutory Parliamentary Commission to examine the Public Accounts which by 1787 had published 15 reports. Its eleventh report, published a fortnight before Pitt took office, advising on what was needed to put the country in a position to reduce the National Debt, has been described as almost seeming to be the text upon which Pitt was to found his financial and economic policy.[17] Pitt had already assisted Shelburne in this general drive for increased economy and efficiency in government. Even the reviled Fox–North Coalition established a Parliamentary Committee of Inquiry into smuggling.

All this was exploited by Pitt, who also consulted authorities such as Dr Price and Adam Smith outside government and the professional experts within it.[18] On the Sinking Fund project for example, Pitt had available the eleventh report of North's Public Accounts Commission, three pamphlets by Dr Price, with whom he also entered into correspondence and who provided him with four alternative schemes, various proposals sent in to the Treasury and the short-lived French scheme of 1785. His proposals were hardened up in discussion with friends and advisers – Pretyman (then his secretary), Grenville and perhaps Lord Mahon among the former, and among the latter, men of business such as Jenkinson, who was sent a copy in January 1786 with a request for his views and an injunction to maintain the utmost secrecy, George Rose at the Treasury, and Richard Frewin of the Customs, while the Cambridge mathematician George Atwood was called in 'to reduce the plan . . . to system and order'.[19]

The sheer extent of Britain's financial problems impelled Pitt to act quickly and energetically. He inherited a state income of £12.7 million and expenditure of £23.5 million in 1783. The long-term funded National Debt had escalated from £124.3 million before the start of the American War to £213 million, with further short-term unfunded borrowings of £19 million. Pitt's immediate priorities were to eliminate the current deficit so as to avoid incurring further debt, to clear short-term debts and to build up a surplus of income over expenditure which could be directed towards reducing the enormous long-term debt, whose annual charges now absorbed almost three-fifths of state income and whose scale undermined financial confidence by raising fears of national bankruptcy.

Attempts to raise income were restricted by the national preference for indirect taxation on items of consumption rather than direct taxation on earnings and by the belief that the acceptable limits of indirect taxation had just about been reached. He followed traditional methods by small taxes on a range of consumer goods in 1784–6, operating on the margins of success by trial and error, but nevertheless prepared to sacrifice popularity in doing so. Some taxes he had to withdraw in the face of public protest (those on ladies' ribbons, hop-planters and a pit-head levy on coals in 1784, that on cotton in 1785), but enough succeeded to give him the extra £900 000 he needed to fund a new long-term loan which both bridged the 1784 deficit and also assimilated most of the outstanding short-term debt. More adventurous was his decision to follow up former enquiries by slashing Customs duties on smuggled items, in the hope of securing a longer-term increase in income from a greater trade through legitimate routes. A successful experiment with tea by the 1784 Commutation Act led to its extension to rum in 1785 and to wine and brandies in the Commercial Treaty with France in 1786.[20]

Since he was operating at the existing tax margins, Pitt also sought to increase revenue by improving efficiency in the collection of existing taxes. The Customs were strengthened by the 1784 Hovering Act, extending their authority to search vessels off the coast, by the 1786 Manifest Act and by the simplification of their procedures in the 1787 consolidation of duties. Far more politically contentious was the transfer of collection of some duties to the more efficient Excise, starting with wines and spirits in 1786. Transfers from the Stamps and Excise Boards, in 1785, focused collection of the assessed taxes in the more cheaply administered Taxes Board, and by a Treasury minute of the same year he reorganised their local collection, instituting vetting and training of local surveyors, banning the use of deputies, extending the number of inspectors so as to abolish general surveyors, establishing a system of promotion and ensuring supervision by a new examiner's department within the Taxes Office in London. All of these measures helped to increase state revenue, which Pitt claimed in 1792 had risen by about £4 million since 1783 (subsequent calculations put the figure at nearer £6 million). He attributed over £1 million of the increase to his new taxes, about £1 million to his measures against smuggling and fraud and £2 million to a general increase in the wealth and prosperity of the country. He modestly understated his own part in re-establishing financial confidence, mentioning his 1786 Commercial Treaty with France, but giving the credit for the unexpectedly rapid growth of British trade after the American War to the enterprising spirit of the people and to the growing strength of British credit and capital accumulation, fostered by internal tranquillity under the blessings of a sound constitution.[21]

Besides seeking to increase income, Pitt also sought ways to cut expenditure without damage to government, in order to achieve a surplus to be applied to his major priority of reducing the National Debt. There were quick savings from reducing the armed forces after the American War, though he took a courageous decision not to go as far as he might so that he could rebuild the fleet. He looked to long-term savings by establishing a Stationery Office in 1786 to eliminate the £40,000 which he claimed was wasted by government offices in this field. He sought to raise his 1784 loan as cheaply as possible by asking for competitive sealed tenders, a system to which both North and Shelburne had aspired. He also looked to make economies by the reduction of sinecures and pensions, though he soon found this to be expensive both financially and politically.

All this was essential preparation for his Sinking Fund scheme. By April 1785 he was able to tell the Commons that he expected a £1 million surplus in the following year, which he intended to apply to the reduction of the long-term National Debt. If he ever devised a system which governed his future conduct, this was it. The restoration and maintenance of the credit system, through confidence in the capacity of the Sinking Fund to contain and eventually eliminate the National Debt, became the basis of his financial and economic policy. When introducing his scheme in 1786, he declared that on its success depended all public hopes 'of a full return to prosperity, and that public security, which will give confidence and vigour to those exertions in trade and commerce, upon which the flourishing state of this Country so much depends'. Confidence in a securely based system of public credit was the keystone to confidence in private credit which, he asserted when extending the scheme in 1792, 'has principally tended to raise this Country to its mercantile pre-eminence'.[22]

The idea of a Sinking Fund of taxes allocated to reduce the debt was an old one, initiated by Walpole in 1716, but Pitt transformed it in two ways. Whereas Walpole and his successors had often raided the fund for other uses, Pitt took up the suggestion, urged by Price and recently attempted by the French, to entrust it to a commission with the statutory obligation of invariably applying it to its object. Second, he adopted the idea, pressed by Price since 1772, of ploughing back into the fund the interest payments on redeemed stock, thus enabling it to grow at compound interest (Pitt claimed his annual investment of £1 million would accumulate to £4 million a year in 28 years), so vastly speeding up the redemption of the debt. Popular confidence in the state finances would be restored by the concept that the National Debt could, and by law would, be paid off. Enacted in May 1786 the measure brought him immense popular acclaim. He followed it in April 1787 with a massive simplification of exchequer accounting by consolidating into a single fund, composed of a single duty on each commodity, all the separate fractional duties that had been imposed by previous Ministers for distinct and separately accounted purposes. A prioritised list of state payments from the consolidated fund was established, with the interest on the National Debt first, the Civil List second and current annual expenditure voted by Parliament next. The Act involved the passage of 2,357 separate resolutions which Pitt himself moved. The sheer magnitude of the task had deterred former Finance Ministers, but Pitt's energy and mounting ascendancy over Parliament on financial matters saw him safely through.[23]

. . .

APOSTATE REFORMER OR COMPULSIVE IMPROVER?

Then, however, the momentum slowed. Of the 15 reports of the Public Accounts Commission, Pitt responded to three in 1785, replacing the outmoded Auditors of the Imprests with a statutory Commission for Auditing the Public Accounts, regulating the office of Treasurer of the Navy and establishing a Privy Council Commission to examine fee-taking in all the public offices. His Sinking Fund in 1786 responded to its eleventh report, but after the Commission completed its fifteenth report in 1787 it was given no more work and was dissolved. The Fees Commission examined only 10 of an intended 24 offices before it too was dissolved in 1789 and its completed reports shelved. There was no major frontal attack on sinecures after he came to power.[24] Indeed the lack of energetic legislative follow-up to his early economic reform and parliamentary reform bills has led to accusations about Pitt's commitment to reform ever since. Did he desert reform to maintain the King's support and his hold on power, as Fox thought? Were his reforming ideals defiled by his association with 'trading politicians' of worldly ways of thinking and acting, as Wilberforce believed? Was he the reformer turned reactionary by the French Revolution as nineteenth-century Whigs like Henry Brougham, Lord John Russell and Lord Macaulay asserted?

Many of these interpretations started with a false assumption of what Pitt was originally, and they focused out of all proportion on one aspect of his activities in the early 1780s (his advocacy of parliamentary reform) and misinterpreted another (on trade) into a doctrinaire liberal espousal of *laissez-faire*. The problem for nineteenth-century Whigs and for historians is that they have tended to judge Pitt in terms of nineteenth-century reform and reformers. Pitt, however, was the product of eighteenth-century traditions. He shared the perspective of the True Patriot, described in the 1768 *Essay on Patriotism*, who was to be employed in times of peace and tranquillity 'in mild and moderate endeavours to rectify whatever disorders or corruptions may have crept into either [the laws or the constitution]'. This was not a perspective that was going to produce radical changes. He took things as they were and worked on them. He always believed that the British constitution was the finest in the world. It had brought Britain to its greatness before the American War; it enabled the country to rise again through its own efforts after that disaster. With a proper balance among its component parts it was a source of vigour and vitality which encouraged economic prosperity, cherished and valued, he said in his budget speech in 1792, 'because we know that it practically secures the tranquillity and welfare both of individuals and the public, and provides, beyond any other frame of government which has ever existed, for the real and useful ends which form at once the only true foundation and only rational object of all political societies'. His object, he told the House in advocating parliamentary reform in 1783, was 'not to innovate, but rather to renew and invigorate the spirit of the constitution, without deviating materially from its present form'. In 1791 he was still 'of opinion that our constitution was capable of gradual and temperate melioration and amendment in some few of its principles', but all such improvements were designed to restore the balance of powers to its former purity and might be advanced or retarded according to where at any time the threat to that balance seemed most pressing.[25]

His restless eye led him to interest himself in endeavours at rectification throughout the system. This was a matter of temperament. In his favourite leisure occupations of architecture and landscape gardening, passions inherited from his father, he was a compulsive 'improver'. His Cambridge tutor Pretyman later recalled that Pitt liked in his early life 'to amuse himself with drawing a Plan of the best possible House', and after a tour of the Norfolk great houses at the age of seventeen, 'he drew from memory a plan of one of the largest houses we had seen, with a view of improving it'. Late in his life, Lady Hester Stanhope recollected 'hearing him say he never saw a house, or cottage, or garden, he liked, but he immediately struck out improvements in his own mind'. It was this attitude he brought to government and which he extended widely to all its aspects which came before his eye.[26]

While he could strike out improvements in his own mind, however, it was another matter to put them into practical effect. Once the pressures which impelled his rush of improving activity in the aftermath of the American War eased and recovery began, he fell easier prey to vices of his temperament which impeded practical realisation of his improving schemes. Burges noted 'his quickness and decision on the first view of a subject' but also 'his easiness in being led from it', and the Clerk of the Commons, Hatsell, later lamented that 'It is the curse of Mr Pitt's disposition, to take up a measure eagerly and earnestly, and as soon to quit it.' There were in Pitt's disposition two speeds, fast or slow, and two moods, sanguine enthusiasm or indecisive procrastination.[27]

He was confronted with undoubted obstacles to 'improvement': the prejudices of an eighteenth-century world imbued with customary ways of doing things and not yet indoctrinated into the utilitarian reforming momentum built up in the nineteenth century; the inertia of an aristocratic bureaucracy founded on patronage and perquisite; the smallness of the number of active staff available to administer the country so that smooth administration might be jeopardised by the turmoil of change and their reaction to it; the First Lord of the Treasury's lack of direct authority over the heads of other government departments, who were appointed by and answerable to the King, and might run their own departments as they saw fit. These were formidable obstacles in themselves, but they were made harder to overcome by Pitt's particular approach to them.

First and foremost Pitt's principal object was to secure a budgetary surplus in order to reduce and eventually eliminate the National Debt. All other reforms were subsidiary to this prime commitment. Administrative improvements were means towards that end and were not to be rushed if they clashed with it. In particular many sinecure offices were granted for life by Crown Patent and were considered as property which could not be arbitrarily taken away. The abolition of the two Auditors of the Imprest in 1785, recommended by the Public Accounts Commission, cost £7,000 each by way of compensation, and a further £10,000 in salaries for the officials of the efficient board that replaced them. When the Public Accounts Commission turned to the Customs and in 1786 recommended the abolition of 180 patent and sinecure posts to effect a saving of £31,430, Pitt chose to act more cheaply by attrition instead. By the end of 1792 only one had been revoked and 28 were left vacant either by resignation or by the death of their incumbents. A commission, set up in 1789 to inquire into fee payments to Customs officials, recommended in 1791 their abolition and replacement by salaries, but at a cost of £127,247. With the finances now in surplus Pitt had a bill drafted in 1792 to end the fees to Outport officers for £45,000, but when he had to pay for war in the following year the project was shelved.[28]

Pitt was neither a doctrinaire, nor a systematic and tightly focused reformer. He was quite ready to cast his improving eye over whatever came before him, and as his confidence increased and he began to intervene in more aspects of government in the course of the 1780s, so his improving interests expanded and dispersed. When in 1784 the reforming Comptroller of the Navy, Sir Charles Middleton, requested his intervention with the First Lord of the Admiralty, he responded that 'from what I feel due to Lord Howe's situation, as well as from the personal confidence to which he is entitled, I cannot interfere in the manner you wish'. However by 1787 he was assertive enough to stop Howe from removing Middleton from his office. In the following year Buckingham could speak of Pitt being 'so much used to engross all the business of government', and he certainly sought involvement in significant business of the major offices. Explaining the need to keep his close associate Dundas head of the War Department in 1794, Pitt declared of the alternative, his new ally Portland, that 'nor could I be content . . . to leave that Department to his separate management'.[29]

However, this developing interventionist instinct led him into clashes with the views of departmental chiefs: with the joint Postmasters General when he forced the Post Office in 1784 to accept John Palmer's mail-coach system, which would enable him to increase revenue by raising postal rates; and with the First Lord of the Admiralty when he backed Middleton's proposed reforms of the Navy Board and the dockyards. The first led to his dismissal of the most obstructive Postmaster General, who retaliated by encouraging calls for a parliamentary inquiry into Post Office abuses which Pitt sought to sidestep in 1787 by referral to his Privy Council Commission on the Fees in Public Offices. The second led to the resignation of Howe in 1788, followed by that of Middleton in 1791 after publication of the Privy Council Commission's favourable report on his Navy Board proposals was held up by Pitt's unwillingness to publish the Commission's report on the Post Office, which was implicitly highly critical of his handling of that department.[30]

Pitt had created the Commission on Fees in 1785, with much of its terms of reference drawn from his abortive Public Offices Bill of 1783, but responsible to the Privy Council rather than to Parliament. This has plausibly been interpreted as a sign of Pitt trying to control reform himself rather than surrender the initiative to Parliament, though he might equally have seen this as a more practical way to get changes through, by means of Orders in Council, after the failure of his earlier parliamentary proposals. This was a tactic he used to restrict the slave trade after statutory attempts were defeated in Parliament in the 1790s.[31] The Commission looked to recommendations which would not cause great new expense, so that Pitt willingly renewed it for a further two years in 1787, intending to have its reports considered as a whole by the Privy Council when they were completed. The Post Office report, however, changed all this, and Pitt had it shelved, along with the others that had been completed, and he allowed the Commission to expire with its remit unfinished.[32]

Even when the different projects which Pitt espoused did not clash with each other politically, they undoubtedly clashed in their demands on his time. As has been seen, Pitt's preference was to immerse himself in one issue at a time, and when Parliament was sitting that tended to have priority. This could have damaging effects. The Commons' investigation into the radical societies in May 1794 delayed payment of the first instalment of the Prussian subsidy. The peace debates at the start of the January 1795 session distracted him from the eruption of the Fitzwilliam crisis in Ireland. Windham, desperate for a decision on the French Royalists in late 1797 begged 'your attention, before the Business of Parliament shall call it off', and the ensuing stormy debates on the assessed taxes led, as Dundas remarked, to a sad interruption to all other business, including national defence planning which needed to be put in train without delay. Ministers and officials fought for Pitt's attention. Rose's daughter recalled how angry her father was 'when he could not fix Mr Pitt's attention on business particularly under his management in the House of Commons'.[33] Moreover, even when his attention was caught, the chances for him to shut himself up for ten days, as he did with Dundas and Charles Grant at Wimbledon in the summer of 1792 to master the Bengal land revenues,[34] came rarely – perhaps once or twice a year at best.

. . .

PERSONAL LIMITATIONS AS A
'MAN OF BUSINESS'

Pitt's administrative methods were too personal to ensure the smooth, secure and successful passage of business. There was too much informality in his proceedings. Letters were left unanswered, and his papers in a mess. His cousin Grenville revolutionised the assimilation of information at the Home Office, and then at the Foreign Office, by employing a précis writer, but Douglas was told that Pitt 'will not suffer anybody to arrange his papers, and extract the important points for him', and the Russian envoy, Vorontsov, in allowing Grenville to show confidential papers to Pitt, begged the Foreign Secretary not to leave them with him 'for he will not be able to find them again a day later among the immense mass of papers which reach him from all sides and encumber all his tables and desks'.[35] Pitt preferred to do business directly rather than by correspondence, but he did not keep minutes of his meetings. Most of the trouble in the Fitzwilliam episode arose from his failure to produce a full and generally agreed record of the 15 November meeting. Douglas complained that Pitt kept no minutes of the meetings of the informal committee he assembled to draw up the Union with Ireland, never gave it an official form as a Committee of the Privy Council, and never even acknowledged its existence to Parliament. Pitt followed his enthusiasms. George III 'observed that Mr Pitt was apt to put off laborious and disagreeable business to the last, but then, when forced to it, got through it with extraordinary rapidity, but that this sort of irregular mixture of delay and hurry was the chief cause of his ill-health'.[36]

It may be, as a number of contemporaries argued, that he was handicapped by coming to power so soon. He brought with him the energy and fresh mind of a young man, but three disadvantages were posited. First, he was unversed in business. This made him the more prepared to proceed informally – which got him into trouble. The original arrangement with Palmer was accepted verbally on Pitt's behalf by Pretyman. In consequence, there was a prolonged battle with the Post Office over his status and remuneration, and equally there was no clearly established line of responsibility. Palmer understood that he was directly accountable to the Treasury, and this occasioned both personal and official problems within the Post Office that finally led to his dismissal in 1793, with Pitt having to provide a £3,000 per annum pension in compensation. Moreover, '[Pitt's] ignorance of both the substance and forms of business when he came into office,' thought Burges '. . . threw him into the hands of improper people.' He was dependent on men versed in business to bring his ideas to reality: both Dundas, whose proud boast was that he never allowed any letter requiring a reply to remain unanswered for more than a day, and George Rose quickly acquired an influence on him, as later did his far more methodical cousin Grenville. Burges thought him 'led by Grenville and Dundas'.[37]

Second, Grenville believed that his cousin's early entry into office left him little opportunity to enlarge his mind by the study of general and philosophical principles which, together with experience, conferred real wisdom on a statesman. Addington asserted that he was hardly ever seen with a book in his hand after his accession to power. When he did read it was for relaxation, and the books 'always to be found upon his table in the midst of finance and political papers', which 'strewed' his apartment at Holwood or Walmer, or which he took if compelled by the weather to travel in his coach, were Latin and Greek classics, especially Homer and Horace.[38] Instead, experience was the greater influence, and experience made Pitt a super-pragmatist. He told Sheridan in 1794 that:

> My experience is a good argument against your theory. It is not . . . by attending to the dry, strict, abstract principles of a point, that a just conclusion is to be arrived at in political subjects . . . Wisdom is gained in politics, not by any one rigid principle, but by examining a number of incidents; by looking attentively at causes, and reflecting on the effects they have produced; by comparing a number of events together, and by taking, as it were, an average of human affairs. This is the true way to become wise in politics; not by adopting that false philosophy which seeks perfection out of that which is imperfect in its nature; which refers all things to theory, nothing to practise.[39]

He came to power, in Ehrman's words, 'eager, as a young man should be, for large proposals and noble reforms'. He looked for general systems and comprehensive solutions to problems. But few of his all-embracing schemes succeeded. When his Irish Commercial Propositions got into trouble he resorted to expedients. Grenville felt that his 'fondness in every difficulty for complicated expedients, which his genius suggested and combined with unexampled facility, was to the last among the failings of his character'. Ireland, as he was forced to admit in 1794, 'had hitherto been, and must yet continue, a government of expedients'. He read Adam Smith's *Wealth of Nations*, but in 1800, against Grenville's protests, preferred state intervention to ameliorate the corn crisis. At a dinner party in 1796 he declared that there was no wisdom in establishing general rules or principles in government or policy. Such pragmatism often got him through immediate difficulties, but it also limited his ability to maintain a consistent strategic approach to issues.[40]

in class?

Third, there was considerable agreement that he came to office before he sufficiently understood mankind. Windham felt that he had thereby lost 'the opportunities of seeing men and manners, except as a minister, not the most favourable way of seeing men'. The MP Nicholls thought 'his mind was confined to the details of business, before He had sufficiently acquainted himself either with Politicks or men, – in the large view in which both ought to be studied', and Sinclair considered that he 'came too soon to power, before he had acquired political knowledge and experience, without which no man can be a successful minister, more especially in times of difficulty'. Pitt undoubtedly suffered from his awkwardness in personal relations outside his intimate circle. Richmond blamed his 'shyness of . . . disposition which when there has been any little rub knows not how to bring matters to rights again'. This made it much more difficult for him to deal with the personal clashes thrown up by his style of government. Windham thought a period in the army, such as his father had experienced, would have given him a greater knowledge of the ways of the world. Burges considered that his innocence made him open to flattery and that 'his high idea of himself made him blind to the impositions of his designing advisers'.[41]

These limitations on Pitt's style of government by enthusiasm made it harder for him to sustain that enthusiasm when prolonged difficulties emerged. He tried to anticipate and resolve all potential problems in advance, but his enthusiasm sometimes blinded him to practical realities. Wilberforce admired 'the clearness of his conceptions' and his 'extraordinary precision of understanding' which enabled him to allow full weight to every opposing consideration and argument, but, he added, 'You always saw where you differed from him and why. The difference arose commonly from his sanguine temper leading him to give credit to information which others might distrust, and to expect that doubtful contingencies would have a more favourable issue than others might venture to anticipate.' Those attempting to press on him facts that he did not wish to hear might be swept aside. The Irish administration repeatedly stressed Irish sensitivities on the Commercial Propositions, but he persisted in believing that all could be arranged if the Irish Parliament accepted the principle of reciprocity 'Which I cannot allow myself to doubt'. Alternatively objections might be laughed off – 'quizzed away' in the eighteenth-century jargon. Windham complained in 1797 that 'quizzing was made a vile part of the present system, and that when anything could be quizzed away, it was considered as completely got rid of'.[42] Yet equally Pitt could suddenly lose enthusiasm for what he was doing, become uncertain and drop the measure. Wilberforce thought 'dilatoriness and procrastination, his great vices'. His method of sounding friends and experts on his ideas provided much opportunity for others to dissuade or deflect him. Burges wrote of his 'want of judgement when to push or when to relinquish doubtful matters'. Old Earl Camden thought him 'too much under the influence of anyone who is about him, particularly of Dundas', while Spencer later told Dundas that 'You know by experience how open he is to be influenced by friends whose minds are not of sufficient strength and calibre to lead a mind like his.'[43] However Pitt the pragmatist never felt so distressed by procrastination as Wilberforce the idealist. The premier who thought that patience was the greatest political virtue had found by experience that much could be achieved in the course of time that could not be rushed at any one moment – he was ready to accept delay and use it as a weapon rather than see it as a sign of defeat.[44]

The compulsive desire to involve himself in all major aspects of government which he developed in the first five years of his administration, together with the oscillating pressures occasioned by his habits of business, subjected him to strains which increasingly made him more susceptible to two vices which further impeded both his capacity to do business and his judgement: 'wine and love of flattery [were] the great weaknesses of his private life', noted Burges. He depended on the affection of his friends, even perhaps the adoration of younger acolytes like Canning, to sustain him. Also in the mounting strains of the 1790s he began to drink more heavily and this started to impinge on his business routine. The first time that he was noticeably drunk in the Commons seems to have been in early 1793, while Canning noted after a large dinner at Pitt's in December 1794 that 'The dinner was pleasant enough – and a considerable quantity of wine was discussed – so much port by Pitt himself particularly, that I think we left him a little unfit for business.'[45]

As regards his government policy, Pitt had no overall programme of reform. He considered improvement wherever it caught his eye and fitted it in to his business as best he could. If it met with initial rebuff then its chances drastically lessened, though it was always possible that should opportunity offer it might be revived in modified form later. His was less a programme than an attitude of mind. He adhered throughout to a high-minded belief in virtuous government. He would not make money from his office, and he expected similar standards of probity from others. He eventually sided with the Opposition's demand for the impeachment of the former Governor-General of India, Warren Hastings, in 1786–7, not just because a fine he had levied had been 'beyond all proportion exorbitant, unjust and tyrannical', but because Hastings had taken presents 'which appeared to him to justify the impeachment, though it had stood alone'. Financial misdemeanours were his *bête noire*.

In 1793 he dismissed a Treasury official who had solicited money from two people under his examination, 'feeling it impossible that you should any longer remain in the office of trust which you now hold', and in 1796 it was his intervention that was decisive in the expulsion from the Commons of a supporter who had been cashiered for embezzling the funds of his militia regiment. When, faced with retirement, his supporters in the City of London offered him £100,000 to help repay his debts, he refused it for fear that, 'if it should be his lot to be in Office again, he should fancy that every person he saw upon business from the City was one to whom he was under pecuniary obligation'.[46]

It was not in Pitt's temperament to be a doctrinaire or systematic reformer. He lacked the single-minded dedication of a Wilberforce. He was too pragmatically aware of political needs and possibilities: willing, for example, to defend sinecures as a necessary means of rewarding long or distinguished service to the country; ready to reward deserving colleagues amply. Except when the pressures were on, in the early and late years of his first Ministry, he lacked the reformer's impulsion of urgency. He was too much the dilettante, interested in all aspects of government, so that if he met obstacles in one area, he readily turned to another. On the whole his attention span was small, responding to wherever the pressure was greatest at any given time, and favouring matters that could be easily isolated, analysed and for which a permanent solution could be attempted. Government problems seldom come so fortunately gift-wrapped!

. . .

THE CHANGING PACE OF IMPROVEMENT

It has been frequently claimed that there was a watershed in his administration between 1789 and 1792, brought about by the French Revolution and which turned the reforming Pitt into a reactionary. However the pace had already slackened noticeably from 1787, coinciding with Britain's return as a major player to the international stage. Instead of spending the summer of 1787 examining another area to improve, Pitt was absorbed in the Dutch Crisis. In the following summer, there was a crisis in the Baltic as well as the need to start focusing on the next general election. The Regency Crisis then followed. 1790 saw the Nootka Crisis and mobilisation against Spain, while between 1788 and 1792 there was also the ongoing distraction of the feud with Thurlow, at his most obstructive on reform issues, and then war intervened from 1793.

This is not to say, however, that his interest in reform came to a full stop. The years 1788–92 were those when he was most engaged in parliamentary efforts to abolish the slave trade, and from 1789 to 1791 he shared in Grenville's reform of the government of Canada. The only issue that he publicly renounced because of the revolutionary situation was parliamentary reform from 1790. But he had already despaired of acceptable change when even his piecemeal efforts were checked in 1789, and he always declared his intention to return to the issue in better times. Moreover, he endeavoured throughout good times and bad to sustain and advance the financial reforms essential to his aim of removing forever the threat of national bankruptcy, the basis on which all future national improvement depended. He responded quickly to the costs of the Nootka armament with a financial package that put him in a position, in 1792, to take steps to further improve his Sinking Fund system with a one-off payment of £400,000 into the Fund, an annual £200,000 extra, and the provision in each new loan for 1 per cent of the sum raised to be used as a Sinking Fund towards its redemption. He extended measures to improve the revenue collection by transferring tobacco duties from the Customs to the Excise in the years 1789–90. He revived his early anti-smuggling drive in the years 1799–1800, with the creation of the Thames river police and the establishment of enclosed London docks. In 1794 the Crown Lands Department was remodelled in the light of the reports of an Inquiry into Crown Land and Forest Revenue set up in 1786. Even the shelved reports of the Fees Commission were finally considered by the Privy Council in 1792, sent to the departments for comment, and in six (out of ten) cases acted upon over the next eight years: the Treasury and Post Office in 1793, the Secretaries of State's offices in 1795, the Navy Board (where many of Middleton's proposals were at last accepted) in 1796, and the Admiralty and Victualling offices in 1800. The pace was slower than in the early hectic years of his administration, and the improvements made were piecemeal and partial in comparison with the breadth of the enquiries instituted in the 1780s, but nevertheless they did not come to a stop.[47]

In fact the ensuing war eventually reinvigorated the reforming impulse. It helped produce a second freer-trade Commercial Treaty, within the wider 'Jay Treaty' of 1794 settling differences between Britain and the United States. Pushed through by Grenville, with Pitt's backing, against the opposition of Hawkesbury, it was as significant in the circumstances of the 1790s as was the Commercial Treaty with France in the 1780s.[48] War again revitalised scrutiny of the government finances. The dramatic growth of fee incomes from increased government business in wartime resurrected public protest at a time of increased taxation, stimulating

Pitt into showing that something was being done to stop profit taking by government officials. In 1797 he intervened in the Office of the Secretary at War (a department untouched by the Commission on Fees) to put an end to the excessive fees accruing to its officials.[49] Although he set up the 1797 Commons Committee on Finance as a sop to forestall greater demands from back-benchers for economic reform in the government offices, Pitt nevertheless was willing to see certain improvements go forward on its recommendation, such as the abolition of the Salt Tax Board and its amalgamation into the Taxes Office. Similarly a Privy Council committee on coinage, set up in 1798 to forestall parliamentary moves in this field, eventually resulted in a major improvement in the production and quality of the coinage.[50] Reform continued, but the sheer scale of the Revolutionary and Napoleonic Wars from 1793 to 1815 increased jobbery far faster than Pitt could or would quell it, and, during his second Ministry, this precipitated the beginnings of a major popular radical movement in revulsion against the administrative system he had sought to sustain by improvement.[51]

The war indeed precipitated the two most fundamental reforms of the era: the introduction of major direct taxation, and the Union with Ireland. Pitt did not shy away from tackling the biggest issues when the need arose or he thought the time was right. In the late 1790s he was at last prepared to think radically, at least on a temporary basis, to increase the tax revenue so as to keep the National Debt under control. He needed to maintain confidence in his Sinking Fund system and thus preserve public and private credit. Expecting a short war, he contented himself with financing its costs through loans between 1793 and 1797, simply raising sufficient new tax income by traditional means through indirect taxes to service interest payments and Sinking Funds for the new loans. However he was faced in 1797 by the prospect of the war continuing, and the National Debt dramatically escalating. By then, loans could only be obtained by offering stock at high rates of discount. For the 1797 loan, double the amount of interest-bearing stock had to be created to raise the sum intended. With real rates of interest thus ruinously high and the size of the debt rocketing, Pitt consequently looked instead to switch towards raising as much as possible of the necessary supplies by taxes within each year, in order to diminish the size of the loans required. This led him at last to defy popular prejudices by increasing direct taxation.

In the parliamentary session 1797–8 Pitt selected payment of the assessed taxes as an indicator of personal property, and increased their rates on a graduated scale according to past payment. He told Canning that the merit of the scheme was that it was a half-measure – just median between the old system practised for so long and a new one, which he believed could not be practised either then or at any other time on so large a scale as the occasion required. He followed this in 1798 with a plan to allow those paying the land tax to buy themselves out of it over five years through buying back National Debt stock, the interest on which would be sufficient to replace their land tax dues, while the capital of the debt would thus be diminished. These makeshifts, however, were only partially successful, and so in the session 1798–9, taking advantage of the new patriotic upsurge, he at last went the whole way and produced his famous direct tax on incomes, completing the switch to a principle which, he told the Commons in November 1797, was 'new in the financial operations of this country, at least for more than a century'. In this way he hoped to retain national financial confidence. By continuing the new tax for as long as necessary after the war, he calculated that the National Debt could still be paid off in 33 years of peace.[52]

The war thus led Pitt into substantial financial innovation. It also led him into constitutional improvement, when the Irish rebellion of 1798 at last provided him with the justification he needed to push through the political Union with Ireland. He had long believed Union the surest solution to the problem of relations with that kingdom, but had hitherto despaired of ever seeing it accomplished. War did not end Pitt's interest in improvement. Instead it moved his improving attentions to issues of war management, which now became more significant, and it led to changes in the state's financial system, in its bureaucracy (with the creation of new offices such as a Secretary of State for War, an Aliens Office and a Transport Board), and in the constitutional relationship between Britain and Ireland. If personal limitations meant that he failed to achieve much of what he initially undertook – to the disappointment of contemporary zealots and later commentators – nevertheless, in both what he attempted and what he actually achieved, he was by far the most 'improving' Premier of the eighteenth century.

. . .

NOTES AND REFERENCES

1 *Parl. Hist.*, vol. 35, col. 970; Bodleian Library, Burges Mss, Box 73–4, Notes on Pitt; Wheatley (ed.), *Wraxall*, vol. 5, p. 83; Rosebery (ed.), 'Tomline's estimate', *Monthly Review*, August 1903, p. 28; A.M. Wilberforce (ed.), *Private Papers*, p. 71.

2 L.G. Mitchell, *Charles James Fox* (Oxford, 1992), pp. 183, 193; PRO, PRO30/58/1, Grenville to Pitt, 26 Feb. 1794; Browning (ed.), *Leeds Memoranda*,

pp. 94, 160; Ehrman, *Pitt*, vol. 3, pp. 46–50. (This episode can be more precisely dated from National Library for Scotland, Minto Papers M24, Elliot to his wife, 7 June 1797 – Dundas urged Elliot, who had contested the Speakership in 1789, to delay taking a peerage.)

3 Ehrman, *Pitt*, vol. 2, p. 19, vol. 3, pp. 844–5.

4 Cave (ed.), *Diary of Farington*, vol. 9, p. 3458; Sinclair, *Correspondence*, vol. 1, p. 99; Fordyce to Dundas, 1 Sept. 1789, quoted in Ehrman, *Pitt*, vol. 1, p. 326, n. 1; Wheatley (ed.), *Wraxall*, vol. 4, pp. 427–8; Bickley (ed.), *Glenbervie Diaries*, vol. 1, p. 149.

5 Bodleian Library, Burges Mss, Box 73–4, Notes on Pitt; A.M. Wilberforce (ed.), *Private Papers*, p. 62; Sinclair, *Correspondence*, vol. 1, p. 99; Bickley (ed.), *Glenbervie Diaries*, vol. 1, p. 128.

6 Countess Granville (ed.), *Private Correspondence of Lord Granville Leveson-Gower* (1916), vol. 1, pp. 5–6.

7 A.M. Wilberforce (ed.), *Private Papers*, p. 66; Rosebery (ed.), 'Tomline's estimate', *Monthly Review*, August 1903, p. 30; Stanhope, *Pitt*, p. 40; Ehrman, *Pitt*, vol. 1, p. 326, n. 1; R. Thorne (ed.), *The History of Parliament. The House of Commons 1754–1790* (1986), vol. 4, p. 815.

8 HMC, *Kenyon*, p. 518; HMC, *Fortescue*, vol. 1, p. 357; Cave (ed.), *Diary of Farington*, vol. 9, p. 3458.

9 C. Wyvill, *Political Papers* (1794–1804), vol. 4, p. 23; Stanhope, *Pitt*, vol. 1, p. 250; Garlick and Macintyre (eds.), *Diary of Farington*, vol. 3, p. 730; Lord Colchester (ed.), *The Diary and Correspondence of Charles Abbot, Lord Colchester* (1861), vol. 1, p. 44; Rosebery (ed.), 'Tomline's estimate', *Monthly Review*, August 1903, p. 30; Jupp (ed.), *Canning Journal*, pp. 28–30; Bickley (ed.), *Glenbervie Diaries*, vol. 1, p. 72; Ehrman, *Pitt*, vol. 1, pp. 578–9; BL Loan, 72/38, f. 44.

10 Rosebery (ed.), 'Tomline's estimate', *Monthly Review*, August 1903, p. 31; R.I. and S. Wilberforce, *Life*, vol. 1, p. 265, vol. 2, p. 86; Hogge (ed.), *Auckland Corresp.*, vol. 3, pp. 114, 331; Pellew, *Sidmouth*, vol. 1, pp. 156–7.

11 Rose was with Pitt at Holwood when he heard of his friend Eliot's death, R.I. and S. Wilberforce, *Life*, vol. 2, p. 236; Pellew, *Sidmouth*, vol. 1, pp. 192–3; Hogge (ed.), *Auckland Corresp.*, vol. 3, p. 385; HMC, *Fortescue*, vol. 3, pp. 382–4; Leeds Central Library, George Canning Papers, Bundle 30, Pitt to Canning, 23 Oct. 1797; Ehrman, *Pitt*, vol. 3, pp. 99–106.

12 Jupp (ed.), *Canning Journal*, pp. 43–5, 64, 92, 154–6; Granville (ed.), *Leveson-Gower Corresp.*, vol. 1, pp. 172, 456.

13 A.M. Wilberforce (ed.), *Private Papers*, pp. 66, 79; R.I. and S. Wilberforce (eds.), *The Correspondence of William Wilberforce* (1846), vol. 1, p. 9; John Rylands Library, Eng. Ms 907, Dundas to Pitt, 4 Jan. 1800; Bodleian Library, Burges Mss Box 73–4, Notes on Pitt.

14 Ehrman, *Pitt*, vol. 1, pp. 119–21, 189–95, 443–66; M. Fry, *The Dundas Despotism* (Edinburgh, 1992), pp. 111–29; HMC, *Rutland*, vol. 6, p. 125; Wheatley (ed.), *Wraxall*, vol. 5, pp. 76–7. Only an Indian financial issue was likely to captivate him. See p. 87 above and n. 34 below.

15 Stanhope, *Pitt*, vol. 1, p. 233; Lord Ashbourne (ed.), *Pitt, some chapters of his Life and Times* (1898), p. 93; *Pitt/Rutland Corresp.*, p. 49; Add. MSS, 69,141, p. 41.

16 Rosebery (ed.), 'Tomline's estimate', *Monthly Review*, August 1903, p. 26.

17 J.E.D. Binney, *British Finance and Administration 1774–94* (Oxford, 1958), p. 112.

18 Binney, *British Finance*, pp. 262–82; Ehrman, *Pitt*, vol. 1, pp. 239–81.

19 Binney, *British Finance*, pp. 110–13; Ehrman, *Pitt*, vol. 1, pp. 260–7; BL Loan, 72/38, f. 58; Hutton (ed.), *Burges Corresp.*, p. 68.

20 For a fuller discussion of Pitt's financial and administrative achievements in the 1780s see Ehrman, *Pitt*, vol. 1, pp. 239–326; Binney, *British Finance*, *passim*; P. Harling, *The Waning of 'Old Corruption'. The Politics of Economical Reform in Britain, 1779–1846* (Oxford, 1996), pp. 42–55.

21 *Speeches*, vol. 2, pp. 40–7.

22 *Ibid.*, vol. 1, p. 300; vol. 2, p. 44.

23 Binney, *British Finance*, pp. 109–16; *Speeches*, vol. 1, pp. 299–319; Ehrman, *Pitt*, vol. 1, pp. 260–71.

24 Harling, *Waning of 'Old Corruption'*, pp. 58–63; J.R. Breihan, 'William Pitt and the Commission on Fees, 1785–1801', *HJ*, vol. 27 (1984), pp. 59–81.

25 *Speeches*, vol. 1, pp. 72–5, vol. 2, pp. 46–7; *Parl. Hist.*, vol. 29, col. 400; vol. 30, col. 606.

26 Rosebery (ed.), 'Tomline's estimate', *Monthly Review*, August 1903, p. 30; Lord Stanhope (ed.), *Notes and Extracts of Letters referring to Mr Pitt and Walmer Castle* (1866), p. 19.

27 Bodleian Library, Burges Mss, Box 73–4, Notes on Pitt; Add. MSS, 34,445, f. 15 (Hatsell wrote in 1804 not 1798, cf. K. Feiling, *The Second Tory Party* (1938), p. 165).

28 Binney, *British Finance*, pp. 32–3, 204; Ehrman, *Pitt*, vol. 1, pp. 289–90.

29 NRS, *Letters and Papers of Charles, Lord Barham*, (ed.) Sir J.K. Laughton (1906–11), vol. 2, p. 190; *L.C.GIII*, vol. 1, p. 355; HMC, *Fortescue*, vol. 1, p. 350, vol. 2, p. 595.

30 Ehrman, *Pitt*, vol. 1, pp. 293–8, 313–17; NRS, *Barham*, vol. 2, pp. 317–50, vol. 3, p. 56.

31 In 1798 and 1805 he issued Orders in Council to restrict the slave trade to conquered and reconquered colonies when parliamentary efforts had failed.

32 Breihan, 'Commission on Fees', pp. 59–81; Harling, *Waning of 'Old Corruption'*, pp. 62–3.

33 *Windham Papers*, vol. 2, p. 62; BL, Althorp Mss, '1st LORD ADM 29', Dundas to Spencer, 7 Jan. 1798; Harcourt (ed.), *Rose Diaries*, vol. 1, p. 213.

34 C. Ross (ed.), *Correspondence of Charles, First Marquis Cornwallis* (1859), vol. 2, p. 215.

35 R.R. Nelson, *The Home Office 1782–1801* (Durham, NC, 1969), p. 59; Colchester (ed.), *Abbot Diary*, vol. 1, p. 45; HMC, *Fortescue*, vol. 6, p. 259.

36 Bickley (ed.), *Glenbervie Diaries*, vol. 1, pp. 149, 337.

37 Fry, *Dundas Despotism*, p. 132; Bodleian Library, Burges Mss, Box 73–4, Notes on Pitt.

38 Add. MSS, 69,139, p. 3; Pellew, *Sidmouth*, vol. 1, p. 152; Add. MSS, 37,416, f. 373ff; Rosebery (ed.), 'Tomline's estimate', *Monthly Review*, August 1903, p. 31.

39 *Speeches*, vol. 2, p. 199 (7 April 1794).

40 Ehrman, *Pitt*, vol. 1, p. 195 (drawing on Walter Bagehot, 'William Pitt', in R.H. Hutton (ed.), *Biographical Studies* (1881), pp. 141–2); Add. MSS, 69,141, f. 41; Bickley (ed.), *Glenbervie Diaries*, vol. 1, pp. 34, 152; PRO, PRO30/58/3, Grenville to Pitt, 24 Oct. 1800.

41 L. Horner (ed.), *Memoirs and Correspondence of Francis Horner* (1843), vol. 1, p. 315; Garlick and Macintyre (eds.), *Diary of Farington*, vol. 2, p. 486; Sinclair, *Correspondence*, vol. 1, p. 99; HMC, *Bathurst*, p. 707; Bodleian Library, Burges Mss, Box 73–4, Notes on Pitt.

42 A.M. Wilberforce (ed.), *Private Papers*, pp. 61–2; *Pitt/Rutland Corresp.*, p. 57; D.R. Schweitzer, 'The failure of William Pitt's Irish Trade Propositions 1785', *PH*, vol. 3 (1984), pp. 129–45; Malmesbury (ed.), *Diaries*, vol. 3, p. 590; Garlick and Macintyre (eds.), *Diary of Farington*, vol. 2, p. 540.

43 Ehrman, *Pitt*, vol. 3, p. 429; Bodleian Library, Burges Mss, Box 73–4, Notes on Pitt; R.I. and S. Wilberforce, *Life*, vol. 1, p. 233; BL, Althorp Mss G44, Spencer to Dundas, 13 Nov. 1801.

44 Stanhope, *Pitt*, vol. 4, p. 407.

45 Bodleian Library, Burges Mss, Box 73–4, Notes on Pitt; Ehrman, *Pitt*, vol. 1, p. 585, vol. 2, p. 461, vol. 3, pp. 80–2, 92–7; Jupp (ed.), *Canning Journal*, p. 159.

46 *Speeches*, vol. 1, pp. 367, 369–70; Rose, *Pitt and Napoleon*, pp. 107–8; Thorne (ed.), *Commons*, vol. 3, pp. 737–8; Rosebery (ed.), 'Tomline's estimate', *Monthly Review*, August 1903, pp. 33, 34–5.

47 *Speeches*, vol. 2, pp. 34–8; Binney, *British Finance*, pp. 76–83; Breihan, 'Commission on Fees', pp. 72–4.

48 S.F. Bemis, *Jay's Treaty* (1923), *passim*; Ehrman, *Pitt*, vol. 2, pp. 513–14.

49 Harling, *Waning of 'Old Corruption'*, pp. 63–80; Breihan, 'Commission on Fees', pp. 77, 79–80.

50 Ehrman, *Pitt*, pp. 14–16.

51 Harling, *Waning of 'Old Corruption'*, Ch. 4.

52 P.K. O'Brien, 'Public Finance in the Wars with France 1793–1815', in H.T. Dickinson (ed.), *Britain and the French Revolution 1789–1815* (1989), pp. 165–87; R.A. Cooper, 'William Pitt, Taxation and the Needs of War', *Journal of British Studies*, vol. 22 (1982), pp. 94–103; Leeds Central Library, Canning Papers, Bundle 30, Pitt to Canning, 25 Oct. [1797]; Ehrman, *Pitt*, vol. 3, pp. 99–109, 358–65; *Parl. Hist.*, vol. 33, cols. 1361–9; *Speeches*, vol. 3, p. 175; *Parl. Hist.*, vol. 34, col. 1060.

Chapter 5

'THE THEATRE OF FUTURE FAME':
PITT AND THE HOUSE
OF COMMONS

. . .

'I WANT TO SPEAK IN THE
HOUSE OF COMMONS'

A principal factor in enabling Pitt to become, and remain for so long, the Prime Minister was the dominance he acquired over the House of Commons. He was early attuned to the significance of the Commons for a political career. His tutor reported him as saying in 1766 (aged seven): 'I am glad I am not the eldest son; I want to speak in the House of Commons like Papa.' He told a French host during his tour in 1783 that 'The part of our constitution which will first perish, is the prerogative of the King, and the authority of the House of Peers.' In debating a new constitution for Quebec in 1791, Pitt told the Commons that aristocracy was 'the essential link that held the branches together, and gave stability and strength to the whole'. Nevertheless it was a passive role that he envisaged for it, reflecting 'lustre on the Crown' and lending 'support and effect to the democracy'. The Crown provided authority and dignity, but it was 'the democracy', he contended, that gave vigour and energy to both.[1] He remained in the Commons all his adult life, advising his rising follower Castlereagh in 1802 to stay in that House 'which *he* thought should be the theatre of future fame'.[2]

No politician could lead the House of Commons without speaking ability and this was universally regarded as Pitt's greatest parliamentary asset. Horace Walpole, who heard Chatham in his prime, thought that 'Pitt had not the commanding brilliancy of his father nor his imposing air and person; but his language was more pure and correct, and his

99

method and reasoning better.'[3] At times he could reach supreme oratorical heights. His opponents, Fox, Windham and Grey, walking home after his speech against the slave trade on 2 April 1792, all agreed that it was 'one of the most extraordinary displays of eloquence they had ever heard'.[4] Pitt particularly excelled his father in his ability to explain financial business to the House, and in his application as a debater.

One of Pitt's main tasks as First Lord of the Treasury and Chancellor of the Exchequer was to get the government's financial business through Parliament, and a capacity for lucid financial exposition was a major instrument towards securing parliamentary and public confidence in a Ministry. Lord North had been a particularly lucid, clear and able financial presenter, but Wraxall, who heard both present budgets, subsequently judged that 'Lord North could sustain no comparison with the late Mr Pitt.' Pitt's exposition of his 1784 budget was 'in a manner at once so voluminous, accurate and masterly, as to excite universal admiration'. Lady Gower enthused in the next session that 'Mr Pitt has gained himself great credit by his last two or three speeches . . . so perfect a knowledge of the Commerce, Funds, and Government of the Country that one must imagine to hear him on these subjects that he had the experience of fifty years.'[5]

Pitt's speeches carried authority. He did not write them out in advance. Rather, he exploited his capacity to assimilate and retain information. At most he assembled a few notes of the heads of subjects for inclusion. On the day of the introduction of his Sinking Fund proposals in 1786, he went over the financial details in the morning, and then settled on the plan of his speech in his mind during a solitary quarter-of-an-hour walk in the park before dinner just before going to the House. His ability to present extensive financial detail from memory made a deep impression on his audience, as it apparently demonstrated his depth of knowledge. Within a very short time he became the unchallenged Commons master on matters of public finance.[6]

The Foxite MP, John Nicholls, admitted in 1796 that Pitt was 'superior in debate to any member of Parliament of this day'. Such superiority did not come without effort. Pitt attended the Commons assiduously. His style was the reverse of the easy laxity of his masterly predecessor North, who slept or feigned sleep during debates. Pretyman recorded that 'He was always attentive to the debate as it proceeded, and listened with care to every speaker, remembering the observation of his illustrious father, that something was to be learnt from the speech of the dullest country gentleman that ever spoke in the House of Commons.'[7] He made brief notes for reply, but again the prodigious memory came into play. Nicholls conceded that:

The arrangement of his matter is as regular as a studied composition; and he has the happy art of introducing his answers to the principal points of argument of his opponents, each in its proper place, thereby giving them full effect. He seems to have apprehended and to have matured the whole subject of each debate, and to leave little to chance; and his speeches have an uniform strength. Of perception he is as quick as Fox; of invention of momentary argument not so fertile; but the equal vigour which he maintains throughout his speeches, overmatches the occasional springs of exertion of his opponent, who is always irregular and often weak.[8]

Another opponent, the Duke of Bedford, explained to Lady Bessborough that:

orator

if I could imagine the purest, most correct, forcible, and eloquent language spoke in the most harmonious voice and animated manner, seizing with incredible quickness and ingenuity all the weak parts of the opposing arguments, and putting the strongest ones of his own in the most favourable point of view, that I should then have some faint idea of what Mr P's speaking was. He said it was the most fascinating thing he ever heard. That in general he thought Mr Pitt plain in his person, but towards the end of an interesting speech that he look'd beautiful.[9]

All agreed that his speeches were 'equal [i.e. strong argument throughout, no lapses]', and wonderfully fluent: 'never a moment's hesitation for a word'; 'a regular flow of expression, never requiring to go backward to correct himself but proceeding with an uninterrupted stream of delivery'; 'every sentence uttered by Mr Pitt was so regular and correct as if to appear formed in his mind before it was expressed, – on the contrary Mr Fox often plunged into the middle of a sentence and found his way through it as well as he could'. Fox himself admitted that 'although he himself is never in want of words, Mr Pitt is never without the very best words possible'.[10] Pitt himself ascribed his fluency to the particular early training he received from his father: 'it was his custom in the morning to construe his author, Virgil or Livy, to his tutor, Mr Wilson; and in the evening, after tea, to translate the same passage freely, with the book open before him, to his father, and the rest of the family'. Chatham instructed him to stop 'where he was not sure of the right word to be used in English, until the right word came to his mind, and then proceed', and in this way over the course of time the right words came naturally to him. His renowned clear and sonorous elocution, delivered in a 'deep, bell-toned voice', came again from Chatham's early coaching in getting him daily to recite passages from the best English poets, usually Shakespeare and Milton.[11]

Yet for all that Pitt was 'without rival as a Parliamentary speaker in arrangement and elocution', there was also an element of the street-fighter in his make-up that ruffled opponents, and occasionally embarrassed his own supporters when they saw it loosed upon unfortunate lesser opponents. Horner spoke of 'that bitter freezing sarcasm which every body agrees is his most original talent', and Windham objected that 'He takes not the grand path suited to his post as Prime Minister, for he is personal beyond all men; pointed, sarcastic, cutting; and it is in him peculiarly unbecoming. The Minister should be always conciliating; the attack, the probe, the invective, belong to the assailant.' That was not, however, how Pitt played the game, nor would he readily retract wounding words once spoken, so that cutting remarks led to challenges to duels from Grey and from Tierney (shots were exchanged with the latter without effect in 1798).[12] It is perhaps little wonder that so many MPs were in awe of him.

. . .

LEARNING THE ARTS OF PARLIAMENTARY MANAGEMENT

Most MPs looked on Pitt with awe rather than affection. For a man who led both the government and the Commons for nearly nineteen years – the second-longest incumbency in British history – Pitt had an extraordinary management style, unique for a successful eighteenth-century Prime Minister in that he disdained the assiduous wooing of back-benchers and borough patrons employed by his predecessors. His friend, Lord Camden, lamented his 'want of *little attentions*' towards his supporters.[13] An eyewitness, Wraxall, described how:

> From the instant Pitt entered the doorway of the House of Commons, he advanced up the floor with a quick and firm step, his head erect and thrown back, looking neither to right or left, nor favouring with a nod or a glance any of those individuals seated on either side, amongst whom many who possessed five thousand pounds a year would have been gratified even by so slight a mark of attention.[14]

This image is abundantly confirmed by others, such as Sir Nathaniel Dance MP, who complained that Pitt 'would scarcely acknowledge a bow'.[15] Pitt failed to make up for it in other ways. Daniel Pulteney MP, in 1785, reported hearing members complain 'that they never supported any minister a fortnight before in their lives without one dinner at least in the time, and it seems in this great duty of a good minister Pitt has almost deserved an impeachment'. When in 1788 Pitt was having trouble with the East India Company interest in Parliament, Lord Bulkeley heard that 'a few dozen of claret, and two or three dinners' might have settled matters, but that Pitt and his political managers, the Treasury Secretaries Rose and Steele, 'vote such company boars not deserving of such notice'.[16]

The most frequently voiced complaint against the Minister, however, was his failure to answer letters. This threatened damaging consequences as the effects rippled down the clientage networks by which British politics were run. The Duke of Hamilton protested in 1791 that this treatment made him 'appear in an odd point of view to those who press me to ask favours, and who look up to me as the channel through which those favours are to come', while Lord Bulkeley thought it 'unhandsome and unkind', adding that Pitt 'must be the best judge, whether such personal inattentions can ensure the continuance of zeal and activity in his interests of those who plague themselves with counties and boroughs'.[17] Bulkeley thought Pitt in more danger of desertions during the 1788–9 Regency Crisis through his 'inattention to these trifles' than from anything else. Citing one MP who complained of never having one letter answered since Pitt came to power, he pointed out the needs of MPs on this score since 'the constituent will not believe the member's assiduity until he sees a real or ostensible answer'. The veteran Cheshire county MP, Sir Richard Cotton, threw up his seat 'in a pet' in 1796 after three applications for a tax collectorship at Nantwich for a friend went unanswered, while Camden blamed Lord Darnley's defection, in 1804, on Pitt leaving two notes from Darnley without any answer.[18]

These 'personal inattentions' stemmed from the amount of business he took on himself, from his attitude to Party, and to the shyness of a young leader of older men. Wilberforce thought him 'one of the shyest men I ever knew'. To strike up a relationship with him was not easy, particularly for those in awe of his achievement. Jeremy Bentham met him in late 1781 and wrote that:

> in his conversation there is nothing of the orator – nothing of that hauteur and suffisance one would expect; on the contrary, he seems very good-natured, and a little raw. I was monstrously frightened at him, but when I came to talk with him, he seemed frightened at me.[19]

This shyness, and even awkwardness, thought Wilberforce, produced effects which were mistaken for a stand-offish pride. In this respect Pitt was less well equipped than any of his most successful predecessors.

Contemporaries thought that he had been thrown too young into the Premiership, before he had acquired a knowledge of the world, and that he never had time to acquire it thereafter.[20] He lacked the earthy urbanity of Walpole, the plain man's painstakingness of Pelham, the easy affability of Lord North. His small talk was limited by the lack of an ear for music, or an eye for drawing and painting, or a wide reading of modern literature and poetry. He had an aggravating habit for more earnest colleagues of making a joke of – 'quizzing away' – unpleasant matters that he did not wish to consider.[21] All this compounded his difficulties in handling patronage matters where demand greatly exceeded supply and he was consequently required to soothe personal sensitivities. Delaying decisions or avoiding reply was too ready a way out. Nothing made him so bilious, he told Camden, as political 'Arrangements'.[22]

There was much truth in James Burges's verdict on 'his total unfitness to be leader of a party'. The Duke of Leeds, in a later comparison of Pitt and Fox, also wrote that:

> As leaders of a Party there is scarcely a competition (in point of management) that can possibly be urged. Mr Fox is without doubt the best leader of a party that the memory of any man living or the history of this country ... can afford us ... [Fox] lives *with* as well as *by* his connections, attentive to the discipline, even to the smallest minutiae of the corps he commands, no local interest of an individual composing that corps is to be an object of indifference (witness all turned up at Brooks Club to rally against the Rochdale Navigation which had injured Lord Derby's property).

In consequence the followers of Opposition were much better drilled and better collected for active operations than the supporters of the Ministry.[23]

Pitt did not believe in this type of Party. He always described himself as an *'independent Whig'*. For him the term 'Whig' denoted a general adherence to 'the principles of liberty settled at the [1688] Revolution' and not membership of a formed and disciplined political Party.[24] His father had established his independence from the 'Old Corps' Party connections of the great Whig aristocratic grandees, and Pitt did likewise. His parliamentary reform proposals would have made the House of Commons more independent of Crown influence, but they would also have made it more independent from Party domination by increasing the seats with the widest electorates and diminishing the weight or number of 'rotten' boroughs under the sway of the great aristocratic patrons. He never sought to build up a personal party of his own. An analysis in 1788, after four and a half years in power, put 'The Party attached to Mr Pitt' at fifty-two, of whom no more than twenty would be returned in an election if Pitt was not Premier. It was not until the 1802 election that this could be tested, at which time he retained a personal following of fifty-seven, but this was far too small to ensure a Commons majority without further support.[25]

Pitt did not expect blind obedience from even this personal following. He told one of them, George Canning, that:

> On speculative subjects especially, it was natural for every thinking man to form his own opinion, and very probable that any two men might form opinions totally opposite. A general good disposition towards government was what he hoped to find in me.[26]

In 1788 his friend Wilberforce, who frequently voted against Pitt's war measures in the 1790s and was influential in Pitt's defeat over Melville in 1805, noted that:

> It is undoubtedly the established rule, that all official men are to vote with their principal; but notwithstanding the systematic support of a ministry which has resulted from systematic opposition, the minister is not considered as entitled to require the votes of the inferior members of government except on political questions.

The key political question, on which Pitt demanded total loyalty from all members of his government, was to ask of any measure: 'Is the credit or stability of the ministry at issue?'[27] Hence the successful conclusion of the Regency Crisis was followed by a purge of those who had 'ratted' on him in his hour of need. Sir John Aubrey and Robert Laurie were removed from their posts, while Colonel Alexander Stewart, applying for promotion, was tartly told by Dundas that 'If political support is to be any foundation for military preferment, these occurrences must of necessity have produced other pretensions not inferior to yours.' When Sir John Sinclair opposed government during the 1797 financial crisis, Pitt manoeuvred his removal from the chairmanship of the government-sponsored Board of Agriculture in the following year.[28]

For most parliamentary issues, however, Pitt allowed a free vote. Possibly this was the only practical way he could hold together what was initially a loose, diverse coalition between supporters of the King and a broad spectrum of opponents of the Fox–North Coalition. However the lack of a clearly established Party line, agreed and enforced in advance, left supporters frequently puzzled at his intentions. Pitt's remoteness from the ordinary member threatened to become an unbridgeable gulf of understanding, leading to dissatisfaction, demoralisation and ultimately alienation. The back-bencher Pulteney's letters to his patron, the Duke of Rutland, indicate occasions, as over Beaufoy's motion to repeal the Test Acts in 1787, when Pitt let it be known in advance that he wanted the measure defeated in the Commons. Advance publicity in April 1785, however, still left Pulteney uncertain whether Pitt was 'encumbered or enamoured with . . . this Yorkshire system of [Parliamentary] Reform'. Only after Pitt's bill was defeated and they met in the park did he see that Pitt 'looks as grave as if he had suffered a Ministerial defeat'. Five weeks later Pulteney was explaining to his patron his problem in knowing what line to adopt on the Irish Commercial Resolutions, 'never finding out but with great difficulty what Mr Pitt intends when he first moves any resolution, waiting, as he often does, for Eden's or Fox's conduct upon it'.[29]

This communications failure was perhaps most demoralising for supporters at times of negotiation for junction with parts of the Opposition. Whereas in 1794 the Duke of Portland consulted his closest colleagues on negotiations to join government, Pitt handled everything on his side himself, so that the result, particularly the extent of the offices and honours offered to win the Portland Whigs, came as a shock to Pitt's supporters. Canning noted that 'many, very many, and amongst them some of Pitt's friends in particular, either *grumble* pretty audibly at the distribution of so great a part of the power among the newcomers, or at best, shake their heads and wish that it may answer in the end'.[30]

Pitt's continued silence to his old followers, as the Portland Whigs demanded control of Ireland and then began to purge the ministerialists in Dublin, led to a real crisis of confidence at the start of 1795. Auckland wrote pessimistically in December 1794 that the Cabinet was made up of strange discordant materials, subject to difficulties within and distrusts without. 'It is neither a Rockingham Ministry, nor a Pitt Ministry, nor a Ministry of King's Friends, but it is all three and none of them.'[31] Finally, as news of Fitzwilliam's removals came from Ireland, Pitt's loyal Solicitor-General, John Mitford, felt obliged to warn the Prime Minister of frequently hearing 'the most disagreeable assertions with respect to the conduct of H.M. ministers and particularly of yourself. The present state of affairs sours the minds of the best friends of government.' Three weeks later he attributed this discontent to 'the ignorance in which I believe most of your friends are with respect both to your real situation & your intentions, & their apparent uncertainty whether you are not acting upon the impulse of the moment because you are unwilling to look at the evil in its full extent . . . [Y]our conduct of late has turned some warm friends into cold friends, or perhaps bitter enemies.'[32] It needed the recall of Fitzwilliam, the vigorous anti-radical measures of autumn 1795 and the simultaneous abandonment of the intransigent French Monarchist line of the Portland Whigs in the war, before confidence was restored among his old supporters.

Pitt's second ministry differed little from the first in this problem. The Speaker of the Commons, Charles Abbot, noted on 28 March 1805 that there had been no declaration yet from Pitt of the part he would take over the Tenth Report of the Committee of Naval Enquiry, which had censured his First Lord of the Admiralty and old friend, Lord Melville (Dundas). The rest of the Cabinet were unacquainted with what Pitt intended and in the Commons there was 'much dissatisfaction among the general supporters of the Administration'. The surprise junction with Addington's party in the previous December led to protests even from those close to him such as Camden and Tomline, and the defection of influential borough owners Lord Stafford and an old friend, William Lowther, now Lord Lonsdale, and their MPs.[33]

A major consequence of this communication gap, explained Pulteney, was that:

> from having no immediate intercourse with the generality of the House of Commons here, he is as ignorant of their opinions on particular ques- tions as if he was minister of another country . . . His living and convers- ing with a very small circle and acting only on abstract principles will, I foresee, involve him at some time or other in difficulties, from which no minister of this country can be free without more extensive information.[34]

His early defeats as leader were the result of failures in management. He underestimated the responsiveness of MPs to constituents' opposition to taxes on coal and cotton in his 1784 budget, which he subsequently had to retract or modify. In attempting to deprive Fox of his popular power base, he persisted in a scrutiny of the 1784 Westminster election beyond the patience and sense of fair play of MPs, who finally voted against him in March 1785 and returned Fox. A month later Pitt was beaten again, on parliamentary reform, principally because parliamentary prejudice and, judging from the paucity of supporting petitions, the opinion of the country was against reform, but also because his remoteness from ordinary MPs prevented him from communicating his genuine personal commitment to the issue.

These results seem to have unnerved him in his most important par- liamentary business of the 1785 session – steering the Irish Commercial Propositions through the Commons. Pulteney commented that 'His whole conduct proves he can only be minister with an independent

House; and the very proofs they give of their independence . . . startles him so much that he is too much frightened for some time to bring questions before them where he is equally sure of decisive majorities in his favour.'[35] By failing to push the Propositions decisively, he gave time for the Opposition to stir up resistance and then made so many concessions and amendments to the plan that it was subsequently rejected by the Irish Parliament. One final major defeat, over the Duke of Richmond's fortifications programme in 1786, was really directed against the unpopular Richmond rather than Pitt and only lost on the casting vote of the Speaker, but it showed the lack of tight ministerial discipline when Admiralty MPs voted against the measure. Had Pitt more positively enforced support from all members of government for a government measure he would have secured the requisite majority.[36]

This string of defeats threatened to sap confidence in Pitt's government. In January 1786 the Irish Secretary, Orde, agreed with his old patron Shelburne (now Marquis of Lansdowne) that 'this will be a Session of Tryal for Mr Pitt, and that He will now be shaken, or his Stability confirmed'.[37] A lack of able subordinates, and careless drafting of bills, were weaknesses, but his management style was seen as crucial. Nine months into Pitt's Ministry, the veteran political manager, John Robinson, was warning that 'great abilities alone, or the greatest, will not lead men or can Englishmen be drove, but that address, temper and management must be called in to aid'. Nine months later, Pulteney thought that:

> the old plan of Lord North, and afterwards of the Coalition, to divide the profits of a Ministry in their several proportions down to the lowest of their adherents, was too well calculated for modern times . . . [I]f Mr Pitt can long persuade the House of Commons to spend their time and fortunes *independently* to support an *independent* Minister in great power and an income of £8,000 a year, it will . . . be such an instance of his eloquence as will raise him above Demosthenes and Cicero.[38]

Pulteney comforted himself that 'The abominable character of the [Fox–North] coalition . . . is still our protection', and others too, including Fox himself, saw hostility to the Opposition as Pitt's salvation in this difficult fledgling period.[39] In the event, however, 1786 turned from a 'Tryal' into a triumph, thanks to his Sinking Fund proposals. He even secured the passage of an excise duty on wines which, as he proudly pointed out to his friend Rutland, 'had nearly overthrown Sir Robert Walpole' – the most powerful of his predecessors.[40] Pitt was developing a management style that did not leave quite so much to the strength of his own debating skills.

. . .

OLD AND NEW IN THE PITT
MANAGEMENT STYLE

Pitt, as he had told Thurlow in 1783, was fully prepared to exert those customary means 'fairly in the hands of Ministers'. In late 1785 he lured over the main Opposition financial expert, William Eden, who had done so much to wreck his Irish Commercial Propositions, with a diplomatic post to negotiate a commercial treaty with France. Twenty peerage creations in his first year of office repaid support given during the establishment of his Ministry. The British peerage in 1786 for the Irish peer and MP, Lord Delaval, who only switched sides to Pitt after the 1784 election, further indicated that there were no permanent exclusions for former opponents and led more to enter into negotiations with the Minister.

Lacking much respect for the sanctity of the old peerage, Pitt was prepared to add to its numbers on a scale far larger than any of his predecessors. To a temporal peerage of 208 in 1783, Pitt made 34 internal promotions and transferred 18 old titles, and he elevated nine Scottish and 22 Irish peers, and 52 commoners – in all, 135 creations or promotions. These included 20 borough owners controlling 41 seats and 65 present or former MPs in his first Ministry, 24 going to county MPs in particular.[41] Wilberforce later complained that what Pitt had done weakened the Commons, by removing from its ranks so many of the wealthiest and most respected landowners of the country. Conversely the Lords were strengthened by their addition, along with many Scottish and Irish peers who made the Upper House more representative of the entire British Isles. However, while Pitt's peerages helped him satisfy the Commons now, they ultimately made the Lords more independent of government control by overwhelming the numbers of the place-holding 'Party of the Crown' in that House.[42]

The hope of places and peerages led nine Northites and four supporters or sympathisers with the Portland/Fox wing of the Coalition to switch sides between 1784 and 1788, before the Regency Crisis and the prospect of a change of Ministry re-polarised support again.[43] Pitt's Regency victory in 1789 and his general election triumph in 1790 enabled him to make altogether more ambitious attempts to negotiate a junction with the Portland/Fox Whigs in early 1791, and with their more moderate Portland wing in the summer of 1792 and spring of 1794. In between he fell back to the tactic of picking off individuals with the lure of offices. Again it was largely the former Northites who took the bait – Loughborough as Lord Chancellor, Sir Gilbert Elliott as commissioner for captured Toulon, Sylvester Douglas as Irish Chief Secretary in 1793. The Portland wing finally agreed to join him in 1794, influenced by the deepening crisis of external war and internal radicalism, but also by Pitt's massive offer of honours and places – five Cabinet seats, the Garter for Portland himself, the Lord Lieutenancy of Middlesex, five peerages and one promotion in the peerage, two Royal Household posts, a pension for Edmund Burke, and the promise of the Viceroyalty of Ireland. Portland brought with him some 62 MPs, leaving Fox with a personal Opposition following of about 55 supporters.[44] Pitt employed this tactic again, more cheaply but ultimately less successfully, in December 1804, when he negotiated the junction of Addington and his followers (about 40 MPs) with his beleaguered second Ministry in return for two Cabinet seats, a peerage for Addington himself, the appointment of three Privy Councillors and a promise of future offices for others.[45]

Three times Pitt had the opportunity to 'make' a Parliament at a general election, and he applied himself to seeking the return of those with 'a general good disposition towards government'. The 1784 election was chaotically managed. The shortness of preparation time, and the inexperience of Pitt and his manager, George Rose, were compounded by the excitements of this unique political crisis, upsetting long-standing local political relationships – fortunately generally in the government's favour. With time enough to prepare for the following general election, Pitt began work in the summer of 1788. He probably had a 1789 election in view, since it became his standard tactic not to let Parliaments run their seven-year course but to forestall the preparations of his opponents by a premature election (a tactic perhaps learned from Lord North, whose snap election of 1780 wrecked his own attempts to find his first seat). That intention was, however, disrupted by the Regency Crisis, and loyalties were left to stabilise again before he went to the polls in 1790 – still a year early. Preparations for the following election began in 1795, supervised again by Pitt, and under the executive management this time of the Treasury Secretary, Charles Long. Scotland on each occasion was largely left to Henry Dundas. As Dundas's influence with the Minister and his patronage resources increased, so did his control over Scotland, where he increased ministerial support (and personal support for Dundas) from 24 of the 45 Scottish seats after the 1784 election to 43 in 1796. This was, moreover, a more disciplined following than Pitt's English support.[46]

Pitt managed English political patronage with the assistance of his former college tutor, George Pretyman, his secretary until created Bishop of Lincoln in 1786, and the Secretaries to the Treasury, George Rose (1783–1801) and Charles Long (1791–1801). Direct Crown control of boroughs had diminished markedly. Pitt told Canning in 1792 that his patronage as a Minister was very small, perhaps as inconsiderable as six seats. Douglas was told in 1796 that the number of seats to which the government could recommend without expense was 'wonderfully reduced' – Pitt and Rose were not aware of more than three.[47] Although he had fewer seats directly under government control and he paid less money directly for others than did his recent predecessors, Pitt nevertheless had the same dealings with borough patrons. These placed seats at his disposal, either in return for favours, or so that Pitt and his election managers might put their way potential candidates willing to pay the going rate to the patron for a seat in Parliament (anything from £2,000 to £5,000). One of the government's main electoral functions was thus to act as middleman, trying to match supporters willing to buy with patrons willing to sell.[48]

The Cornish borough of East Looe, under the proprietorship of the Buller family, was one such case. Just before the 1784 election Pitt appointed the head of the family, John Buller, to the Treasury Board and had his brother, the Rev. William Buller, made Dean of Exeter, since it was 'very much the wish of Dr Butler's [sic] friends'. Dean Buller became family manager of the borough on his brother's death in 1786, and, on the eve of the 1790 election, Pitt wrote to Rose that 'I have made up my mind to offer the Deanery of Canterbury to Dean Butler [sic]; and you will be so good as to inform him of it, contriving at the same time to make sure of the *return* we wish, as far as you can with *propriety*'. Following an initial payment of £400, Buller also received £500 from the secret service funds in 1791, 'in further part of the expenses at East Looe for the whole Parliament'. In 1792 he was made Bishop of Exeter. East Looe's two seats throughout remained at the disposal of government.[49]

To get Canning into the Commons in 1793, between general elections, Pitt turned to a borough patron willing to vacate his seat for a friend of government – at a price. Sir Richard Worsley provided the opening in his seat for Newport, Isle of Wight, in return for being made envoy to Venice. For the following Parliament, Pitt had Canning returned for Wendover, controlled by a close friend, the banker Robert Smith, for whom he secured an Irish peerage in 1796 and an English one the following year.[50]

Secret service expenses for the 1784 elections totalled £32,000 and those in 1790 probably amounted to about £40,000. Although the Opposition was better prepared on the latter occasion, the government as usual prevailed, while the junction with the Portland Whigs, and Fox's stance on the war and the French Revolution, helped produce an overwhelming victory in 1796 (see Table 5.1).

Table 5.1   General election results under Pitt

	Government	Opposition	Independent	Doubtful
1784	315	213		30
1790	340	183	29	6
1796	424	95	29	10

Source: Namier and Brooke (eds.), *Commons*, vol. 1, pp. 92–3; Thorne (ed.), *Commons*, vol. 1, pp. 126, 149.

Pitt's area of political vulnerability was, however, less at the polls, where (except in 1784) constituency politics were relatively static and enough local patrons were willing to deal with the government of the day to ensure that no eighteenth-century Prime Minister ever lost a general election. The main area of potential volatility was from members, once elected. There was a natural tendency to support the King's government, provided it was not particularly unpopular.[51] Of Pitt's predecessors since 1714 only Walpole, North and Shelburne fell through losing the confidence of the Commons (all three through perceived mishandling of wars). After its initial trial of strength, therefore, Pitt's Ministry was not in danger of falling except in special circumstances. The King's illness at the end of 1788 suddenly raised questions of which King, present or future, MPs should support. In the Regency Crisis of 1788–9, the unpopularity of the Prince of Wales came to Pitt's rescue, but in 1804–5 the age of the ailing Monarch, which brought his demise closer, was a growing consideration in the minds of ambitious politicians. In most circumstances, however, Pitt was fighting to get government business through the house rather than for political survival, though too many defeats might have led to a loss of confidence in his competence.

It was important for any eighteenth-century leader of the Commons to have on his side those who chaired its debates, as Pitt discovered by uniquely having two major tied votes decided against him, by the casting votes of Speakers who were not of his choosing.[52] The first, Charles Cornwall, appointed by North from his junior office-holders, also put Pitt on the defensive from the start of the parliamentary struggle in January 1784 by refusing him the floor on the first day, in Wraxall's opinion 'in subversion of all usage'.[53] Pitt was consequently fortunate when Cornwall's timely death at the start of the Regency debates in 1789 allowed him to install his cousin, Grenville, as Speaker. After the crisis Grenville moved on to the Home Office, to be replaced by the Premier's long-standing friend, Henry Addington, son of the Chatham family physician. Faced with a tie on the legacy duty in 1796, Addington used his casting vote in favour of government, and it was Addington's failure to press Pitt into retracting his savage attack on Tierney in May 1798 that led to the latter challenging the Premier to their duel on Wimbledon Common.[54]

Pitt also needed a sympathetic Chairman of the Commons' Committee of Ways and Means which oversaw financial legislation. After the 1784 election, he was able to put in place Thomas Gilbert, formerly land agent to Pitt's cabinet colleague, Earl Gower, and who sat for a Gower-controlled seat, but whose campaigning for economy in government expenditure (besides being a champion of reform of the poor laws) had gained him a reputation as 'demi-courtier, demi-patriot', and harmonised with the Premier's outlook. In 1791 he was succeeded by Henry Hobart, a reliable independent supporter of Pitt. Addington thought him inefficient, but it was only when he was on the point of death in 1799 that he was replaced by the Speaker's conscientious brother-in-law, Charles Bragge. It may be significant of Pitt's sense of the importance of these positions that, in 1789, he was behind the proposal to replace the Speaker's income from fees and allowances of c.£3,000 by a salary of £5,000 (which a sympathetic House raised to £6,000), and that in 1799 the unofficial salary of between £500 and £800 paid to the Chairman of Ways and Means from the secret service fund was replaced by a regular payment by the House of £1,200 at the end of each session.[55]

More was needed to get his business through an independent-minded House, however. Pitt recognised the need for a political society hostess to match the Opposition's formidable array. He planned a series of assemblies, 'to take in everybody', with as hostess his sister Harriot, who came with her husband, Pitt's friend Edward Eliot, to live with him after their marriage in 1785. But Harriot died after a difficult childbirth in 1786. The deficiency was, however, abundantly filled by the irrepressible Jane, Duchess of Gordon, who stepped forward in the late 1780s, and who, with Dundas, drew Pitt's frequent attendance at her soirées into the early 1790s. In addition White's Club acted as a male social club for those who supported the Ministry. Pitt was dining there frequently at the end of the 1780s. It was to White's that Pitt went directly when he returned hurriedly from Cambridge to rally support for Dolben's flagging slave trade regulation bill in 1788. The members of White's proved a pillar of strength in the Regency Crisis when, according to one of them, General Grant, 89 MPs who belonged to the club attended constantly and voted with Pitt. These familiar expedients failed, however, to survive the outbreak of war in 1793, after which his attendance at the Duchess of Gordon's assemblies and at White's became rare.[56]

There was, however, a general acceptance that the Ministry must be made to survive, and alternative ways were found to bridge the gap between Pitt and the generality of MPs. Where Pitt seemed too aloof to supply these needs, MPs turned to others as middlemen with the Prime Minister. Two men in particular played a vital part in smoothing Pitt's relationship with ordinary members. Henry Dundas, 'unaffected, frank, and *jovial*', provided 'more amenity of manner, more placability of temper, more facility of access'. To Wraxall:

> Pitt appeared as if made to withhold, Dundas to confer, Ministerial favours. Many of those recompenses and remunerations denominated in the vulgar language jobs, unfortunately necessary among us in order to keep adherents in good humour, and which flowed from the state fountain in Downing Street, were distributed, not by Pitt, but by the Treasurer of the Navy [Dundas].

Dundas's role was supplemented in the 1790s by the popular Speaker of the Commons, Henry Addington. Nathaniel Dance contrasted Pitt, scarcely acknowledging a bow, with Addington, who was 'all civility'. To Addington fell the anxieties and confidences intended for Pitt's ear, from Addington came encouraging reports of Pitt's reaction to speeches, and Pitt himself used Addington to conciliate applicants disappointed of patronage.[57]

While Dundas and Addington applied themselves to the rank and file, Pitt applied himself in particular to seeking out those with both talents and the same taste for business as himself. Wilberforce remarked 'the kind interest he took in the rising talents of every young public man of any promise whose politics were congenial with his own'. In 1788–9 he backed a new dining club, the Constitution Club, to celebrate the principles of 1688, and intended as 'a good political net to catch young men just launching into the world from college', to counteract the attractive powers of the Opposition Whig Club.[58]

Mostly Pitt found his talent in the chamber and committee rooms of the House, where he could be found listening, commending, encouraging and advising. The new Scottish MP and Advocate-General, Robert Dundas, was told by Pitt after an early speech in 1791 that what he had said was:

> in point of matter and manner more to the purpose than anything he had heard on the subject. In short, he thinks I shall do him good; and in proof of it, I was admitted, by his own desire, to the previous meeting at his house yesterday, of 8 or 10 of his friends, to consider what was to be stated in answer to the expected attack on the bill for appropriating the

unclaimed dividends. He says he never wants me to make a set speech, but wished me to make myself previously master of the business to come on, and not to rise and speak on it, unless I feel inclined, and anything occurs which I think myself able to answer.[59]

Pitt's own determination to lead on all occasions – what his friend Henry Bankes described as 'his manly manner of proceeding as a Minister always coming forward to avow his measures and not seeking to shelter himself under the cover of others' – in practice limited speaking opportunities for his young protégés, often to their frustration.[60] The particular public opportunity that he gave them to shine however was in coupling them with older independent back-bench supporters in proposing or seconding the Address in answer to the King's speech at the start of a session. Pitt's record in selecting for this occasion new men not yet in office and many not related to those in office is remarkable, and it stands in contrast to the practice of his predecessors, who called on office-holders or their relatives for this task.[61] Of 34 chosen by Pitt for the 17 Addresses during his first Ministry, two were future Prime Ministers (Addington and Canning), five were future Cabinet Ministers (Ryder [later Earl of Harrowby], Yorke, Castlereagh, Morpeth, Granville Leveson-Gower), and five more became holders of lesser offices (Smyth, Pole Carew, Murray, Wallace and Dickinson Jr). This contrasts with the 26 proposers and seconders under Lord North, of whom only one became a Cabinet Minister, and eight held government offices.

This list moreover does not include another future Prime Minister (Grenville) and future Cabinet Ministers, Mornington (later Marquess Wellesley) and Apsley (later Earl Bathurst), whom Pitt befriended and brought forward in the 1780s, and two more future Premiers, Robert Jenkinson (later Earl of Liverpool) and Spencer Perceval, and Cabinet Ministers, Nicholas Vansittart and Bragge-Bathurst, who served their apprenticeship under Pitt's encouraging eye in the 1790s. The longest-surviving acolyte to come under his tutelage was the Earl of Aberdeen, who nominated Pitt one of his guardians in 1795 and who resigned as Prime Minister in 1856.[62] Pitt raised and trained many of those who would be the rulers of Britain for the next fifty years!

This talented support was attracted by early privileged access to his inner circle. Invited to dine together with his close friends and men of business, they encountered a different Pitt from the public image. The young Canning found Pitt, in company at the head of his own table, to be 'exactly what hits my taste – attentive without being troublesome – mixing in the conversation without attempting to lead it – laughing often and easily – and boyish enough if it should fall in his way, to discuss the history of Cock Robin'.[63] They were allowed to attend meetings of the main government speakers in Downing Street preparatory to debates. Above all they were given open access to Pitt, especially Canning, who thought him in private 'just as I would have him – open, free, ready to answer questions without reserve, or to say without reserve that they were such questions as he cannot at present answer'. Canning found him readily accessible whenever he wanted to discuss the subject of debates in which he wished to participate; Granville Leveson-Gower described how Pitt 'Talked with the most unreserved confidence upon almost any subject, argued and discussed points with us upon which he had any doubts, and made jokes to us about S. Legge etc. as if he was exactly our own age.'[64]

With these kindred spirits Pitt lost his shyness, and they were flattered and won over to great devotion by his uninhibited familiarity. Whereas to those outside the circle he seemed 'devilish close', and Burges could write of 'his apparent hauteur and extreme unease in private society', Canning, when accused of lack of deference because he too publicly showed this private familiarity with the Prime Minister, protested that Pitt 'is in fact a very hearty, salutation-giving, shake-handy sort of person'.[65] Older men too could be caught by this narrowly revealed charm. The parliamentary reformer, Wyvill, could equally say that 'in his deportment in private society there is much ease and affability; he possesses a rich fund of benignity and good nature; and it is not easy to approach him in the freedom of friendly intimacy, without feeling a strong predilection for him'.[66]

Mornington also testified that Pitt 'was a most affectionate, indulgent and benevolent friend, and so easy of access'. His public dominance disappeared in private society, where he 'seemed utterly unconscious of his own superiority and much more disposed to listen than to talk'. Lady Stafford, too, thought 'His unassuming manner is almost as winning as his superior understanding', and Wilberforce equally remembered that 'In society he was remarkably cheerful and pleasant, full of wit and playfulness ... He was always ready to hear others as well as to talk himself.'[67] He stayed loyal to his early friends. 'No man ... appeared to feel more for others when in distress,' remembered Wilberforce, whose public career Pitt helped to revitalise by encouraging him to take on leadership of the anti-slave trade cause in Parliament during his moral turmoil after his religious conversion. In return Pitt was rewarded with their continuing support and affection.[68]

Here was a core of dedicated activists who were essential to Pitt's management of Parliament. He used them to gauge the sense of the House and to influence its debates. We know of considerable preparation in advance of debates. Pitt followed custom by sending a Treasury circular to all supporters with advance warning of the date of the opening of Parliament, with some explanation of the reason why attendance was particularly requested if the timing was unusual.[69] On the evening before the start of a new session, Pitt met his supporters at the Cockpit in Whitehall and read over twice to them the next day's King's Speech and the intended Address in Reply once, introducing his selected proposer and seconder to them.[70] During sessions there were preliminary canvasses of opinion, as in advance of Pitt's parliamentary reform motion in 1785 and before Col. Bastard's motion on naval promotions in 1788.[71] On particular occasions Pitt's intentions were communicated beforehand to his supporters, either by writing to influential figures as in the advance lobbying on parliamentary reform in 1785, or by word of mouth as over his wish to throw out the attempt to repeal the Test Acts in 1787, or by mass meeting when, at the beginning of the Commons battle over the Regency in December 1788, in response to 'wishes expressed to him . . . by several good friends in the House of Commons', Pitt held a special meeting of his supporters at the Cockpit to state the general subject of the King's indisposition and the steps likely to be proposed in Parliament next day.[72] Treasury letters summoned support, though, in the absence of the prospect of material reward from Pitt, Pulteney thought that these did rather more harm than good. Pitt himself wrote to request the attendance of influential figures. When the government seemed likely to be in trouble there was more insistence to the hasty whipping up of attendance of likely supporters, as for example over the East India Declaratory Bill of 1788 when, as General James Grant MP explained in military fashion, 'Mr Pitt never has had such a push made against him; [and] it was thought necessary to call in the outposts, and the auxiliary troops were brought from Scotland'.[73]

Major debates were carefully planned in advance. Major government speakers and also significant lesser figures were gathered in Downing Street to agree the line to be taken. In the 1790s there was a core of about eight to ten regulars – the Cabinet members who sat in the Commons (Pitt, Dundas, Windham); the Crown law officers (the Master of the Rolls, the Attorney- and Solicitor-General); vocal junior Ministers such as Dudley Ryder, and some vocal young supporters on the fringes of government such as Robert Jenkinson and George Canning in 1794–5. Also frequently present was a strong speaker from the newly joined Portland Whigs, Mr Serjeant Adair, as well as a long-time friend of Pitt, former Treasury Secretary and popular MP, Thomas Steele, who had some feel for members' opinions.[74] Tactics for debates were planned down to who was to answer whom. John Scott (Lord Eldon) later recalled how 'Mr Pitt has sent for me on the morning of a day on which a debate was to come on, and said to me, "Attorney-General, you must speak on such a one's motion tonight"', following this with a briefing on the relevant points and concluding, '"There, now you are quite as equal to debate the subject as I am. You must follow Mr So-and-so in the debate".'[75]

For particular business individual experts would be brought in to the preparatory meetings. Tom Grenville, recently returned from a mission to Vienna, advised for the debates on the Austrian loan in early 1795. For financial matters the circle of consultants was much wider. 'A great circle of the House of Commons' was at Pitt's house on 12 December 1790 to discuss the Premier's proposals for paying for the Nootka Sound mobilisation. We have the names of those present for another such meeting, when Pitt's assessed taxes proposals ran into trouble in late 1797. Besides the usual group there were the two Treasury Secretaries (Rose and Long) and a member of the Treasury Board (Sylvester Douglas), other junior office-holders – Sargent, the procedural specialist Bragge and Spencer Perceval (whose speech on 4 January was one of the decisive moments of this episode), vocal back-bench supporters Abbot, Elford and Shaw-Lefevre, and some influential but wavering back-bench loyalists – Burdon, Carysfort, Hawkins-Browne, and Charles Yorke. Pitt outlined his proposed amendments to meet criticisms and stated 'his own most sincere opinion that, as matters now stood, it was absolutely and indispensably necessary to carry through such a measure'.[76]

Pitt was interested in the active, doing members of the House and focused his attention on them rather than on the silent majority, many of whom attended only sporadically. John Sargent, Clerk of the Ordnance (1793–1802) and a former Director of the Bank of England, was a Pitt nominee to the balloted Select Committee on the Public Accounts in 1791, and in 1799 chaired the Income Tax Bill through its committee stage in the Commons. It is perhaps significant of the qualities for which Pitt looked in his active coadjutors, that he described Sargent as 'a man of very clear understanding, of good temper, a sufficiently good speaker and very conversant in business'.[77] Charles Bragge was one of his nominees to the balloted Select Committee on the demands upon the Bank of England in 1797, becoming its chairman, before being appointed chairman of the crucial Commons' Committee of Ways and Means in 1799. Pitt also used a number of back-benchers as very useful opinion formers. Isaac Hawkins-Browne, colliery owner, iron-master and spokesman of the Birmingham-area industrialists, served on four balloted select committees, in 1794, 1797 (public debts), 1799 and 1805

(Tenth Report of the Committee of Naval Inquiry); the Newcastle banker and county MP, Rowland Burdon, and Yorke served on two (1797 [public debts] and 1799). These were the men whom Pitt looked to as sounding boards for his ideas and as back-up to his own efforts in debates.

. . .

CONTROL OF THE COMMITTEE SYSTEM AS THE KEY TO BUSINESS

Pitt had further reason for focusing on the active, doing MPs, because he needed their services to run the Commons through its committee system. Many have failed to appreciate the significance of Pitt's attention to committees. Sylvester Douglas and the King agreed that Pitt was 'apt to pass too much time at boards, committees, etc. on business he might entrust to others'.[78] But it was in the committees that Pitt found men of business to do his work, and where he placed his men of business. The reports we have of Pitt at Commons committees are very different from Wraxall's picture of Pitt entering the main chamber. In 1796 Charles Abbot was a new member serving on his first committee. This was Sir John Sinclair's General Enclosure Committee, which Pitt saw as a possible means of preventing a recurrence of the 1795 corn crisis, and which he consequently attended, along with some of his more prominent friends and supporters. After making some remarks at one meeting, Abbot recorded that at the end:

> Mr Pitt came round the table and talked them over with me. This is the first time that we ever exchanged a word or appeared to know each other, and the first of the Cabinet Ministers who ever spoke to me since I came into Parliament.

After proposing some clauses at a further meeting, 'Mr Pitt told me that I had done more for Sir John Sinclair than anybody had.' Shortly afterwards Pitt sent Abbot a copy of his own Poor Relief Bill, and later sent the man he was using to manage the bill, Sylvester Douglas, to ask Abbot to act as another of its caretakers. When some months later Pitt needed a sympathetic independent chairman of the highly sensitive committee to examine public expenditure he chose Abbot.[79]

Pitt kept a careful control over the membership of all significant committees. On eight occasions he resorted to the unusual measure of a secret ballot to secure the membership he wanted, with lists of government nominees circulated in advance. He first used this expedient in

1786 to set up a committee to ascertain whether there was a sufficient surplus to implement his Sinking Fund scheme, and he had his cousin, Grenville, elected its chairman. Grenville later confessed that he lacked the knowledge and experience to act in this capacity, but he was helped by Pitt and still more by Pitt's newly recruited financial expert, William Eden, neither of whom was on the committee. The committee backed Pitt by showing an £800,000 surplus, though subsequent calculations seem to indicate an actual £1.7 million deficit![80] In 1791 a balloted committee examined the accounts of public income and expenditure. In 1794 it was used to involve some of the Portland Whigs on the Committee of Secrecy as part of Pitt's ultimately successful attempts to bring that party into coalition. In 1797 it was employed for a Committee of Secrecy to examine the outstanding debts of the Bank of England and for the Select Committee on Finance, to examine the public debts. This was to keep Charles Fox out of the most sensitive committees, while admitting a limited number of lesser opponents, and equally to ensure that sufficient of Pitt's men of business and back-bench supporters were appointed to ensure the decisions he wanted. In 1797, Dudley Ryder was appointed to Abbot's committee on the public debts as his minder. Ryder reviewed the drafts of the committee reports with Abbot before they were presented, and, when the committee was reconvened in the next session, Pitt himself worked on the reports with Ryder.[81] In 1799 it was employed again for the Committee of Secrecy into treasonable societies, and in 1805 for committees on the controversial tenth and eleventh reports of the naval inquiry.

Throughout, Pitt used the young men of business he recruited as essential assistants to his leadership. In the 1790s two in particular, Dudley Ryder and Robert Jenkinson, were frequently employed on committees on financial or economic matters. Ryder, eldest son of Lord Harrowby, entered Parliament in 1784 at the age of twenty-two, made his first reported speech in May 1786, but soon impressed Pitt enough to be asked to move the Address in November 1787. The Premier forced the reluctant Carmarthen to take him as Under-Secretary of State at the Foreign Office in 1789–90, moving him to Comptroller of the Household and one of the commissioners of the Board of Control for India in 1790–1, then to his most active post for Commons business – that of Vice-President of the Board of Trade 1790–1801, remunerating him with the semi-sinecure offices of Paymaster General 1791–1800, and Treasurer of the Navy 1800–1. It was Ryder that Pitt asked to be his second for his duel with Tierney in 1798. Ryder chaired the important committees on the corn scarcities of 1795–6 and 1800–1, steering them into justifying the government's policies during those crises and managing associated government measures through the Commons. Jenkinson, eldest son of Lord Liverpool, entered Parliament in 1790, and was employed as a regular junior speaker for government after a maiden speech praised by Pitt in February 1792. A commissioner of the Board of Control 1793–9, member of the Board of Trade 1799, rewarded with the post of Master of the Mint 1799–1801, by the 1799–1800 session he led the list of Pitt's juniors appointed to Commons committees (14 as against Ryder's nine) and managed the London Bread and Flour Company Bill (backed by the Board of Trade to open up the London market) through the Commons.[82]

A Select Committee of the House was an extremely flexible multi-purpose weapon to deploy in the management of the Commons. From its broad composition it had the appearance of being more impartial in its recommendations than direct proposals from government, and, through its collection of evidence, it could pretend to an informed, expert knowledge to which fellow MPs might be expected to defer. It could thus be used to give authoritative backing to Pitt's policies; it was a powerful tool to influence back-benchers. It could be used to deflect criticism of government, as in the 1797 case when Pitt needed to justify his suspension of cash payments by the Bank of England. It could be used to postpone unwanted demands for immediate action as again in the 1797 financial crisis when Pitt faced a reflex demand to abolish sinecures and cut official salaries, or in 1800 when the Corn Committee cooled the mounting demand for price controls.[83] It could be used to enable government to reverse its policy at delicate times without recriminations, as with the 1795 Corn Committee, by which Pitt abandoned interventionism for free trade in the famine of that year and where he was described by an out-manoeuvred opponent as working in 'a sure little junto with Ryder [the committee chairman] and young Jenky [Jenkinson]'.[84]

Select committees could also be used positively to accelerate legislation. Among these were the secret committees of 1794 and 1799, which led rapidly to the suspension of habeas corpus and the banning of seditious societies respectively,[85] but perhaps the best example of the constructive use to which Pitt put the committee system can be seen in the case of the London docks.

In 1796 a committee was formed to inquire into the trade of the port of London. Thirty-six MPs (including Pitt) were nominated to it, plus all members for the City and adjacent counties. It was too unwieldy and, faced with many vested interests, got nowhere until Pitt suddenly woke up to the amount of revenue the Treasury was losing from pilfering or smuggling from ships lying in the river. In consequence in 1799 he nominated a 14-strong select committee, composed to produce results. He sat on it himself and had one of his key men of business, Jenkinson (now Lord Hawkesbury) chair it. It included two Treasury Board members (Douglas and Smyth), two of Pitt's financial advisers (Fordyce and Nicholas Vansittart), two procedural experts (Abbot and Bragge), two close friends and influential Commons speakers (Steele and Wilberforce), two influential back-bench supporters (Hawkins-Browne and Burdon), the Comptroller of the Navy, and the East India merchant, George Vansittart.[86] The results were described by the engineer, Thomas Telford, in 1800:

> I have twice attended the Select Committee on the Port of London, Lord Hawkesbury is Chairman – The subject has now been agitated for four Years and might have been so for as many more, if Mr Pitt had not taken the business out of the hands of the General Committee and committed it to a Select Committee. They last year recommended that a system of Docks should be formed ... [at] ... the Isle of Dogs ... There are now two other propositions under consideration, one is to form another system of Docks at Wapping – and the other to take down London Bridge ... and form a new Port for ships ... between London and Blackfriars Bridges.[87]

The West India Dock Act of 1799 and the London Dock Act of 1800 set up enclosed docks which protected goods and Customs revenues (they were reckoned to have added £800,000 to Customs revenues in the first three years). From Abbot's account of its meetings we can see Pitt setting up the committee and attending its early meetings to get it launched in the direction he wanted, then leaving his experts to bring its deliberations to a satisfactory conclusion, making intermittent personal interventions himself thereafter.[88]

The traditional view of Pitt's handling of the Commons, that he 'pleaded, and left others to muster the support that pleading could not sway',[89] does scant justice to Pitt's own part in producing this supportive effort. He cultivated the active, doing men of business, the most conscientious back-benchers and the opinion formers, and he used them to man the Commons committees – that most effective and influential tool for managing Commons' business and over which he kept a very tight control. He used the reports and recommendations of those committees alongside an organised deployment of a team of pleaders to gain MPs' approval for his measures. It was management by contrived, persuasive influence, rather than by Party discipline, but it proved very effective.

. . .

'TOSS AND THROW HIM AS YOU WILL,
HE ALWAYS LIGHTS UPON HIS FEET'

Nevertheless it should not be assumed that Pitt had an easy time of it in Parliament. There were defections as a result of his 'want of *little attentions*'. Tierney was among perhaps half a dozen in the 1784–90 Parliament. No amount of attention could satisfy the prickly Duke of Northumberland, leading a resentful Pitt to 'have no scruple' about attacking the Duke's hold on his boroughs in the 1796 election.[90] Shelburne (Marquis of Lansdowne) and his followers broke with Pitt on his policy towards the French Revolution.

More significantly, Pitt's policy of seeking to persuade the Commons by argument rather than Party discipline exposed him to back-bench revolts on almost any measure. After the last of his early defeats, on Richmond's fortifications in 1786, he ran into trouble again in 1788, when he struggled to defend Howe's naval promotions and Dundas's Declaratory Bill for India, and when he opposed the impeachment of an Indian judge, Sir Elijah Impey. Grenville lamented that 'It is a dreadful thing for the general strength of Government, to have these sort of doubtful days recurring so often.' A disillusioned 'third Party' of 26 MPs and peers emerged to oppose bad measures and support good ones proposed from whatever quarter. The advent of the Regency Crisis rapidly polarised loyalties again, yet all Pitt's subsequent internal and external triumphs in 1789–90 failed to prevent a dramatic defeat in early 1791 when confidence in his proposed armament against Russia ebbed so fast in the Commons that he quickly abandoned the measure.

Nor did his victory over Thurlow in 1792 or the junction of so much of the former Opposition coalition in 1793–4 leave him entirely secure. In late 1794 a swelling peace movement emerged, in which his friend Wilberforce took the lead and drew other county MPs with him. Shortly after, back-bench hostility to the size of the proposed marriage settlement for the Prince of Wales forced Pitt to confess to the King that he could not carry the measure as originally proposed, and that failure might affect the government's ability to get future business through Parliament as well as impact upon the next election. Pitt's friend Mornington described the 1794–5 session as 'the most unpleasant I ever remember'. However the 1797 session was probably worse, with final defeat on the Continent, successive invasion scares, a run on the banks which led to the suspension of cash payments, mutiny in the fleet, and reaction against a seeming lack of vigour from a sick Pitt. Canning described it as 'a season of storms and tempests', and it was followed by sessions in 1797–8 and 1798–9 in which Pitt had a hard struggle to pass his swingeing new financial measures.

Nevertheless Pitt survived. Time and again he was rescued by his own debating and procedural skills on the floor of the House, aided by the mistakes of his opponents and by his own pragmatic political sense of what the House could or could not be persuaded to accept. His most famous counter-punch in debate was undoubtedly during the Regency Crisis when Fox asserted that Parliament had no right to determine the powers of the Regent and could only decide when power should be transferred to him. Pitt reportedly slapped his thigh, declared to his neighbour that 'I'll *unwhig* the gentleman for the rest of his life', and exploited Fox's claim in order to justify setting up a committee to determine Parliament's rights in the matter, thus enabling him to spin out time in which the King might recover, and also to show himself as the champion of parliamentary rights over hereditary right.[91]

Pitt, by choice, and indeed by the desire of most members, was the most frequent speaker in the Commons.[92] That government success relied much on his performance can be seen from times when he was ill. His notorious 'Angry Boy' speech of 17 February 1782 was on an occasion when Wilberforce described him as 'Stomach disordered, and actually holding Solomon's porch open with one hand, while vomiting during Fox's speech to whom he was to reply'. He got into trouble on the second reading of the Declaratory Bill on 5 March 1788 because, according to Lord Bulkeley, he was 'low spirited, and overcome by the heat of the House, in consequence of having got drunk the night before . . . with Mr Dundas and the *Duchess of Gordon*'. He blundered through his initial statement and was too ill to make amends by speaking at the end of the debate. Nevertheless he had a remarkable capacity to bounce back from such disasters. Four days after his 'Angry Boy' performance he made one of the greatest speeches of his life, while a package of conciliatory amendments quickly restored his majority on the third reading of the Declaratory Bill.[93]

He was skilled in diverting immediate danger by the use of select committees, but he also knew when to bow to the feelings of the House. Time and again he found his way through problems by concession, withdrawing measures such as the Russian Armament in 1791 or the legacy duty in 1796, repealing legislation that had become unpopular such as the 1785 shop tax in 1789 and the 1791 extra malt duty in 1792. After fighting off peace motions in the first part of 1795, Pitt's opening speech at the start of the next session in October was described by Canning as:

magnificent, and its impression upon the House beyond anything that I ever witnessed. His declaration respecting the possibility of treating with the new [French] Government seemed to take a weight off people's minds and set them shouting with approbation . . . Wilberforce and his conscientious followers, the effusion-of-human-blood party, all came back to us, and thus at the end of three years of unsuccessful war, here is Pitt stronger and gaining strength – and Opposition further from their object than ever.[94]

To still objections, amendments were made to the Assessed Taxes Bill of November 1797 and the Income Tax Bill in December 1798. There were indeed those, including the King, who thought he was too prone to making concessions.[95] But it won him the confidence of the House, and this enabled him to achieve a remarkable success rate with measures thought impossible in the past – the extension of the excise in 1786–90, the income tax in 1798–9, the Union with Ireland in 1799–1800 (which went far beyond his failed proposals of 1785). He also got away with some astonishing violations of parliamentary rights on which members were traditionally sensitive – landing Hessian mercenaries in Britain and also creating volunteer companies by direct arrangement with the Lords Lieutenant without consulting Parliament in 1794, directing the Bank of England to make secret financial advances to Austria in 1796, for which he had to persuade Parliament to grant him a retrospective indemnity.

Members tolerated so much partly because of respect for his talents and integrity and partly because of their dislike of Fox as the alternative. Fox struggled hard to overcome the stigmas of his Coalition with North and his India Bill, while his espousal of the cause of the French Revolution and constant opposition to the war ran counter to the majority mood. When he failed to overthrow Pitt during the crisis of 1797, Fox and most of his leading Opposition colleagues stayed away from Parliament as the only form of protest left to them. Only Tierney remained to voice the Opposition case, and, for all the violence of the sarcasm Pitt directed against him and the duel that they fought, he provides a final clue to Pitt's parliamentary success. Lady Holland had it from Tierney himself that when, sometime after the duel, the Comte d'Artois asked why he was not locked up, 'Pitt replied that Mr Tierney was a member of Parliament, a very loyal subject, and respectable in his private character'. 'This was said drily,' she noted, 'and intended as a reproof to a very ill-judged question. Nothing could show a greater want of taste and knowledge of English customs, than to abuse a member of Parliament to the Prime Minister of England.'[96] Pitt's constant readiness to listen to and argue with MPs in debate inside the House, and to defend them outside it; his instinctive parliamentarianism which still had him crying 'Hear, hear' in his deathbed ramblings;[97] made him a champion of the House of Commons at the same time as he was the King's Minister. His ability to keep the confidence of both Court and Commons enabled him successfully to bridge the main pillars of constitutional power in eighteenth-century Britain.

Pitt's sheer resilience, his formidable staying power and incurable optimism enabled him to ride out setbacks. Indeed the defeats seemed to reinforce his position, as MPs were prepared on occasion to sanction more positive policies, feeling that they could limit him when they wished. Fox protested, during the debate on Richmond's fortifications bill in 1786, that defeating the measure would bring neither himself nor his friends one step nearer the acquisition of office or power. Pitt was a Minister:

> who thrives by defeat and flourishes by disappointment. The country gentlemen oppose him on one occasion, only to give him more strength upon another; he is beaten by them upon one subject, only to be assisted by them in a succeeding one; if he falls by the landed interest today, he is sure to rise up by them tomorrow with added energy and renewed vigour.[98]

A frustrated back-bench opponent, Sir Robert Clayton, put it even more succinctly in 1798 when he declared that 'Indeed, the present Minister reminded him of a *Cat*; for toss and throw him as you will, he always lights upon his feet.'[99]

. . .

NOTES AND REFERENCES

1 R. Pares, *George III and the Politicians* (Oxford, 1987), p. 57; *Parl. Hist.*, vol. 29, col. 414.

2 Stanhope, *Pitt*, vol. 1, p. 3; R.I. and S. Wilberforce, *Life*, vol. 1, p. 38; A.M. Wilberforce (ed.), *Private Papers*, pp. 131–2.

3 Steuart (ed.), *Last Journals*, vol. 2, p. 460.

4 R.I. and S. Wilberforce, *Life*, vol. 1, pp. 345–6.

5 Wheatley (ed.), *Wraxall*, vol. 2, pp. 137–8, vol. 3, p. 428; Granville (ed.), *Leveson-Gower Corresp.*, vol. 1, pp. 5–6.

6 C. Headlam (ed.), *The Letters of Lady Harriot Eliot 1766–1786* (Edinburgh, 1914), pp. 139–40. For Canning's account of Pitt's presentation of his 1795 budget see Jupp (ed.), *Canning Journals*, p. 211.

7 Rosebery (ed.), 'Tomline's estimate', *Monthly Review*, August 1903, pp. 25–6.

8 Garlick and Macintyre (eds.), *Diary of Farington*, vol. 2, p. 486.

9 Granville (ed.), *Leveson-Gower Corresp.*, vol. 1, p. 177.

10 Windham (1788) in C. Barrett (ed.), *Diary and Letters of Madame D'Arblay* (1905), vol. 3, p. 473; Abinger in P.C. Scarlett, *A Memoir of the Rt Hon. James, First Lord Abinger* (London, 1877), p. 57; Cave (ed.), *Diary of Farington*, vol. 7, p. 2795 (Sir Francis Baring), vol. 8, p. 2921 (Porson); Abbott (1795) in Colchester (ed.), *Abbot Diary*, vol. 1, p. 23.

11 Rogers, *Recollections*, pp. 177, 184; Stanhope, *Pitt*, vol. 1, pp. 8–9; Garlick and Macintyre, *Diary of Farington*, vol. 6, pp. 2405–6.

12 Granville (ed.), *Leveson-Gower Corresp.*, vol. 1, p. 183; Colchester (ed.), *Abbot Diary*, vol. 1, p. 22; Horner (ed.), *Memoirs*, vol. 1, p. 248; Barrett (ed.), *D'Arblay Diary*, vol. 3, p. 495; Ehrman, *Pitt*, vol. 1, p. 296.

13 Malmesbury (ed.), *Diaries*, vol. 4, p. 314 (21 May 1804).

14 Wheatley (ed.), *Wraxall*, vol. 5, p. 217.

15 Garlick and Macintyre (eds.), *Diary of Farington*, vol. 6, p. 2362. See also *ibid.*, vol. 2, p. 401 quoting Sir George Beaumont MP.

16 HMC, *Rutland*, vol. 3, p. 221; *C.C.GIII*, vol. 1, p. 362.

17 PRO, PRO30/8/141, f. 121; *C.C.GIII*, vol. 1, p. 394.

18 *C.C.GIII*, vol. 2, p. 14; Thorne (ed.), *Commons*, vol. 3, p. 509; Malmesbury (ed.), *Diaries*, vol. 4, p. 314. For other complaints see HMC, *Rutland*, vol. 3, p. 280.

19 Fitzmaurice, *Shelburne*, vol. 3, p. 463.

20 See above p. 90.

21 Garlick and Macintyre (eds.), *Diary of Farington*, vol. 2, p. 540; Malmesbury (ed.), *Diaries*, vol. 3, p. 590.

22 Stanhope, *Pitt*, vol. 4, p. 239.

23 Bodleian Library, Burges Mss, Box 73–4, Notes on Pitt; Add. MSS, 27,916, f. 62.

24 Ehrman, *Pitt*, vol. 1, p. 58 citing Pitt to Westmorland, 26 July 1779 (for similar sentiments on independence see PRO, PRO30/8/12, Pitt to his mother, 27 March 1780); *Parl. Hist.*, vol. 30, col. 606.

25 Aspinall and Smith (eds.), *Eng. Hist. Docs*, vol. 11, p. 253; Thorne (ed.), *Commons*, vol. 1, p. 172.

26 D. Marshall, *The Rise of George Canning* (1938), p. 36.

27 R.I. and S. Wilberforce, *Life*, vol. 1, p. 165.

28 Namier and Brooke (eds.), *Commons*, vol. 3, pp. 33–4, vol. 4, pp. 24, 479–80; R. Mitchison, 'The Old Board of Agriculture (1793–1822)', *EHR*, vol. 74 (1959), pp. 54–6.

29 HMC, *Rutland*, vol. 3, pp. 202, 209, 379.

30 Jupp (ed.), *Canning Journal*, pp. 137–8. For other disgruntled reactions see R.I. and S. Wilberforce, *Life*, vol. 2, pp. 103–4; Hogge (ed.), *Auckland Corresp.*, vol. 3, p. 220.

31 Nat. Lib. Scot., Minto Mss M69, Auckland to Elliot, 21 Dec. 1794.

32 PRO, PRO30/8/170, Mitford to Pitt, 25 Jan., 14 Feb. 1795.

33 Colchester (ed.), *Abbot Diary*, vol. 1, p. 544; Stanhope, *Pitt*, vol. 4, pp. 239–41; Thorne (ed.), *Commons*, vol. 4, pp. 460, 462, 464.

34 HMC, *Rutland*, vol. 3, p. 203 (23 April 1785).

35 *Ibid.*

36 P. Kelly, 'British Parliamentary Politics, 1784–86', *HJ*, vol. 17 (1974), pp. 733–53.

37 Orde to Lansdowne, 24 Jan. 1786 (Bowood Mss), quoted in Mitchell, *Fox and the Disintegration of the Whig Party*, p. 102.

38 BL Loan, 72/29, Robinson to Jenkinson, 24 Sept. 1784; HMC, *Rutland*, vol. 3, pp. 129, 220–1, 224.

39 HMC, *Rutland*, vol. 3, p. 129; Mitchell, *Fox and the Disintegration of the Whig Party*, p. 101; McCahill, *Order and Equipoise*, p. 88, n. 2.

40 *Pitt/Rutland Corresp.*, p. 142.

41 G.C. Richards, 'The creation of peers recommended by the Younger Pitt', *American Historical Review*, vol. 34 (1928–9), pp. 47–54; A.S. Turberville, *The House of Lords in the Age of Reform, 1784–1837* (London, 1958), pp. 47–50, 444–52; McCahill, *Order and Equipoise*, pp. 177, 231.

42 R.I. and S. Wilberforce, *Life*, vol. 1, p. 391; D. Large, 'The Rise of Parties in the Lords 1783–1837', and M.W. McCahill, 'Peerage creations and the changing character of the British nobility 1750–1850', in C. Jones and D.L. Jones (eds.), *Peers, Politics and Power: the House of Lords 1603–1911* (1986), pp. 233–59, 407–32; McCahill, *Order and Equipoise*, p. 231.

43 I.R. Christie, 'The Anatomy of the Opposition in the Parliament of 1784', *PH*, vol. 9 (1990), pp. 50–77.

44 D. Wilkinson, 'The Pitt–Portland Coalition of 1794 and the Origins of the "Tory" Party', *History*, vol. 83 (1998), pp. 252–4; Mitchell, *Fox and the Disintegration of the Whig Party*, p. 247.

45 A.D. Harvey, *Britain in the Early Nineteenth Century* (1978), pp. 155–6.

46 Namier and Brooke (eds.), *Commons*, vol. 1, p. 93; Thorne (ed.), *Commons*, vol. 1, p. 149; D.J. Brown, 'The Government of Scotland under Henry Dundas and William Pitt', *History*, vol. 83 (1998), pp. 265–79.

47 I. Christie, *PH*, 1970, pp. 229–31, 301–9; Marshall, *Rise of Canning*, p. 34; Bickley (ed.), *Glenbervie Diaries*, vol. 1, pp. 67–8.

48 For accounts of the elections see Namier and Brooke (eds.), *Commons*, vol. 1, pp. 87–96; Thorne (ed.), *Commons*, vol. 1, pp. 110–26, 141–50.

49 *L.C.GIII*, vol. 1, pp. 39, 610–11 (the King, always a watchful guardian of bishoprics, nevertheless approved Buller as 'a proper person' to be promoted to Exeter); Harcourt (ed.), *Rose Diaries*, vol. 1, p. 107; Namier and Brooke (eds.), *Commons*, vol. 1, p. 232; Thorne (ed.), *Commons*, vol. 2, p. 70.

50 Thorne (ed.), *Commons*, vol. 5, pp. 200, 650–1.

51 P. Kelly, 'British Parliamentary Politics, 1784–86', pp. 738–40.

52 In 1786 on Richmond's fortifications programme and in 1805 on the motion of censure against Melville.

53 P.D.G. Thomas, *The House of Commons in the Eighteenth Century* (Oxford, 1971), p. 188; Wheatley (ed.), *Wraxall*, vol. 3, p. 256.

54 Pellew, *Sidmouth*, vol. 1, pp. 203–5.

55 Namier and Brooke (eds.), *Commons*, vol. 2, p. 500; Thorne (ed.), *Commons*, vol. 3, pp. 243–4, vol. 4, p. 207; Thomas, *House of Commons*, pp. 72, 286–7, 291.

56 Headlam (ed.), *Letters of Harriot Eliot*, p. 137; Ehrman, *Pitt*, vol. 1, pp. 583–4; Rosebery (ed.), 'Tomline's estimate', *Monthly Review*, August 1903, p. 29, n. 2; HMC, *Fortescue*, vol. 1, p. 342; *L.C.GIII*, vol. 2, p. 14; Ross (ed.), *Cornwallis Corresp.*, vol. 1, p. 446; Garlick and Macintyre (eds.), *Diary of Farington*, vol. 3, p. 794 (this contradicts Ehrman's assertion, in *Pitt*, vol. 1, p. 580, that Pitt made few visits to White's).

57 Jupp (ed.), *Canning Journal*, p. 29; Wheatley (ed.), *Wraxall*, vol. 4, pp. 13–14; Garlick and Macintyre (eds.), *Diary of Farington*, vol. 4, p. 1162, vol. 6, p. 2362; Pellew, *Sidmouth*, vol. 1, p. 189; Thorne (ed.), *Commons*, vol. 1, p. 39, vol. 5, pp. 36, 510; Bickley (ed.), *Glenbervie Diaries*, vol. 1, p. 52.

58 *C.C.GIII*, vol. 1, p. 418; Hutton (ed.), *Burges Corresp.*, p. 126.

59 G.W.T. Omond (ed.), *The Arniston Memoirs. Three Centuries of a Scottish House 1571–1838* (Edinburgh, 1877), pp. 225–6.

60 Garlick and Macintyre (eds.), *Diary of Farington*, vol. 3, p. 696; Jupp (ed.), *Canning Journal*, pp. 269–71; Bickley (ed.), *Glenbervie Diaries*, vol. 1, p. 150.

61 For practice before Pitt, see Thomas, *House of Commons*, pp. 41–2.

62 M.E. Chamberlain, *Lord Aberdeen* (1983), pp. 21–22.

63 Jupp (ed.), *Canning Journal*, p. 30.

64 *Ibid.*, pp. 30, 45, 81–2, 92, 149–50, 192, 200–1, 225; Granville (ed.), *Leveson-Gower Corresp.*, vol. 1, pp. 170, 226–7.

65 Lord Herbert (ed.), *Pembroke Papers* (1950), p. 276; Bodleian Library, Burges Mss, Box 73–4, Notes on Pitt; Jupp (ed.), *Canning Journal*, p. 169.

66 Wyvill, *Papers*, vol. 4, pp. 88–9.

67 Add. MSS, 37416, f. 373ff; Granville (ed.), *Leveson-Gower Corresp.*, vol. 1, p. 123; A.M. Wilberforce (ed.), *Private Papers*, p. 68.

68 A.M. Wilberforce (ed.), *Private Papers*, p. 65; R.I. and S. Wilberforce, *Life*, vol. 1, pp. 139–40, 150–1. Lord Mahon was the most conspicuous defection, drifting away after differing with Pitt on the best form of Sinking Fund and, as Lord Stanhope, taking a pro-French Revolutionary stand in the 1790s.

69 Jupp (ed.), *Canning Journal*, p. 42; Colchester (ed.), *Abbot Diary*, vol. 1, p. 187.

70 The Cockpit meeting was, however, discontinued in 1800 because it was being heavily infiltrated by 'blackguard news writers' and because of the low state of the Opposition: Jupp (ed.), *Canning Journal*, pp. 46, 173; HMC, *Rutland*, vol. 3, p. 276; Colchester (ed.), *Abbot Diary*, vol. 1, p. 162; Granville (ed.), *Leveson-Gower Corresp.*, vol. 1, p. 289.

71 HMC, *Tenth Report, Appendix, Pt VI*, p. 69; *C.C.GIII*, vol. 1, p. 377.

72 HMC, *Kenyon Mss*, p. 519; Anson (ed.), *Grafton*, pp. 398–9; HMC, *Rutland*, vol. 3, p. 379; Browning (ed.), *Leeds Memoranda*, p. 178.

73 HMC, *Rutland*, vol. 3, p. 220; HMC, *Kenyon Mss*, p. 521; Ross (ed.), *Cornwallis Corresp.*, vol. 1, p. 374.

74 Jupp (ed.), *Canning Journal*, pp. 194, 200–1, 254–5. For earlier instances of meetings see *L.C.GIII*, vol. 1, p. 23; Omond (ed.), *Arniston Memoirs*, p. 266.

75 Twiss, *Eldon*, vol. 1, p. 314.

76 Jupp (ed.), *Canning Journal*, p. 201; R.I. and S. Wilberforce, *Life*, vol. 1, p. 285; Colchester (ed.), *Abbot Diary*, vol. 1, p. 123.
77 Thorne (ed.), *Commons*, vol. 5, p. 96.
78 Bickley (ed.), *Glenbervie Diaries*, vol. 1, p. 149.
79 Colchester (ed.), *Abbot Diary*, vol. 1, pp. 48–51, 92.
80 *Journal of the House of Commons*, vol. 41, 9 March 1786; Add. MSS, 69,139, f. 31; Ehrman, *Pitt*, vol. 1, pp. 262, 275.
81 Colchester (ed.), *Abbot Diary*, vol. 1. pp. 93, 95, 116, 120–3.
82 Hogge (ed.), *Auckland Corresp.*, vol. 3, pp. 349–50; Namier and Brooke (eds.), *Commons*, vol. 3, p. 388; Thorne (ed.), *Commons*, vol. 4, pp. 300–3, vol. 5, pp. 76–7; *Journal of the House of Commons* 1799–1800, *passim*.
83 Ehrman, *Pitt*, vol. 3, pp. 9–10, 16, 293; Colchester (ed.), *Abbot Diary*, vol. 1, pp. 91–2; Roger Wells, *Wretched Faces: Famine in Wartime England, 1793–1801* (Gloucester, 1988), pp. 243, 245–7.
84 Hogge (ed.), *Auckland Corresp.*, vol. 3, pp. 349–50; Wells, *Wretched Faces*, pp. 184–95.
85 Ehrman, *Pitt*, vol. 2, p. 395, vol. 3, pp. 304–5.
86 *Journal of the House of Commons*, vol. 51, 16 March 1796, vol. 54, 1 May 1799.
87 Quoted in J. Pudney, *London's Docks* (1975), pp. 25–6.
88 Colchester (ed.), *Abbot Diary*, vol. 1, pp. 177–8, 207.
89 R.G. Thorne, 'William Pitt', in Thorne (ed.), *Commons*, vol. 4, p. 807.
90 Harcourt (ed.), *Rose Diaries*, vol. 1, p. 200.
91 Stanhope, *Pitt*, vol. 1, pp. 5–6.
92 Thorne (ed.), *Commons*, vol. 1, p. 344.
93 R.I. and S. Wilberforce, *Life*, vol. 1, p. 26; *C.C.GIII*, vol. 1, pp. 358–61; Ehrman, *Pitt*, vol. 1, pp. 454–5.
94 Quoted in *L.C.GIII*, vol. 2, pp. 415–16, n. 5.
95 Not least the King – see *L.C.GIII*, vol. 2, p. 548, Stanhope, *Pitt*, vol. 3, p. xi.
96 Earl of Ilchester (ed.), *The Journal of Elizabeth, Lady Holland* (1908), vol. 2, p. 50.
97 Stanhope, *Pitt*, vol. 4, p. 381.
98 *Parl. Hist.*, vol. 25, col. 1154.
99 *The Senator*, vol. 21, p. 145, 5 Dec. 1798.

Chapter 6

'THE IMPRESSION AND EFFECT OF NUMBERS ON OUR SIDE':

PITT AND THE PEOPLE

. . .

THE APPEAL TO 'THE PUBLIC AT LARGE'

As a Patriot minister, independent of the corruption of Court and the faction of Party, Pitt needed the backing of popular support to sustain his political strength. In his 21 February 1783 speech, he directly appealed to 'the public at large' for approval, and the public rallied to establish him in power in the crisis of early 1784. He remained constantly alive to the need to 'have the Impression and Effect of Numbers on our Side' and developed a remarkable instinct for what he could ask of the nation. The popularity and public confidence that Pitt earned in the 1780s served him well in the troubled years of the 1790s when his skill at manipulating public opinion, his willingness to call for public assistance and his success in attracting a supportive response made him the most formidable minister that opponents, themselves seeking public support, could have encountered.

Public support had to be earned, however. Pitt entered Parliament as member for a closed 'rotten borough' and without contact with the wider public until he joined the agitation for parliamentary reform. He soon acquired a reputation as a reformer, winning the enthusiastic support of the Rev. Christopher Wyvill, energetic leader of the influential Yorkshire Association. Pitt's object, as he declared when he became the first government leader to introduce a parliamentary reform bill into the house in April 1785, was to produce 'a house of commons between whom and the people there should exist the same interest, and the most perfect sympathy and union'. He claimed that the most glorious periods of the country's history occurred when the people had most confidence in the Commons and that house most confidence in their Ministers. Purity of the representation was the only reliable source of such confidence.[1]

He accepted that occasionally bright characters, with integrity and virtue, rose above the general corruption and depravity and 'forced both parliament and people to countenance their administration'.[2] He had his father in mind, but it was the role to which he himself aspired. Throughout his life he strove to maintain just such a character as his one sure way to secure public support. His personal disdain of titled rank or financial profit was an essential part of his public persona. His little regard for the old aristocracy was made abundantly clear by the way he swelled the peerage with new creations. His niece claimed that he privately declared the revolutionary Tom Paine 'quite in the right' in his view of the vice and folly of the upper class. When his proud friend, Lord Abercorn, boasted that the greatest perfection of the human figure was not in the labouring classes but in the aristocracy, Pitt cut him down with the sarcastic interjection, 'That may be owing to the new nobility'![3] The much-coveted social cachet of the Garter he left to his brother. His father's reputation had been made as 'the Great Commoner' and he determined to remain both a commoner and plain 'Mr Pitt'. His 'magnanimous contempt of money' when he disdained to take the sinecure Clerkship of the Pells in 1784, wrote Wraxall, 'extorted universal applause' and 'operated throughout his whole life, and even beyond the grave, by its effect on Parliament and the nation'. A biographer in 1789 eulogised how 'With a true and genuine patriotism, unrivalled save by his immortal Sire, he has received no remuneration, no favor, no honor. He has secured to himself no pension, no place, no reversionary grant, no royal promise.'[4]

Throughout his adult life Pitt was in debt – not through wild expenditure, but through inattention to personal gain. His meagre patrimony frightened him out of an early fascination for gambling, and he likewise shunned the turf, in both of which aristocratic vices his rival Fox indulged so recklessly. When Premier he built no palace as Walpole had done at Houghton, acquiring instead only a modest country villa in Kent. His accounts show horses as his major extravagance, and Ehrman believes he was probably being cheated on these (though his friend Mornington later recalled his fondness for 'exertion on horseback', and anecdotes of his galloping and fast-driving in the 1780s indicate a taste for speed which did not come cheap).[5] He supported his mother when her pension was in arrears in the 1780s, but neglected his own finances. Yet, when he was threatened with losing office in the Regency Crisis, he rejected a proposed subscription of £100,000 by City merchants, and there was talk of returning again to practising law to sustain himself.[6] Only in 1792 did he at last defer to the King's insistence and accept the Wardenship of the Cinque Ports. The £3,000 annual income of this largely sinecure office relieved his hard-pressed personal finances (next year he had to assign to his banker Coutts his £4,000 salary as First Lord of the Treasury), but his predominant motive was probably his political need for a decisive signal of royal favour to confirm his victory over his rival Thurlow.[7] Although he worried over the public reaction to the rewards he obtained for his acquisitive relatives, he nevertheless managed to maintain his own personal character for integrity as the man of virtue who gained neither money nor rank from government. When his friend Dundas was impeached for financial malpractice in 1805, Pitt's niece overheard Kent farmers calling the Premier 'the only honest man amongst them, and the only public man with clean hands'.[8]

Besides his integrity, it was his youth that caught the popular imagination. He did not reach thirty until 1789. Early prints and ballads satirised his youthfulness by calling him 'Master Billy', and he was popularly referred to as 'Billy Pitt'. His Yorkshire supporters in 1795 were 'Billy-men'.[9] By the 1790s knowledge of his over-indulgent drinking habits became widespread and the butt of satirical verses and cartoons, but he was fortunate that Fox's rash politics and peccadilloes furnished a far more vulnerable target for the savagery of caricaturists than he. He did not neglect this advantage. James Sayers was rewarded with the sinecure office of Marshal of the Court of the Exchequer for his highly effective demolition of Fox during the India Bill crisis. James Gillray gave Pitt his distinctive cartoon image: Pitt lined the walls of his Kent villa with Gillray's prints and gave him a government pension in 1797. He was perhaps fortunate to come to power as the golden age of political caricature reached its peak, so that he became the most caricatured Premier of the century and the one consequently of whom the generality of the public probably had the clearest visual image.[10]

. . .

PARAMETERS OF PITT'S POPULARISM

The prints however could still be critical of him, for, much as he desired public support, he was determined to be no mere tool of public opinion. In 1784 he sought and won an independent rather than a popular seat (Cambridge University, which he held till his death). He offered independent rather than popular leadership, and this indeed became a major element in the confidence the public placed in him – he would no more be run by the people than by the King or by Party. From the start of his Ministry he showed himself willing to risk short-term unpopularity for the sake of long-term advantage – 'no light effort,' thought Grenville, *in class* X

'for a youthful mind elate with the recent testimony of popular affection and confidence'. There were tax riots against him in Westminster in June 1785 and his coach was stoned in November, but he made light of these as the work of apprentices.[11] He seems to have treated such attacks as a hazard of the British political system, to be met by a firm determination to persevere. He answered the popular outcry against his swingeing increase in the assessed taxes in 1797 by insisting that, while he would give due weight to the influence of public opinion, 'it never was the principle of the constitution, that the representatives of the people should shift with every breath of popular desire'. It was not his idea of public duty 'that the legislature should consult the popular opinion at the expense of public safety'.[12]

While this attitude won him many admirers, it also lost him some of his early popular support. First to be disillusioned were Protestant Dissenters who backed Pitt in 1784 in the expectation that he would imitate his father, who had supported their campaign for civil rights in 1772. Pitt held no strong religious beliefs: 'he was so absorbed in politics,' explained his evangelical friend Wilberforce, 'that he had never given himself time for due reflection on religion'. He had no great affection for the Church of England, thinking requests for ecclesiastical preferment his greatest plague and its right to tithes in kind one of the greatest impediments to agricultural improvement. Like his father, Pitt believed in assuring full civil and legal property rights to Protestant Dissenters, and his sense of justice led him further; being willing to override Anglican alarm he helped through Mitford's Act to extend the civil rights of English Catholics. In Ireland he was prepared to go further still for the Catholic majority.[13]

Nevertheless when in 1787 the English Dissenters mounted a campaign to repeal the Test and Corporation Acts, which legally confined public office to members of the Church of England,[14] Pitt declared his opposition and three times, in 1787, 1789 and 1790, helped defeat attempts at repeal. His motivation, as he admitted, was one of expediency: he believed in the utility of an Established State Church. When he consulted the bishops in 1787, he found only two in favour of repeal and he had no wish to alarm and jeopardise the Church of England or its popular support. On a proposal in 1794 to repeal the religious tests on officers in the armed forces, Pitt advised his sympathetic protégé Canning:

> to reflect how very large a part of England the Church of England party were, how very great a value they attached to this particular question (which he would confess he thought comparatively speaking of very little importance) – and how rash it would be in a young man, just entering

into political life, and likely to become and continue a public character –
to do anything *unnecessarily*, that might prejudice so large a party of the
people against him.

Pitt was faced with upsetting one of the two sides. When he bowed to
the bishops' opposition to repeal and subsequently to his proposals to
commute tithes to a money rate, he lost much of his earlier Dissenting
support. However his decisions bore abundant dividends in the 1790s,
when the Church of England clergy were at the forefront of the propaganda campaign against revolutionary ideology and acted as local col-
lectors for the 'patriotic contribution' of 1798, while the laity rallied to
'Church and King' against those disappointed Dissenters who turned to
demands for parliamentary reform and who praised the French Revolution's removal of religious barriers to political participation.[15]

Many parliamentary reformers were similarly disillusioned when he
abandoned his efforts in that field as the public demand melted away.
Whereas he had been supported by 35 petitions in 1783, only 12 backed
him in 1785. After the defeat of his motion in that year, the very success
of his efforts at government economy and the advancement of national
prosperity made the nation 'generally disinclined to any great Parliamentary change', as his ally Wyvill ruefully admitted in 1787.[16] For a few
more years Pitt struggled on with piecemeal reform of electoral practices, backing measures limiting the length of polls and scrutinies (1785),
preventing voting by occasional inhabitants of cities and boroughs (1786),
and in 1788 getting through the bill of his brother-in-law Mahon (now
Earl Stanhope) for the better management of county elections after it had
been three times rejected by the Lords. However an outcry from electors
at the extra expense produced 24 hostile county petitions and forced its
repeal in 1789, after which Pitt's remaining zeal at last evaporated.
From 1790 onwards he opposed new proposals while still asserting his
long-term commitment to parliamentary reform.

He hoped for a time when moderate reform could be achieved by
general consent, and in which opponents' fears at the danger of innovation might be overcome. That time however was not in the immediate
aftermath of the revolution which broke out in France in 1789, and which
diverted the reform movement into a different direction – towards the
universal suffrage that he had ruled out earlier.[17] While Pitt's 1785
proposals would have added copyholders to the county electorate, he
had looked to make the Commons more representative by extending the
number of more representative seats, rather than by any substantial
widening of the franchise. When thwarted reformers accused him of
apostasy, he retorted that his proposals had been intended to reinvigorate

and stabilise the old constitution, whereas many of those urging reform in the 1790s saw it as a means to replace that constitution with a French or American republican model. For reform to take place without revolution required the agreement of those already within the political nation, and there was no sign of this in the 1790s (as the large majorities against Grey's motions in 1793 and 1797 proved). Pitt contended that demand for reform was a minority movement and to impose it on the majority might demoralise them, encourage the extremists and lead to further, more revolutionary steps. This was not the view of Wyvill, who broke with him in the 1790s, but it was undoubtedly the view of the majority of the political nation. Lady Holland, wife of Fox's nephew, admitted that Pitt was as popular in resisting Grey's reform proposals in 1797 as he had been in proposing them himself years before.[18]

He came to develop a shrewd feel for the national mood, but it was often more by instinct than by direct contact. He confessed in 1800 that he was 'Inexperienced himself in country affairs, and in the condition of the poor' and hence 'diffident of his own opinion' on that subject.[19] He lacked the common touch to handle people *en masse*. He found public ceremony uncomfortable. His niece, Hester Stanhope, asserted that sometimes in his later years she was 'obliged to pinch his arm to make him not appear uncivil to people'. He was equally discomposed by the applause of a mob: 'what a fright I was in', was all he told her after a cheering crowd pulled his carriage through a country town on his way to the King at Weymouth.[20] However he was fortunate that Treasury business brought him into regular contact with so many different representatives of the economic life of the nation. Even there he got off to a bad start as delegations of Navy Bill holders, race horse owners and Manchester and Glasgow cotton manufacturers complained of his 'great superciliousness', 'great want of politeness' and cavalier treatment of their representations against his 1784 budget. He was forced to make concessions to all three aggrieved groups, though he was too late to stop the cotton manufacturers joining a hostile General Chamber of Manufacturers, alarmed by the threat of Irish competition in his Irish Commercial Propositions. On these, too, he botched his public relations, announcing a readiness to hear from vested interests, but pressing ahead before a wave of opposing petitions arrived. Again he was forced into making concessions to the indignant manufacturers.

Nevertheless he had the capacity to learn from his mistakes. He was careful to prepare his ground before his 1786 commercial negotiations with France by consulting individual manufacturing interests on this sensitive issue, though he deliberately refused to talk to the General Chamber, which he regarded as an illegitimate combination, and he was delighted when it collapsed after its members differed over the resultant Anglo-French commercial treaty. Thereafter he worked hard at exploiting this new-found advantage, readily receiving delegations from individual interest groups in Downing Street. Indeed he became probably the most accessible Prime Minister of the eighteenth century to commercial lobbying.[21] The MP Charles Abbot was told in 1796 that 'In his reception of the merchants, when they wait upon him, he is particularly desirous of satisfying them that his measures are right. Lord Hawkesbury [President of the Board of Trade], on the contrary, entertains them with telling them what he knows of their business, instead of hearing what they have to tell him.'[22]

He could be disarmingly honest. When challenged as to his knowledge of the extent of the national gold stock, at a meeting with the Governor of the Bank of England in 1795, 'he really took shame to himself for having never formed any idea on that subject so as to lead him to judge of it with any accuracy'. His mercantile visitors were impressed by the plainness of his dress and his absence of rank and ceremony. '[T]here is no fashion about Pitt's person and manner, . . . he appeared like a man come from a college,' reported the chairman of a delegation of wine merchants, also remarking how 'he has a habit when attentive of pushing up his under lip, and drawing down the corners of his upper lip in the form of whiskers'. Pitt requested a regular statement of their situation and wishes. One cotton manufacturer was struck by the knowledge which his prodigious memory enabled him to build up: 'One would suppose that man had lived in a bleaching ground all his life.' His behaviour towards a delegation against his proposed cotton tax in 1796 was far different from that to their counterparts in 1784: 'He proposed questions, and their answers and statement of objections were so convincing that finally Mr Pitt told them He would neither tax the manufacture in the loom, nor the raw material, Cotton. He expressed his sense of the great support government had received from the County of Lancaster.'[23]

This accessibility on business matters smoothed relations with the all-important City of London, assisted also by the activities of vital intermediaries. Pitt never had a close friend at the heart of City politics to play the role that William Beckford had with his father, but he had personal friends well connected in the City. Dundas had close ties with the tight-knit Scottish commercial community in London, his second daughter being married successively to two Scottish bankers. This Scottish group played an important part in the control that Dundas established among the Court of Directors of the East India Company in the 1790s. Vital too was Pitt's warm friendship with the London and

Nottingham banker, Robert Smith, which began in Goosetree's Club and in their common zeal for parliamentary reform in the early 1780s. When Pitt became Warden of the Cinque Ports, he made Smith Governor of Deal Castle, adjacent to his own residence at Walmer, according to Pitt's snobbish niece 'to have somebody near at hand, who could take off the bore, and the expense too, of entertaining people from London'. Although Smith gave up his banking partnership when Pitt made him an Irish peer in 1796, then an English peer as Lord Carrington in 1797, he retained his contacts with the City that Pitt found so useful.[24]

Pitt's popularity in the City was helped by his willingness to open opportunities for lesser merchants and bankers, and for newcomers outside the older institutional establishment. Rather than allotting loans to government favourites, he invited competition by sealed tender. When he did show a preference in the mid-1790s, it was to a consortium led by a newcomer, the Scottish former Parisian banker, Walter Boyd, whose financial imagination matched Pitt's immense wartime needs. Although Pitt came to power as defender of the East India Company, he had his clashes with the big City institutions. The old ruling 'Indian interest' in the Company was reminded of his independence and ultimate authority over them by the impeachment of Warren Hastings (1786) and by the 1788 Declaratory Act; while he clashed with the Bank of England over his appropriation of unclaimed dividends in 1790 and the effect of his payments abroad on its bullion balances in the mid-1790s. Nevertheless the political and financial stability he achieved in the 1780s won the confidence of all. In June 1787 the rumour of his impending resignation saw stocks fall $3\frac{1}{2}$ per cent in a quarter of an hour, while during the Regency Crisis of the following year, Sir William Young recorded 'as an eyewitness to the temper of men at the Royal Exchange, and Lloyd's Coffee-rooms, never did Administration stand so high in the opinion of the moneyed and commercial world: throughout the city, the fears of losing Pitt from the finance make as much of the regrets of anticipation, as fears of losing the King from the throne'.[25]

Pitt showed himself as generally protective of City interests, in 1793 persuading Parliament to take the unprecedented step of offering loans to help merchant houses through the credit crisis following the outbreak of war with France. He was attentive to nursing City support. Although he did not fill the Lords from 'the alleys of Lombard Street . . . and . . . the counting-houses of Cornhill', as Disraeli later alleged, he did nevertheless bestow lesser favours.[26] In recommending a baronetcy for Sir James Sanderson in November 1794 he told the King that 'it will probably produce a very good effect in the City'.[27] Sanderson (Lord Mayor 1792–3) and another staunch supporter, Sir William Curtis (Lord Mayor 1795–6), were key players in keeping the City loyal to Pitt during the difficult year of 1795. This alliance of mutual convenience between Pitt and the City was shown to its greatest effect in the panic rush on gold in February 1797, when Pitt's drastic decision to suspend cash payments was immediately endorsed by a meeting of leading merchants at the Mansion House, who unanimously agreed to accept banknotes as legal tender, thus helping to secure his political and their financial salvation.[28]

The usefulness of the City of London to Pitt was not just in its financial muscle, but in its influence on the commercial community throughout the country. Pitt's own network of friends and supporters also used their influence locally, and, like all his predecessors, Pitt resorted to the media to get his message across. He believed in increasing the information government made available to the public, and accorded Parliament a central role by encouraging the growing practice of the Commons from the late 1770s, of printing parliamentary bills and committee reports for public consumption. The Irish trade papers of 1785 have been described as the first substantial block of Commons' sessional papers to be printed in something approaching the modern manner. Pitt wrote optimistically that 'It will be difficult for malice or faction to find many topics calculated to catch the mind of the public, if the nature of the measure is fairly stated, and sufficiently explained in its true light.' The first report of the Committee of Secrecy on the radical societies in 1794 indeed became a best seller, reprinted by Debrett. There were 14 published reports on the slave trade in 1790 and four more in 1791; two reports, an appendix and a supplement of the Committee of Secrecy in 1794; six reports and an appendix on the high price of corn in 1795–6 (and six more in 1800); and 36 reports of the Committee on Finance in 1797–8. This deluge of information played a significant part in the political awakening and involvement of the reading public in the late eighteenth century. It has been said that 'To print a bill was to invite public participation in the debate', and by the 1790s the Commons were ordering the printing of almost all public bills. Pitt abandoned his Poor Bill after being swamped with letters of informed criticism when it was published in December 1796.[29]

He found Parliament a useful tool for influencing opinion. The King's Message at the start of a session, or his own budget speech, provided opportunities to broadcast good news to the country. Conversely when in the autumn of 1793 the war with France took a bad turn, he told the Speaker that he hoped to avoid calling Parliament until after Christmas, but 'If attempts to make any bad impression in the country seem likely to be successful, we certainly must meet at all events.' Parliament was a safety valve where the debate could be focused in a forum over which he had more immediate influence. During the grain crisis of late 1800 he thought 'nothing so likely to prevent the progress of discontent and internal mischief as what we have more than once found effectual, and cannot too much encourage the public to look up to – a speedy meeting of Parliament. Even if no important legislative measure could be taken, the result of parliamentary enquiry and discussion would go further than anything towards quieting men's minds, and checking erroneous opinions.' When Parliament met, he ensured the creation of a committee of investigation which produced a report endorsing the steps taken by government to deal with the crisis.[30] Indeed, Opposition leaders thought they would put him at a disadvantage by staying away from Parliament in 1797, because 'the loss of a theatre in which he could defend his measures, would deprive him of opportunities of ascertaining, as well as leading the publick opinion'.[31]

Pitt's debating skills put him in an ideal position to capitalise on the recently won freedom of the press to publish parliamentary debates. William Windham described his debating style as so clear and to the point 'that it appeared to be his only object to explain to the people through the medium of the reporters, the matter on which he spoke'.[32] Like all governments, Pitt's was attentive to the press. Of the £1,239 it spent on the press to secure his triumph in the first eight months of 1784, £229 went to the printer Stockdale 'for various pamphlets and publications', £200 'to persons for writing in the newspapers', and the rest subsidised three of the eight London daily and three of its nine thrice-weekly newspapers. Pitt's brother-in-law, Lord Mahon, acted as his press agent, 'indefatigable', according to William Woodfall, in pressing reports of his speeches on editors 'in such a manner as to render a refusal impossible'. In 1788 Woodfall was printing Pitt's main speech on the Regency five days before Fox's, and it was claimed that 100,000 copies of the speech were also printed for distribution in the country. The escalating battle for the press over the Regency Crisis and the 1790 election, saw the Treasury subsidising seven and the Opposition six of the 14 London dailies by 1792. At that point Treasury subsidies, including payments to letter writers and pamphleteers, nearly equalled the £5,000 a year which Walpole averaged in the last ten years of his ministry. The Treasury then changed tactics. At the end of 1792, it established two new daily papers, the *Sun* and *True Briton*, more responsive to its management, abandoning direct subsidies to the rest shortly afterwards. These two, together with a thrice-weekly, were then regularly delivered by the Post Office, at Treasury expense, to respectable provincial newspapers for further dissemination of the message.[33]

Handling the press was a task which Pitt usually left to others. Grenville later asserted that his speeches on the Sinking Fund in 1786 and in answer to Bonaparte's peace overture in 1800 were the only two that Pitt ever corrected for the press, though the short-hand reporter Montague claimed that Grenville and Mornington asked him to take down Pitt's 1792 budget speech, which Pitt then corrected (it was published in the newspapers and separately as a pamphlet). Among Pitt's other speeches published in pamphlet form, there are also claims that he corrected that of 31 January 1799 in favour of Union with Ireland which appeared in two versions, one of which ran to at least seven editions. The importance of pamphleteering did not escape him – both Burges in 1792 and Auckland in 1795 acknowledged his help and advice for pamphlets they wrote.[34]

Pitt's energetic efforts between 1784 and 1787 to restore confidence in the state finances, re-establish general commercial confidence and resurrect international respectability, all carefully publicised via Parliament and the press, secured his popularity. His measures to reduce sinecures were widely welcomed. The hostility of the Glasgow cotton manufacturers rapidly evaporated at the prospect of his Sinking Fund to pay off the National Debt, while the City too welcomed its effects in raising the value of stocks and giving stability to credit.[35] When he added the diplomatic triumph of overthrowing French influence and restoring a pro-British regime in Holland in the autumn of 1787, the young Minister was raised, in Wraxall's estimation, 'to an unprecedented point of general confidence'.[36] A brief economic recession and the outcry against his East India Declaratory Act were hiccups in 1788, but the ensuing Regency Crisis of 1788–9 served to remind the public of Pitt's merits compared with his likely successors. His adroit handling of the Crisis, which enabled him to present himself as defender both of the King and of the rights of Parliament, climaxed by the King's recovery, had the result that, according to Lady Stafford, 'Mr Pitt, popular as he has been for these last five Years, never was in such high Estimation as he now is.'[37]

This accrued fund of popular goodwill was vital in enabling Pitt to withstand the extraordinary conjunction of events which dramatically changed the political situation in the 1790s: a turbulent brew of radical reform agitation, reinvigorated and extended by the French Revolution; a prolonged, unsuccessful and exhausting war with Revolutionary France; and disruptive economic fluctuations stemming from war, inflation, and increasingly severe harvest failures in 1792, 1794–5 and 1799–1800. Any one of these alone would have created law and order problems. Cumulatively they made the 1790s a period of recurrent crises which would have stretched any government.[38] The growing tax burdens of the war re-kindled attacks on corruption and expense in government, all the more resented when that government failed to bring the war to a successful conclusion. War induced a credit crisis and rush of bankruptcies in 1793, a run on gold which forced the abandonment of the gold standard in 1797, and together with the effect of bad harvests on the home market occasioned repeated boom/slump oscillations in manufacture and commerce. The manpower demands of the war occasioned anti-crimp (impressment) riots in London in 1794 and 1795 and anti-militia riots in parts of Ireland (1793), England (1796) and Scotland (1797). The worst famines of the century in 1795–6 and 1800–1 saw soaring food prices and produced extensive food rioting, while inflation made the 1790s the worst period of recorded labour disputes of the century.[39] These recurrent economic and social discontents found a political outlet by periodically swelling the ranks of those demanding parliamentary reform, an end to the war and an end to Pitt's ministry. In late 1795 a crescendo of popular agitation led to the King's carriage being assailed by an angry mob at the opening of Parliament. In spring 1798 insurrection broke out in Ireland.

In this popular turmoil, when old opponents from the traditional political classes and newly awakened radical activists from the middling and lower classes alike looked to rally popular support against Pitt's government, they found Pitt ready and able to deploy his skill and experience in mobilising public opinion against them.

· · ·

INVOKING PUBLIC INVOLVEMENT IN POLITICS

Unlike former governments, Pitt was successful in securing the support of the bigger and more open parliamentary constituencies at elections. It was Fox's dictum that 'Yorkshire and Middlesex between them make all England', but, except for one Middlesex seat briefly lost between 1790 and 1794, Pitt won and held all four of those weightiest county seats. In 1784 he zealously backed Wilberforce's efforts to win Yorkshire by rushing information to him for the decisive county meeting, on 25 March, and assiduously lobbying those with electoral influence in the county to secure his election as county MP. He attached particular importance to the 12 county and borough seats of the populous London metropolitan area, devoting to them £14,000 of the £31,848 spent by the Crown on the 1784 elections and winning nine seats. Although two were lost in 1788–9, one was regained in the 1790 election and eight held in 1796. His desire to be seen as the popular choice was taken to extremes in Westminster, the biggest and most prestigious open borough in the country. There, in 1784, one of Pitt's candidates, the naval hero and family connection, Lord Hood, easily topped the poll, but Fox was narrowly re-elected to its second seat in a dirty, tumultuous contest (which absorbed £9,000 of the Crown's expenditure on the metropolitan seats). Pitt, reluctant to relinquish the opportunity for his biggest popular triumph of all, stopped the return and embarked on a scrutiny of the votes in a prolonged but ultimately unsuccessful attempt to deprive Fox of his popular power base.[40] Westminster nevertheless remained an important symbol for the Premier. When his unpopular shop tax contributed towards the loss of Hood's seat in another turbulent contest in 1788, Pitt repealed it in the following year and, on the eve of the 1790 general election, came to an agreement with the Opposition to end this cripplingly expensive battle by supporting only one candidate each for Westminster in future. Rather than risk losing all, Pitt opted to ensure an equal footing in this key popular constituency.[41]

Pitt excelled previous Prime Ministers in the frequency and success with which he continued to invoke public support between elections. He was the first Premier to bring public pressure on Parliament by means of petitions demanding reform for which he acted as spokesman, and he did so twice. The first occasion was in relation to parliamentary reform in 1785, and the second over the abolition of the slave trade, when he stood in for the sick Wilberforce in 1788, and, backed by over 100 petitions, urged the need for parliamentary consideration. In the latter he also used his position to supply information for the public from the Customs House registers and through a Privy Council committee report on the trade. The movement to abolish the slave trade, with its network of local agents and committees operating in concert with a central London committee, rousing the public by travelling speakers, press propaganda and petitioning campaigns, has been described as the prototype for nineteenth-century reform organisations. The active and vocal support of the Prime Minister surely helped this movement to establish itself so quickly and widely. Pitt spoke in its favour each time the Commons debated the matter in 1789 and 1791; in April 1792, backed by 519 petitions involving up to 400,000 people, it occasioned one of the greatest speeches of his life, subsequently issued as a pamphlet by the abolitionist press.[42] In 1792 the Commons agreed to the gradual abolition of the trade, though its supporters blocked the measure in the Lords.[43] The number of anti-slave trade petitions in 1792 was by far the greatest yet submitted on any occasion, and even Pitt was shaken by the volume. At a time of renewed radical movement for political reform, and against a background

of direct popular action in Revolutionary France, he admitted that it was 'a bad precedent to establish'. Nevertheless, when his 'Two Acts' of 1795 restricted methods of public protest, he still maintained the public's right to petition Parliament.[44]

Petitioning, however, was the least way by which Pitt invoked public support. His greatest successes came from addresses to the King. Lord North had provided the example with a Royal Proclamation which produced 158 addresses supportive of his American policy in 1775, but it was Pitt who used this instrument with the greatest success, in early 1784. The struggle over Fox's 1783 India Bill was ideal material for arousing the public. Its attack on chartered rights brought Pitt extensive City support for the first time. The East India proprietors formed a defence committee which lobbied chartered corporations throughout the country for a wider backing, while the initial City address, supporting the King's decision to change his Ministers, provided the lead for the country. Pitt's supporters added their local efforts, but the defence of the Constitution against attack by a corrupt coalition of parties was an attractive cause that enabled the movement to acquire its own momentum.[45] The reformer, Major Cartwright, claimed in the following year that the Fox–North Coalition was overthrown '"BY THE VOICE OF THE PEOPLE" declaring in favour of Mr Pitt, in whom they hoped to find an able and upright servant'.[46] From the first address by the City of London on 16 January 1784 to the last, 'from Your Majesty's most faithful and loyal subjects, proprietors of land in the County of Orkney' on 7 April, 191 declarations of public support for the King and Pitt were printed in the official *London Gazette* as against only eight in favour of the Coalition.[47]

Having used this weapon successfully in his greatest hour of need, Pitt resorted to it in subsequent moments of peril. During the Regency Crisis in 1788–9 Ministers looked to a new wave of addresses, 'presented from all parts to the Regent, to continue the Government'. From the first calls on 26 December up to 19 January 1789, 45 addresses of support were received from towns and boroughs, with more in preparation, while their opponents were still struggling even to begin. Again Pitt overwhelmingly won in the battle of public addresses, and he basked in the reflected glory of the 756 loyal addresses to the throne which welcomed the King's recovery in the spring of 1789.[48] Perhaps this sort of success, together with the burgeoning prosperity of the rapid economic recovery from the American War, made him complacent about any impact from the French Revolution for nearly three years after its outbreak. He told the Commons in May 1791 that 'he could not think the French revolution, or any of the new constitutions, could be deemed an object fit for imitation in this country, by any set of men', and in September he assured the alarmist Burke to 'depend on it we shall go on as we are, until the day of judgement'.[49] However, when faced with mounting public alarm at the growth of popular radical societies distributing inflammatory propaganda, his first step was to issue a Royal Proclamation, on 21 May 1792, against 'proceedings tending to riots and tumults' and calling for action against seditious libels. Again he secured an immediate response. On 13 June a delighted Grenville declared that 'Our Addresses are going on swimmingly.' By 1 September supportive addresses had been received from 71 British counties and 315 towns and cities.[50]

In this and other ways, Pitt's response to the pressures of the 1790s was preconditioned by his experiences of the previous decade. He knew that government could not sustain itself without popular support. It had few coercive means that were independent of popular participation. His government's efforts to establish a London police force were defeated in 1785. He did manage to establish a police force in Dublin in 1786, and finally got a much reduced measure for the metropolis (excluding the City itself) through Parliament as the Middlesex Justices Act in 1792, but overall, government still ultimately depended on the public to provide information for prosecutions and to act as local constables, militia and juries. As early as 1784 he advised the Irish Secretary that 'the Government can never be carried on to any good purpose by a majority *in Parliament alone*, if that Parliament becomes generally and lastingly unpopular. We may keep the Parliament, but lose the people', and in 1800 he told the Commons that 'If the mass of the people were disloyal, the means of Parliament . . . would be ineffectual.'[51] He knew he needed public support and he was confident enough to call upon it.

There were three strands to his consequent policy when confronted by popular agitation in the 1790s, all of which had precedents in the 1780s either in his advice to the Lord Lieutenant facing popular disturbances in Ireland in 1784 and 1786, or in his own mobilisation of popular support. First, government could 'never make its stand effectually till it gets upon right ground'. He advised Rutland to be prepared to yield on reasonable points, even at the risk of incurring the imputation of weakness. Sources of complaint should be ascertained and a sincere disposition to give just redress held out, while making clear a firm determination to do no more. Second, while that was happening, care should be taken 'to hold up vigorously the execution of the law as it stands (till altered by Parliament), and to punish severely (if the means can be found) any tumultuous attempt to violate it'.[52] Third, he would seek popular backing for the lead given by government.

. . .

MAKING A STAND UPON RIGHT GROUND

In 1784 he felt it an indispensable duty 'not to struggle but in a *right cause*'.[53] In contrast to the 1780s, however, that right cause in the 1790s was not a reformed British Parliament. Pitt regarded this as the demand of a minority whose revolutionary fringe, as happened in France and elsewhere, would gain encouragement from concessions which would also demoralise loyalists. For all the vociferousness of the reformers, Grey's reform proposals in May 1793 attracted only 36 supporting petitions, of which only 12 came from England (no more than Pitt attracted in 1785) and the rest from Scotland. Pitt questioned whether 'in order to please a few individuals, [we are] to hazard the consequences of producing alarm and distrust in the general body?'[54] Yet while in 1792, 1793 and 1797 he determinedly opposed parliamentary reform in Britain, he was prepared to concede it in Ireland by pressurising the reluctant Protestant Ascendancy into admitting the Catholic majority into the franchise in 1793. Confronted with agitation from the latter he told Dundas that 'the dilemma is certainly a cruel one, as it is impossible to yield to force or menace, and yet there is too much reason to think that they have been provoked and may be continued from not affording a prospect of reasonable and honourable concessions'.[55] Pitt also persisted with other liberal causes where he felt justice required changing the law. He backed Acts giving civil rights to Catholics in England (1791) and Ireland (1792) – the latter of which stimulated Catholic demands for the vote – and in 1791–2 he supported Fox's Act transferring from judges to juries the decision in cases of libel, a cause for which his father had formerly struggled.

The 'right ground' on which he hoped to take his stand was the prosperity and economic growth which had obliterated the demand for parliamentary reform in the previous decade, and in his widely publicised budget speech of February 1792 he associated growing prosperity with the beneficial liberties of the British Constitution. When driven from a prosperous peace by the outbreak of war with France and by grain scarcity, he was pragmatic enough to see that, however great were the long-term economic virtues of Adam Smith's *laissez-faire* philosophy, the political need was for government intervention to provide immediate relief. In contrast to inflexible hard-core economic rationalists within government, like Grenville and Portland, he was ready to try eclectic short-term remedies – issuing public loans to merchants suffering from the credit crisis in 1793; government purchases in the international corn market to ease the famine of 1795; the creation of a state-sponsored London Flour Company to beat down the market prices in 1800. He used traditional measures of meeting the food crises by banning food exports and offering bounties or guaranteeing minimum prices to encourage grain importers.[56]

Even where he upheld the fashionable contemporary theories of market forces, he sought to temper them with humanity. His Ministry secured protection for the funds of the Friendly Society movement, the biggest working class self-help organisation of the eighteenth and nineteenth centuries (far more numerous than trade unions), when his Treasury Secretary, George Rose, steered through a Friendly Societies Act in 1793. He opposed setting a minimum wage for labourers in 1796 and 1800, but instead attempted a comprehensive solution to poverty by a new Poor Law, based on 'an extensive survey of the opinions of others'.[57] He advocated provision of relief before (and to prevent) destitution. He was in favour of the wage supplement schemes of outdoor relief already being adopted by magistrates, such as the Berkshire meeting of JPs at Speenhamland in 1795. He wanted family allowances, 'schools of industry' to provide work training, and contributory parochial pension funds for sickness, infirmity and old age along the lines of the benefits provided by Friendly Societies. His proposals were defeated by their high cost at a time of increased rates and taxes.[58]

It is not insignificant that most of Pitt's more successful actions to provide 'just redress' for complaints took place before or just after the onset of war in 1793. Thereafter projects for economic or social reform foundered because their cost or their complexities exceeded the money or the time he had available to focus on them amidst the demands of the management of the war. For example, he provided a small annual grant of £5,000 to set up an advisory Board of Agriculture in 1793, and he repeatedly considered commutation of the tithe (1786, 1792, 1795, 1798, 1800–1) and general enclosure legislation (1796, 1800) as ways of promoting a more prosperous and productive agriculture.[59] However, as soon as the distress of famine was removed by good harvests in 1793 and 1796–8, he returned to more pressing priorities of the war effort. Long-term economic remedies ultimately depended upon his ability to win a secure peace, and to eliminate the National Debt and the taxes which serviced it.

· · ·

THE BALANCE OF LAW AND LIBERTY

The limited legislative solutions to the problems of the 1790s made him the more wary in the second strand of his policy – prevention of disorder by the vigorous enforcement of the law. It has long been debated whether the repressive measures that Pitt introduced during the war with Revolutionary France were an overreaction to events. Such was the view of the Foxite Opposition and many reformers at the time, and of those since who have portrayed the radical reform movement as at heart predominantly peaceful, patriotic and the way to a democratic future, or who wrote before twentieth-century British governments introduced repressive wartime controls way beyond Pitt's conception. Such critics have always sought to separate the British radicals from events in France and the war with the French Revolution, but Pitt could not afford to make such distinctions. He was engaged in a war with a revolutionary power which was seeking to extend its revolution in Europe. The popular radical societies never hid their ideological sympathy with the French Revolution. They sent congratulatory addresses on French military success in 1792 and loudly opposed war as an attempt to suppress French liberty. It is perhaps unsurprising that Pitt was unwilling to go to any great lengths in seeking fine distinctions between the principles of British radicals and French revolutionaries.

Nevertheless he remained acutely conscious that he had to balance steps to secure the Constitution with a due regard for the liberties of the subject. Maintaining as he did that the beneficial effect of the British Constitution stemmed from its 'union of liberty with law', and that in the war with France they would 'stand or fall by the laws, liberties, and religion of our country',[60] he could not afford too readily to use the law to suppress liberty. He had to justify his measures as necessary and temporary sacrifices for the long-term defence of British freedoms.

He had earlier declared his belief that discontent would be 'ultimately checked by its own excess, and by the steadiness of Government', provided that no provocation or pretext was afforded.[61] In the event the loyalist 'Terror' against radicals in the localities far exceeded any government 'Terror' administered through the Home Office and the Crown law officers from London.[62] Ministers were appalled by the 'Church and King' riots against radical Dissenters in Birmingham in 1791, rushing in troops to restore order, and law officers to prosecute the rioters (17 trials and three executions followed).[63] Pitt seems to have been embarrassed by the persecuting zeal of the Scottish judiciary, judging by his slowness in coming forward to defend them in 1794 against attack in the Commons, where he restricted himself to the legality rather than the fairness of their decisions. He was certainly scandalised by the savage brutality of the ultras of the Protestant Ascendancy in Ireland towards the disaffected Catholic population. When one of their number, Lord Clare, tried to justify their behaviour in the Lords in 1798, Pitt turned to Wilberforce 'with that high indignant stare which sometimes marked his countenance, and stalked out of the House'. He insisted that troops sent against the Irish rebellion in 1798 should not become involved in the intemperate cruelty of the Irish loyalists towards the rebels, which he urged the Lord Lieutenant to resist.[64]

During the debates on the suspension of habeas corpus in May 1794, he declared that 'prosecution, in no instance, ought to extend beyond what the real necessity of the case required'.[65] Yet alarmed loyalists were demanding decisive government action against sedition and subversion, and if he did nothing they might either become demoralised or take matters into their own hands – in either case government would lose control of the situation. During the panic in the autumn of 1792 Pitt told Dundas that from the anxious impression arising everywhere it 'becomes so important, in Point of Appearance, to show that We are attending to them'.[66] But he had also to beware of an excessive reaction that might arouse sympathy and support for the radical extremists. A considerable publicity campaign, based on the reports of the Parliamentary Committee of Secrecy, was mounted in 1794 to justify the suspension of habeas corpus, and even then suspension was confined only to those suspected of treasonable practices and limited to nine months, with renewal requiring further parliamentary approval. In fact suspension, with one renewal, lasted only until 1 July 1795, and was not reintroduced until 21 April 1798, to be successively renewed until March 1801. The notorious Treasonable Practices and Seditious Meetings Acts of 1795 required renewal after three years.[67]

Pitt's concern not to alienate public opinion meant that his measures were marked by restraint rather than intemperance or panic. During November 1792 he discussed with Grenville and Dundas almost all the measures that were adopted over the next seven years, but they were held back to be introduced piecemeal when occasion required.[68] Habeas corpus was not suspended until May 1794, and again in April 1798. Penalties for seditious libel were not increased until November 1795. Pitt disliked the new popular radical societies of the 1790s and thought of banning them in November 1792. He thought their plan of universal suffrage and annual elections 'wild, visionary and mischievous'. He considered them potentially dangerous because of their assiduous propagandising among the lower ranks, whose education, habits of life and means of information made them 'indisputably the least capable of exercising sound judgement' on public affairs, and because their membership from among the lower classes gave them 'the means of unbounded extension, and concealed within itself the seeds of rapid increase'. He suspected their leaders of republicanism and French Revolutionary

Jacobinism. Spies were sent to report on their meetings. Their modes of protest were restricted by the suppression of their projected national convention in 1794, and by controls placed upon mass meetings and public lectures in 1795. Their leaders were charged and tried whenever they were thought to be going too far. Nevertheless Pitt did not move to ban any societies until April 1799, when he named five as illegal after another Secret Committee of the Commons decided that there was enough evidence of their involvement in the 1798 Irish rebellion and in treasonable collusion with the French.[69]

Throughout, Pitt remained sensitive to what he could or could not do. He never resorted to overt censorship. In November 1792 he wrote to Dundas that:

> It has . . . struck me as possible (without any interference on the Liberty of the Press) to make it highly Penal for any person to print papers on any Political Subject, who had not previously entered his Name as a Printer at some Public Office, and to require that all who should so enter, should at the same time find substantial security to be forthcoming in case of any legal process against them.

Yet even this limited measure was not introduced until 1798–9. Freedom to publish was maintained, subject to consequent action under the law where the definition of sedition and the penalties for it were not increased until November 1795. Even the King admitted that 'there is so great a jealousy of any infringement of what is called the liberty of the Press, that it is a chord that must be touched with great delicacy'.[70]

Pitt was also responsive enough to modify restrictions where he thought objections were reasonable. He eventually reacted to the frequent strikes in the 1790s by introducing a general Act against combinations (trade unions) in 1799. This was intended far more as an industrial than a political measure – another attempted comprehensive solution in an area where there had been many Acts for individual trades, and it was largely modelled on the Papermakers Act of 1796. Yet he was prepared to respond to a flood of workingmen's petitions against the 1799 Combination Act by recasting it in 1800, to incorporate provision for arbitration of disputes and strengthen provisions against employers' combinations too, receiving a letter of thanks for his efforts from 'The Managing Committee of the Journeymen of this Country'.[71]

Pitt declared it his 'mild and forgiving policy to separate the misguided from the criminal'. He sought to drive a wedge between the moderates who distanced themselves from the violence in France and accepted the limitations that Parliament imposed on their activities, and the irreconcilable extremists who after 1795 developed a conspiratorial, underground, extremist fringe, more republican, often looking to revolutionary France for help, and which in Ireland helped to produce the insurrection of 1798.[72] Like the rest of the Draconian legislation of eighteenth-century England with its plethora of capital offences, 'Pitt's Reign of Terror', as the radicals branded it, was intended to deter rather than punish. Only two people were executed for treason in England and Scotland and no one was prosecuted under the 1795 Treasonable Practices Act. There were far fewer prosecutions for sedition in the 1790s (200) than against Jacobites by governments earlier in the century. In his speeches Pitt assailed the bloody French Revolutionary Reign of Terror; he had no intention (and no capacity) to repeat it in Britain. When he put the leaders of the London radical societies on trial for treason in October 1794, for planning to hold an illegal convention,[73] he obeyed the subpoena of a former reforming ally, Parson Horne Tooke, to attend as defence witness and had it reluctantly extracted that he himself had attended a reform convention of delegates in 1782. When the rigid requirements of the treason law – an overt act against the king – led to the acquittal of the first three accused, the government dropped charges against the others and made the most of the contrast between state prosecution before a jury at the Old Bailey and before the Revolutionary Tribunal in Paris. If the definition of treason was subsequently sharpened and penalties for seditious libel increased, they still allowed room for criticism of his policies, and he stressed that his so-called gagging Acts of 1795 retained the right to petition Parliament, so that he still had to fight a public battle against attacks on his war policy, including a new petitioning campaign for peace in early 1797.[74]

. . .

MOBILISING LOYALISM

All this was necessary to retain and mobilise public support – the main strand of Pitt's defence against disorder at home and the French Revolution abroad. Initially he looked to the efforts of the leaders of the local communities and, ultimately, to the people themselves. This strategy was activated with the May 1792 Proclamation, and thereafter Pitt, Dundas and Grenville repeatedly asserted the need to mobilise public support in defence of the Constitution and the country. In November 1792 Pitt was sure that 'the bulk of the people here, and certainly the higher and middling classes are still sensible of their Happiness and eager to preserve it', and in May 1793 he believed that 'ninety-nine out of a hundred of the people of England' were warm in their support of the Constitution 'and so far from wishing to touch it with an innovating hand, are prepared to defend it against every attack'. What was needed was a means by which, in Dundas's words, 'the Body of the well affected to the Constitution' could take 'an open and active and declared part to check the first appearance of Sedition'.[75] It was a need that called into action one of Pitt's major strengths, for among the leaders of eighteenth-century Britain his adroitness at rousing public opinion was only ever matched by his father.

This can be seen especially in his reaction to the creation of the Association Movement in November 1792.[76] When the growing agitation of the radical societies began to cause alarm and despondency among loyalists, Pitt was quick to seize upon an advertisement in the London press announcing the formation of an 'Association for the Preservation of Liberty and Property against Republicans and Levellers' and urging others to form similar societies. On the day after its publication he summoned the Association's originator, John Reeves, to Downing Street, and induced him to reissue his proposals in a way that could become the basis of a national loyalist movement acceptable to and clandestinely assisted by government. Pitt's declared intention was to set up similar societies in the City of London, Westminster and Southwark, with the possibility of smaller societies being formed around them, and then to procure similar declarations in 'the Counties and great Towns in England'. He urged Dundas to do the same in Scotland. Grenville, in alerting his brother in Buckinghamshire, indicated the government's wish to target the middling orders in particular: 'A few persons of rank cannot be kept out of it [Reeves's Association], but we mean it to consist of merchants and lawyers, as a London society, and that the example should be followed in each county or district – including as many farmers and yeomen as possible.'[77]

To activate the loyalties of the public in this way was a major new step that required careful handling. Whereas addresses were one-off instruments usually organised by the local leaders of established institutions in Church and State, the new Associations were to be more lasting organisations primarily intended to detect and prosecute sedition and with a composition which potentially took them beyond the immediate supervision of the traditional local rulers. Pitt was wary of creating a popular loyalist movement out of his control. He wanted one tending 'to uphold instead of to weaken the Authority of regular Government'. A further advertisement, issued by Reeves's Association but dictated by Pitt and Grenville, 'more carefully and precisely' defined the objects to which they wished to confine the movement. Government involvement was concealed. 'We mean not to let it be known that it comes from us,'

Pitt told the absent Dundas. In return for his co-operation Reeves was promised free publicity in the government-subsidised press and free use of the postal service to disseminate loyalist publications. The revised declaration was published in the London press on 26 November. It specified the prime functions of the Associations as to discover and bringing to justice seditious libellers, and to circulate 'useful writings'. They should 'always act in subordination to the Magistrate and the Executive Government, and in their aid and support, and not otherwise'. Rather than meeting as a full society twice a week as originally proposed, business should be left to a small elected committee, the full Association assembling only at long intervals to receive the committee's reports, pass accounts and if necessary renew subscriptions. 'In this Way,' explained Pitt, 'We hope to avoid the Inconvenience of much Public Discussion at Numerous Meetings, and yet have the Impression and Effect of Numbers on our Side.'[78]

Amid rumours of a plot to spark a rising in London, Pitt issued a new Royal Proclamation calling out part of the militia on 1 December.[79] This drew a further 64 supportive addresses printed in the official *London Gazette*, and provided the final stimulus to bring the public forward. By 18 December the Foreign Office Under-Secretary, Burges, claimed exultantly that 'the whole country is forming itself into associations'. Reeves subsequently claimed 2,000 were formed, and even more recent conservative estimates put the number at between 1,000 and 1,500. The government target of middling class participation was met, and recent studies have shown that the catchment of the Associations even extended into the lower orders of society.[80] This demonstration of mass support greatly strengthened the government's hands, both internally and in its concurrent confrontation with the French Republic. Although many Associations, having served their purpose, faded away in the course of 1793, many also continued, and others were subsequently formed – in Manchester eight more in 1794 in response to the threat of invasion and the Secret Committee's report on radical activities, and a further five in 1795. During the London riots against recruiting crimps in August 1794, the magistrates were instructed to alert the chairmen of Associations in their districts to be ready to give assistance if required. The Nottingham Constitutional Association was still in existence campaigning in support of the 'Two Acts' in February 1796, while the Manchester Bull's Head Association was still setting a lead in the patriotic mobilisation of 1798.[81]

The methods which served Pitt well in the 1780s were also brought into play in the struggle for the passage of the Treasonable Practices and Seditious Meetings Acts of 1795. With London aroused to a fever-pitch of excitement by the radical societies and the parliamentary Opposition,

Pitt assembled troops sufficient 'to keep in awe, or to disperse any mob, however numerous, that may be assembled', until the bills were passed.[82] However he knew that the battle had to be won by persuasion rather than coercion.

Westminster's Pittite MP, Lord Hood, its leading landowner, Lord Belgrave, 'and many friends of government' attended and neutralised a public meeting called by Fox and the Opposition on 16 November. In Yorkshire opponents called a surprise county meeting and Pitt rushed Wilberforce up from London to present the government case, lending his own carriage when Wilberforce's could not be got ready in time, and sending after him extra information for his speech. This was effort well spent. Yorkshire was the biggest and most influential county in the country, and not only did Wilberforce carry the meeting, but he returned to London with a supportive petition to Parliament with 7,000 signatures, and addresses to the King from the county freeholders and from the woollens towns of Leeds, Halifax, Bradford, Huddersfield and Barnsley.[83] Pitt's opponents chose to take their popular ground on petitions to Parliament against these measures and the *Commons Journals* record 88 petitions received against the bill. However, the Premier's declaration of his willingness to negotiate peace with any lasting French government on honourable terms neutralised one underlying cause of discontent, so that even on his opponents' ground Pitt's supporters raised 70 petitions. Meanwhile on his own ground of addresses Pitt was supreme. Royal Proclamations on 31 October and 4 November drew 530 loyal responses printed in the *London Gazette* expressing their abhorrence of the attack upon the King, of which 169 specifically added their support for Pitt's two bills, while none declared against them. Despite all the Opposition's furore, Pitt won the battle for public support. One of his opponents, Francis Place, admitted many years later that 'Infamous as these laws were, they were popular measures. The people, ay, the mass of the shopkeepers and working people, may be said to have approved them without understanding them. Such was the terror of the French regicides and democrats.'[84]

The war with France created a need to raise a martial spirit in a British civilian population traditionally hostile to standing armies. The mobilisation of the English militia in late 1792 was followed in 1793 by the successful imposition of a militia system on the Irish population. Ministers reckoned on Catholic acquiescence after their concessions of 1792–3, and, though there were initial riots against balloting (the unpopular eighteenth-century equivalent of conscription), an Irish militia was established and took the early brunt of the fighting against the 1798 rising. Scotland in the absence of a militia initially raised nine volunteer home defence Fencible battalions for the duration of the war, and another 16 when invasion threatened in 1794. This threat led Pitt to appeal in March 1794, through the county Lord Lieutenants, to 'gentlemen of weight and property' in England to raise and finance extra companies of infantry and troops of Fencible cavalry to supplement the militia, and part-time volunteer yeomanry cavalry to act as counter-invasion forces and to suppress internal disorder, and infantry companies intended chiefly for local coastal defence. The appeal raised 5,000 supplementary militia-men and 6,000 Fencibles, while within a year 48 yeomanry cavalry and 119 volunteer infantry units were formed.[85]

Lord North's government had been reluctant to call for volunteer support when invasion last threatened in 1779, for fear of strengthening the local influence of Opposition leaders and of creating pressure groups for constitutional reform, but Pitt had no such inhibitions.[86] He was careful to consult local interests, commissioning Lord Radnor to sound out the reaction of the Berkshire Grand Jury before going public with the scheme. His preference early in the war was to expand the militia, which was subject to military discipline when on service, and hence more likely to be controllable by regular authority than civilian volunteers.[87] In 1796–7 Ministers further put through Parliament proposals to treble the English militia to 90,000 and to raise a 20,000-strong provisional cavalry from those who paid the horse tax. This was followed by the establishment of a Scottish militia system, for which Dundas prepared the ground in 1794 by the creation of county Lord Lieutenants on the English model. These levies by ballot have been described as 'easily the largest requisition of military manpower the British state had ever made'.[88] They were pressed through in spite of more riots against balloting in Lincolnshire and East Anglia in late 1796 and in parts of Scotland in 1797. Only Ministers confident of their standing in public opinion could have carried through such measures, and Pitt succeeded by some adroit political manoeuvring. Abortive peace overtures demonstrated that the war must continue. He consulted with MPs who were militia officers. He withdrew an unpopular proposal to levy gamekeepers to serve as sharpshooters, and in 1798 he abandoned the provisional cavalry, but he got his supplementary English militia and a Scottish militia. By April 1798 there were 131,000 militiamen and Fencibles in arms.[89]

Much of the facility to mobilise the public depended on Pitt himself and his ability to retain public confidence. In 1795–7, as in 1784–5, polarisation of opinion produced the most overtly hostile (as well as some of the most strongly supportive) public reactions of his career. An anti-recruitment riot threatened his house in Downing Street in July 1795, but again he made light of it, reassuring his mother that 'that which visited my window with a single pebble was really so young and so little versed in its business, that it hardly merited the notice of a newspaper'. When the King's carriage was attacked in October, Pitt was also met by 'hissing and execration'. He was more concerned when the radical orator, John Gale Jones, threatened histrionically at a mass protest meeting against the 'Two Acts', on 12 November, that Ministers would answer with their heads for advising such punitive measures. Pitt was recorded by Wilberforce as expecting 'a civil broil' and saying that 'My head would be off in six months, were I to resign.'[90] In December, while emotions were still riding high, a group of men pelted him with mud while he was riding in St James's Park and one tried to seize his horse's bridle. In June 1796 Downing Street was again invaded by a crowd which had to be dispersed by soldiers.[91]

In order to keep the public 'on side' as the war dragged on from bad to worse, he began to equivocate with his announcement in late 1795 of his willingness to negotiate with the French. As he explained to his brother, Chatham, in September 1796, if he was to persuade the public to make the immense efforts necessary to support the continuance of the war he had to 'satisfy the country that we have done enough towards general peace'.[92] For a while this worked. An abortive overture in February 1796 cleared the way for the 1796 campaign. An unsuccessful negotiation in Paris in October–December facilitated his massive augmentation of the militia and enabled him to make a direct appeal to the public for an £18 million 'Loyalty Loan' in December, which was subscribed within four days, with Pitt, Dundas and Grenville setting an example by subscribing £10,000 each.

This stop-go war policy however eventually began to produce a downward spiral of public morale. European defeats precipitated a further bout of peace petitions in spring 1797 which, although often answered by counter-petitions in favour of the war by his supporters, led him to risk breaking his government by forcing through another overture to the French, which resulted in further peace negotiations at Lille in the summer.[93] The failure of the Lille negotiations in September 1797 created a crisis of popular confidence, for the stringent financial measures that Pitt had now to propose to enable the war to continue were deeply unpopular, sparked a new round of protest meetings and unsettled loyalist opinion. This time, as one Pittite MP admitted, 'The friends of government have not exerted themselves nor attended any of these meetings.'[94]

Pitt and his colleagues had to work hard towards 'raising people's spirits'. They seized upon the timely defeat of the Dutch fleet at Camperdown in October and turned it into a nation-wide celebration, with captured flags marched through the streets by a detachment of sailors and ceremonially laid up in St Paul's in a Day of National Thanksgiving on 19 December. Pitt himself suggested the text for the sermon.[95] Just how much needed to be done was shown when his carriage was hissed and pelted in the churchyard at St Paul's, and he returned home under military escort in a friend's carriage.[96]

Part of the effort was a new project for 'keeping the public mind right upon all subjects by the press', developed by the Foreign Office Under-Secretary, Canning, in consultation with Pitt.[97] The caricaturist Gillray was recruited with a £200-a-year pension to produce anti-invasion and anti-Opposition prints. To reinvigorate the government's own flagging supporters a new weekly satirical journal, the *Anti-Jacobin Review*, was set up, to which Pitt himself anonymously contributed six articles and some satirical poetry. Three articles in November, another in January 1798 and a fifth in April explained his financial measures, and one on 2 July detailed the improved state of the war between autumn 1797 and summer 1798.[98] Other members of government also contributed articles, and Grenville was soon exclaiming in delight that 'It is quite new for us to have so much advantage in writing, and particularly in squibs in which we now beat the Enemy out and out.'[99]

To get his tax demands through Parliament, Pitt adopted a proposal of Speaker Addington to invite voluntary higher contributions from those best able to pay. This was turned into a means of stimulating a public display of patriotism by soliciting voluntary contributions from the nation at large. Pitt threw himself wholeheartedly into the endeavour. He successfully cajoled the complaining George III to set the example by contributing a third of his Privy Purse income, and gave a lead himself by giving one-fifth (£2,000) of his own income, urging his colleagues to do likewise. Sensitive to accusations that government officials were profiting from high fee income from the war, he virtually compelled the two biggest beneficiaries, the Tellers of the Exchequer, to donate the excess of their wartime over their peacetime fees. As he hoped, and as Lord Auckland soon confirmed, contributions of this magnitude from members of the government had 'an excellent effect in quieting the complaints of others' who had to give no more than a tenth of their income in increases to their assessed taxes.[100]

And suddenly the idea took off, as the public again rallied behind the Premier. Renewed threat of invasion, and the shock even to former sympathisers with the Revolution when the French suppressed the historic liberties of neutral Switzerland, fuelled a patriotic upsurge. By April 1798 Grenville could report 'the wonderful change that has taken place here' due to Swiss business but even more to Pitt himself, who at last abandoned all prevarication about peace and firmly came out for determined resistance to the French menace.[101] French atrocities had at last given him the strongest, appropriately Patriotic, 'right cause' on which he could take his stand. Speaking in April in support of the King's Message calling for resistance to the threatened invasion, he declared that the British people were 'contending for liberty, for order, for property, for honour, for law, for religion, and even for existence'.[102] In consequence the patriotic contribution became a means by which rich and poor alike could actively participate in the national resistance to the enemy. By the time subscriptions closed in February 1799, £2.2 million had been donated.[103]

Equally remarkable was the degree of military fervour which was now aroused in the public. Half the new English militia was mobilised against invasion in February 1798, and the rest in April. In the crisis of 1798 the militia colonels themselves came forward and volunteered to waive statutory restrictions on their service in order to go to Ireland to help suppress the rising. That year also saw Pitt and Dundas switch their emphasis for home defence from extracting compulsory service in the militia to volunteering, to which they found an enthusiastic popular response. Dundas circulated the Lord Lieutenants in April 1798 on the importance of extending 'as widely as possible, that feeling of confidence that will naturally result from men of every description being placed in a situation to take, in their respective stations, an active part in the defence of the country'. He called for fresh volunteers, and his Defence of the Realm Act in April also required the listing of all males between the ages of 16 and 60, not engaged in military activity, who were willing to volunteer their services in the event of invasion. The new appeal more than doubled volunteer numbers in four months to 116,000. Between May and August 1798 some 264 volunteer companies, 80 yeomanry cavalry troops and 275 armed associations were approved by the Crown. The new units were largely town based and, because the call was now directed at all householders, the patriotism and local pride of lower social classes was invoked rather than the more limited appeal to 'gentlemen of weight and property' of 1794. Urban units were typically composed of retailers, skilled workers and artisans, and yeomanry cavalry of tenant farmers and rural tradesmen. Urban propertied Dissenters formerly critical of government and opposed to the war now took their stand as natural leaders in their local communities in heading the defence against invasion. 'Church and King' gave way to King, Country and Town/Locality in forging a corporate national unity out of renewed local unities. If local pride gave these urban units an independent identity and culture from the dominant county élite, patriotism led the vast majority of them to declare a willingness to serve away from their own immediate locality within their regional military district, and almost 10 per cent were prepared to go anywhere in Britain.[104]

Pitt's militia expansion of 1796–7 and call for volunteers in 1798 was a state arming of the civilian population to an extent (about a quarter of a million) which had never been contemplated, much less achieved, before. The number of volunteers reached 146,000 in 1801 and 380,000 at the peak of the invasion scare of 1803–4 in 'simply the greatest popular movement of the Hanoverian age'.[105] Its most vocal advocate was Pitt. Unlike some of his supporters, and the more hesitant Addington Ministry of 1801–4, he was ready to call upon popular loyalty and unafraid of arming the masses. In 1803–4 he set an example by raising three battalions of Cinque Ports' Volunteers and became Colonel of the Trinity House Volunteers. He never lost confidence in the patriotism of the British people.[106]

. . .

KNOWING 'THE PEOPLE OF ENGLAND'

Throughout his life Pitt retained his belief in the importance of approaching the public for support. He had his father's example before him of the strength this gave to any politician or minister. Needing the strength of popular support behind them, since each disdained to work up their own political party, they developed a skill in achieving wider national support than politicians tied to distinctions of Party. The onset of war gave Pitt the opportunity to exploit to the full his earlier carefully cultivated image as the disinterested Patriot Minister working for the good of his country in its time of need. As a Patriot appealing for patriotism, his calls for national unity eventually led in July 1794 to the conservative half of the Opposition joining government, and in 1798 to a great patriotic rallying of almost the whole nation. He extended his means of rallying the public to his side from addresses to active participation in civilian associations, patriotic subscriptions and contributions, and finally to military volunteering. Fundamentally Pitt believed that so long as he set the example of virtuous patriotism, the people would back him, and during his first Ministry – in 1784, 1788–9, 1792, 1795 and 1798 – they regularly came to his aid.

In contrast to others more timorous and doubting, he was confident that he could appeal to the public and get a supportive response. In 1803 he told Parliament that:

Much has been said of the danger of arming the people. I confess that there was a time when that fear would have had some weight; but there never was a time when there could have been a fear of arming the whole people of England ... I never, indeed, entertained any apprehensions from a patriot army, regularly officered ... From an army to consist of the round bulk of the people, no man who knows the British character could have the least fear.[107]

He remained attentive to public mood swings and was alert to opportunities to guide it in directions he wished it to take (as with the 1792 Association Movement). Admittedly he was helped by circumstances. The disastrous American War had disillusioned the public about the factional party struggles of the 1760s and 1770s, and it responded willingly to the independent Patriot leadership that Pitt sought to represent, particularly when the nation was again brought under threat during the 1790s. But it was his own aptitudes which enabled him to keep his hold on both Parliament and the people. Lady Holland, wife of Fox's nephew, wrote in 1797 that Pitt 'knows what is called the people of England – a very different thing from knowing mankind – better than anybody'.[108]

. . .

NOTES AND REFERENCES

1 *Speeches*, vol. 2, pp. 225–6, 237–8.

2 *Ibid.*, p. 238.

3 C.L. Meryon (ed.), *Memoirs of the Lady Hester Stanhope as related by herself in conversation with her physician* (1845), vol. 2, p. 32; Garlick and Macintyre (eds.), *Diary of Farington*, vol. 6, p. 2436.

4 *Speeches*, vol. 1, p. 238; Wheatley (ed.), *Wraxall*, vol. 3, p. 227, vol. 5, p. 54; Add. MSS, 70,827, Mss Life of Pitt, p. 403.

5 Add. MSS, 37,416, Wellesley's Memoir, 22 Nov. 1836; Pellew, *Sidmouth*, vol. 1, p. 38; Ehrman, *Pitt*, vol. 1, pp. 585, 588.

6 Ehrman, *Pitt*, vol. 1, pp. 595–603; Stanhope, *Pitt*, vol. 2, pp. 16–17.

7 For the Wardenship see Dundas's letter to Pitt of 5 August 1792 (PRO, PRO30/8/157(1), f. 118) and its representation in the pro-Ministerial press in L. Werkmeister, *A Newspaper History of England, 1792–1793* (Lincoln, Nebr., 1967), p. 107.

8 Stanhope, *Pitt and Walmer*, pp. 17–18; A.M.W. Stirling (ed.), *Pages and Portraits from the Past: being the private papers of Sir William Hotham* (1919), vol. 2, p. 246.

9 R.I. and S. Wilberforce, *Life*, vol. 2, p. 125.

10 The indexes to vols. 4–7 of F.G. Stephens and M.D. George, *Catalogue of Political and Personal Satires ... in the British Museum* (1978) show Pitt

PITT AND THE PEOPLE

included in 756 prints (compared with 397 for his predecessor North). See also *ibid.*, vol. 5, pp. 736, 739; Ehrman, *Pitt*, vol. 1, p. 591.

11 *L.C.GIII*, vol. 1, pp. 164–5; HMC, *Rutland*, vol. 6, pp. 216–18; Headlam (ed.), *Letters of Harriot Eliot*, pp. 116–17.

12 *Speeches*, vol. 3, pp. 248–9.

13 P. Kelly, 'Radicalism and Public Opinion in the General Election of 1784', *BIHR*, vol. 45 (1972), pp. 76–80, 82–3; R.I. and S. Wilberforce, *Life*, vol. 1, p. 95; *Pitt/Rutland Corresp.*, pp. 13, 175–7; HMC, *Rutland*, vol. 3, p. 314; *L.C.GIII*, vol. 2, p. 539, n. 3; Ehrman, *Pitt*, vol. 2, pp. 84–5, 221–2, 424–5, vol. 3, pp. 177–8, 827–8; HMC, *Fortescue*, vol. 2, p. 13.

14 In practice Parliament annually absolved violations, particularly in local government, by all Dissenting sects except Unitarians.

15 Ehrman, *Pitt*, vol. 2, pp. 57–73; G.M. Ditchfield, 'The Parliamentary Struggle over the Repeal of the Test and Corporation Acts', *EHR*, vol. 89 (1974), pp. 551–77; Jupp (ed.), *Canning Journal*, p. 98.

16 Wyvill, *Papers*, vol. 4, pp. 32–3.

17 G.M. Ditchfield, 'The House of Lords and Parliamentary Reform in the 1780s', in Jones and Jones (eds.), *Peers, Politics and Power*, pp. 327–45; HMC, *Kenyon*, p. 525; *Parl. Hist.*, vol. 28, col. 469; *Speeches*, vol. 1, pp. 77, 225, 232–7, vol. 2, pp. 89–92, 143–56, vol. 3, pp. 127–40.

18 *Parl. Hist.*, vol. 31, col. 532; *Speeches*, vol. 2, pp. 89–92, 144–56, vol. 3, pp. 127–40; Ilchester (ed.), *Journal of Lady Holland*, vol. 1, p. 102.

19 Quoted in J.R. Poynter, *Society and Pauperism . . . 1795–1834* (1969), pp. 75–6.

20 Meryon (ed.), *Memoirs of Hester Stanhope*, vol. 1, p. 73.

21 P. Langford, *Public Life and Propertied Englishmen, 1689–1798* (Oxford, 1991), p. 205.

22 Colchester (ed.), *Abbot Diary*, vol. 1, p. 45.

23 Sir John Clapham, *The Bank of England. A History* (Cambridge, 1970), vol. 1, p. 267; J.M. Norris, 'Samuel Garbett and the Early Development of Industrial Lobbying in Great Britain', *Economic HR*, vol. 10 (1957–8), pp. 450–60; W. Bowden, 'The Influence of the Manufacturers on some of the early Policies of William Pitt', *AHR*, vol. 25 (1919–20), pp. 18–36; Garlick and Macintyre (eds.), *Diary of Farington*, vol. 1, p. 481, vol. 2, pp. 631–2; Pellew, *Sidmouth*, vol. 1, pp. 151–2.

24 Meryon (ed.), *Memoirs of Hester Stanhope*, vol. 1, pp. 70–1.

25 Add. MSS, 34,426, f. 93, Cunningham to Eden, 18 June 1787; *C.C.GIII*, vol. 2, p. 17.

26 Langford, *Public Life*, p. 314; B. Disraeli, *Sybil* (1845), Bk. 1, ch. 3 (1980 edn., p. 44). Much attention was given to the Irish peerage conferred in 1789 on Sir Sampson Gideon, Christianised and landowning eldest son of the most prominent Jewish banking family of mid-century, and to Pitt's friend Smith. Pitt pointed out that Gideon had already earned the social cachet of county MP for ten years (HMC, *Rutland*, vol. 3, p. 333) while Smith gave up his banking partnership on his peerage.

27 *L.C.GIII*, vol. 2, p. 275.

28 *Annual Register . . . for 1797*, vol. 39, p. 9.

29 *Pitt/Rutland Corresp.*, p. 57; S. Lambert (ed.), *House of Commons Sessional Papers of the Eighteenth Century* (Wilmington, Del., 1975–6), vol. 1, pp. 31, 53, 71; Poynter, *Society and Pauperism*, pp. 75–6.

30 Pellew, *Sidmouth*, vol. 1, pp. 107, 264.

31 Lord Holland (ed.), *Memoirs of the Whig Party during my time* (1852), vol. 1, p. 92.

32 Garlick and Macintyre (eds), *Diary of Farington*, vol. 5, p. 1973.

33 A. Aspinall, *Politics and the Press c.1780–1850* (1949), pp. 6 (and corrigenda), 66–83, 163–6, 421, 444; *L.C.GIII*, vol. 1, p. 118; Werkmeister, *Newspaper History*, pp. 19–41, 172.

34 Rogers, *Recollections*, p. 188; Colchester (ed.), *Abbot Diary*, vol. 1, p. 75; Ehrman, *Pitt*, vol. 2, pp. 212–13, n. 6; Nat.Lib. Scot., Minto Mss, M69, Auckland to Elliot, 2 Nov. 1795.

35 P. Kelly, 'British and Irish politics in 1785', *EHR*, vol. 90 (1975), p. 547.

36 Wheatley (ed.), *Wraxall*, vol. 5, p. 55.

37 *C.C.GIII*, vol. 2, pp. 17, 41; J. Derry, *The Regency Crisis and the Whigs 1788–9* (Cambridge, 1963), pp. 127–32; L. Colley, 'The Apotheosis of George III', *Past and Present*, no. 102 (1984), p. 122; Granville (ed.), *Leveson-Gower Corresp.*, vol. 1, p. 14.

38 The extent of the threat to the political system and its inherent strengths on which an active premier could call are well set out in articles by Roger Wells and Ian Christie in M. Philp (ed.), *The French Revolution and British popular politics* (Cambridge, 1991), pp. 169–226.

39 C.R. Dobson, *Masters and Journeymen: a prehistory of industrial relations 1717–1800* (1980), pp. 20–9, locates nearly one-third of all labour disputes between 1717 and 1800 as taking place in the decade of the 1790s.

40 R.I. and S. Wilberforce, *Life*, vol. 1, pp. 55–64, vol. 2, p. 133; A.M. Wilberforce (ed.), *Private Papers*, pp. 6–8; *L.C.GIII*, vol. 1, pp. 116–18; P. Kelly, 'Pitt versus Fox: The Westminster Scrutiny, 1784–85', *Studies in Burke and His Time*, vol. 15 (1972–3), pp. 155–62; Ehrman, *Pitt*, vol. 1, pp. 217–23.

41 Stanhope, *Pitt*, vol. 2, pp. 52–3.

42 *The Speech of the Right Honourable William Pitt on a Motion for the Abolition of the Slave Trade in the House of Commons on 2 April 1792*.

43 Ehrman, *Pitt*, vol. 1, pp. 387–402; S. Drescher, *Capitalism and Anti-Slavery* (1986), pp. 67–88; J.R. Oldfield, *Popular Politics and British Anti-Slavery. The mobilisation of public opinion against the slave trade 1787–1807* (Manchester, 1995), pp. 1–62.

44 Malmesbury (ed.), *Diaries*, vol. 2, p. 464; *Speeches*, vol. 2, p. 327, 334–5, speeches of 10 and 17 Nov. 1795.

45 Wheatley (ed.), *Wraxall*, vol. 3, pp. 253–4.

46 *A Nottinghamshire Farmer to his brother Freeholders* (1785), p. 7, quoted in Kelly, *BIHR*, vol. 45 (1972), p. 84.

47 *London Gazette*, Jan.–May 1784 (the total addresses probably exceeded 200 since on two occasions the *Gazette* did not have room to print them all); Cannon, *Fox–North Coalition*, pp. 185–90; D.R. McAdams, 'Addresses to the King and the Fox–North Coalition', *Huntington Library Quarterly*, vol. 35 (1971–2), pp. 381–5; Wheatley (ed.), *Wraxall*, vol. 3, pp. 214, 253, 337.

48 *C.C.GIII*, vol. 2, pp. 17, 41; Derry, *Regency Crisis*, pp. 127–32; Colley, 'The Apotheosis of George III', p. 122.

49 *Parl. Hist.*, vol. 29, col. 400; Pellew, *Sidmouth*, vol. 1, p. 72.

50 *C.C.GIII*, vol. 2, p. 209; R.R. Dozier, *For King, Constitution and Country. The English Loyalists and the French Revolution* (Lexington, 1983), ch. 1.

51 Lord Ashbourne (ed.), *Pitt, some chapters of his Life and Times* (1898), p. 89, Pitt to Orde, 19 Sept. 1784; *Parl. Hist.*, vol. 35, col. 726.

52 *Pitt/Rutland Corresp.*, pp. 174–5.

53 *Ibid.*, p. 47.

54 *Speeches*, vol. 2, p. 151.

55 Ann Arbor, Michigan, Pitt Papers, to Dundas, 8 Nov. 1792.

56 Wells, *Wretched Faces, passim*.

57 *Speeches*, vol. 2, p. 373 (12 Feb. 1796).

58 Poynter, *Society and Pauperism*, pp. 62–76; Ehrman, *Pitt*, vol. 2, pp. 471–5, vol. 3, p. 297; Rose, *Pitt and Napoleon*, pp. 79–92.

59 *Pitt/Rutland Corresp.*, p. 175; Ehrman, *Pitt*, vol. 2, pp. 84–5, 468–9n., vol. 3, pp. 177–8, n. 2; HMC, *Fortescue*, vol. 6, p. 357; Ashbourne (ed.), *Pitt Chapters*, p. 340.

60 *Speeches*, vol. 2, p. 46 (17 Feb. 1792), vol. 3, p. 174 (10 Nov. 1797).

61 *Pitt/Rutland Corresp.*, p. 35.

62 C. Emsley, 'Repression, "Terror" and the Rule of Law in England during the Decade of the French Revolution', *EHR*, vol. 100 (1985), pp. 802–3; A. Booth, 'Popular Loyalism and Public Violence in the North West of England 1780–1800', *Social History*, vol. 8 (1983), pp. 295–313.

63 HMC, *Fortescue*, vol. 2, p. 136; *L.C.GIII*, vol. 1, pp. 551–2; A. Goodwin, *The Friends of Liberty* (1979), p. 182.

64 R.I. and S. Wilberforce, *Life*, vol. 2, pp. 297, 327; Ehrman, *Pitt*, vol. 3, p. 168.

65 *Speeches*, vol. 2, p. 207.

66 Ann Arbor, Michigan, Pitt Papers, to Dundas, 8 Nov. 1792.

67 An extension of treason to attempts to force the King to change his measures or Ministers or to overawe Parliament ran until the end of the next session after the death of George III: Emsley, 'Repression, "Terror"', pp. 810–25.

68 Pitt's notebooks are in PRO, PRO30/8/198, ff. 108v–112v and his letters to Dundas are in the Pitt Papers at Ann Arbor, Michigan. Dundas's letters to Pitt are in PRO, PRO30/8/157(1). Grenville's letters to Buckingham are in *C.C.GIII*, vol. 2, pp. 221–31 and in the Stowe Mss at the Huntington Library (STG, Box 39). See also J. Mori, 'Responses to Revolution: the November crisis of 1792', *Historical Research*, vol. 69 (1996), pp. 284–305. The only major absentees from consideration were the Acts against seditious meetings of 1795 and against seduction of the armed forces and the

administration of illegal oaths in 1797 – which met particular circumstances not apparent in 1792.

69 *Speeches*, vol. 2, pp. 192–211, 335, vol. 3, pp. 403–12.

70 Ann Arbor, Mich., Pitt Papers, to Dundas, 8 Nov. 1792; *L.C.GIII*, vol. 2, p. 485.

71 J. Moher, 'From suppression to containment: Roots of trade union law to 1825', in J. Rule (ed.), *British Trade Unionism 1750–1850. The formative years* (1988), pp. 74–84; Ehrman, *Pitt*, vol. 3, pp. 297–303.

72 *Speeches*, vol. 3, p. 407; R. Wells, *Insurrection. The British experience 1795–1803* (Gloucester, 1983).

73 This was again consistent with his attitude in the mid-1780s when he urged that a proposed parliamentary reform convention in Ireland in 1784, which might rival the Irish Parliament, be referred to the judges for an opinion, with government interposition if it met and claimed legal authority. Ashbourne (ed.), *Pitt Chapters*, pp. 93–5.

74 C. Emsley, 'An aspect of Pitt's "Terror": prosecutions for sedition during the 1790s', *Social History*, vol. 6 (1981), pp. 155–84; Emsley, 'Repression, "Terror"', pp. 813, 819, 822–23; Dozier, *King and Country*, p. 169.

75 Ann Arbor, Mich., Pitt Papers, to Dundas, 15 Nov. 1792; *Speeches*, vol. 2, p. 150: 7 May 1793; PRO, PRO30/8/157(1) Dundas to Pitt, 22 Nov. 1792.

76 The following paragraphs are based upon M. Duffy, 'William Pitt and the origins of the loyalist association movement of 1792', *HJ*, vol. 39 (1996), pp. 943–62.

77 Ann Arbor, Mich., Pitt Papers, to Dundas, 25 Nov. 1792; *C.C.GIII*, vol. 2, p. 229.

78 Ann Arbor, Mich., Pitt Papers, to Dundas, 25 Nov. 1792; *The Times*, 26 Nov. 1792.

79 *C.C.GIII*, vol. 2, p. 230; C. Emsley, 'The "London Insurrection" of December 1792: Fact, Fiction or Fantasy?', *JBS*, vol. 17 (1978), pp. 66–86.

80 Add. MSS, 34,446, f. 161; Dozier, *King and Country*, pp. 61–2; H. Dickinson, 'Popular conservatism and militant loyalism 1789–1815' in Dickinson (ed.), *Britain and the French Revolution* (1989), pp. 115–16; N.E.J. Strange, 'Manchester loyalism 1792–1798', Manchester University MPhil thesis, 1990, pp. 96–102.

81 R.R. Nelson, *The Home Office, 1782–1801* (Durham, N.C., 1969), p. 118; Strange, 'Manchester Loyalism', pp. 89–95; M.C. Pottle, 'Loyalism and patriotism in Nottingham 1792–1816', Oxford University DPhil thesis, 1988, p. 29.

82 *L.C.GIII*, vol. 2, p. 422; PRO, HO42/35 minute by Pitt, 14 Nov. 1795.

83 Garlick and Macintyre (eds.), *Diary of Farington*, vol. 2, pp. 403–6; R.I. and S. Wilberforce, *Life*, vol. 2, pp. 117–33.

84 Add. MSS, 27,810, f. 91, to Harrison, 15 Feb. 1842.

85 J.R. Western, 'The county fencibles and militia augmentation of 1794', *Jnl. of the Soc. for Army Historical Research*, vol. 34 (1956), pp. 3–11; Dozier, *King and Country*, pp. 154–5.

86 S. Conway, 'The politics of British military and naval mobilisation 1775–83', *EHR*, vol. 112 (1997), pp. 1186–9; J.R. Western, *The English Militia in the Eighteenth Century* (1965), pp. 217–18.

87 J.E. Cookson, *The British Armed Nation 1793–1815* (Oxford, 1997), p. 26; Dozier, *King and Country*, pp. 138–54.

88 Cookson, *British Armed Nation*, p. 36.

89 *Ibid.*, pp. 7, 49, 68; *C.C.GIII*, vol. 2, pp. 255–6; Western, *English Militia*, pp. 219–26.

90 R.I. and S. Wilberforce, *Life*, vol. 2, p. 114: Diary, 16 Nov. 1795.

91 HMC, *Rutland*, vol. 3, pp. 216–17; *L.C.GIII*, vol. 1, pp. 164–5, vol. 2, p. 416, n. 1; Headlam (ed.), *Letters of Harriot Eliot*, pp. 116–17; Stanhope, *Pitt*, vol. 2, pp. 323–4; J. Stevenson, *Popular Disturbances in England, 1700–1832* (2nd edn., 1992), pp. 214–15, 218.

92 Stanhope, *Pitt*, vol. 2, p. 382.

93 J.E. Cookson, *The Friends of Peace* (Cambridge, 1982), pp. 158–62.

94 Granville (ed.), *Leveson-Gower Corresp.*, vol. 1, p. 188.

95 NRS, *The Spencer Papers*, (ed.) J. Corbett, vol. 2, p. 196; Ashbourne (ed.), *Pitt Chapters*, p. 345.

96 Stevenson, *Popular Disturbances*, p. 218; Garlick and Macintyre (eds.), *Diary of Farington*, vol. 3, p. 953.

97 Leeds Central Library, Harewood Mss, Canning Diary, 17 Oct 1797.

98 A.D. Harvey, *William Pitt the Younger 1759–1806: A bibliography* (1989), pp. 33–4.

99 Add. MSS, 70,927, to Mornington, 9 Jan. 1798.

100 *L.C.GIII*, vol. 3, p. 13; Hogge (ed.), *Auckland Corresp.*, vol. 3, pp. 385–6.

101 Add. MSS, 70,927, to Mornington, 11 April, 3 May 1798, 1 June 1799.

102 *Speeches*, vol. 3, p. 275.

103 D.G. Vaisey, 'The pledge of patriotism, Staffordshire and the voluntary contribution, 1798', *Collections for the History of Staffordshire*, 6 (1970), pp. 209–23; Add. MSS, 70,927, Grenville to Mornington, 3 April 1798.

104 A. Gee, 'The British volunteer movement 1797–1807', Oxford DPhil thesis, 1981, pp. 53–4, 71, 72, 109–10; Cookson, *Friends of Peace*, p. 143; J.E. Cookson, 'Political Arithmetic and War in Britain, 1793–1815', *HJ*, vol. 32 (1989), pp. 868, 872; Cookson, *British Armed Nation*, pp. 69–73.

105 *Ibid.*, p. 66.

106 *Ibid.*, pp. 67–8; *Speeches*, vol. 4, p. 247.

107 *Speeches*, vol. 4, p. 247.

108 Ilchester (ed.), *Journal of Lady Holland*, vol. 1, p. 102.

Chapter 7

'TO DIMINISH THE TEMPTATION TO WARS OF AMBITION':

PITT AND THE POWERS OF EUROPE

. . .

TOO INEXPERIENCED TO MEDDLE MUCH IN FOREIGN AFFAIRS

Pitt came to power in a country shaken by a war in which it had found itself friendless, threatened with invasion and forced to concede home rule to Ireland and independence to America. Many years later Grenville still recalled 'the deep despondency of my country in the sacrifice of that immense territory, and I partook of these apprehensions of distress and ruin which so great a loss had universally diffused'. Many in Europe considered the British defeat as terminal. 'Farewell to the esteem and riches of England,' wrote Emperor Joseph II of Austria to his brother, Grand Duke Leopold of Tuscany, who concurred that 'This great power, which held France in balance, [is] fallen entirely and forever; all respect and force lost, . . . descended to the status of a second-rank power, like Sweden or Denmark.'[1]

This disaster had enabled Pitt to shine in the reflected glory of his father's great victories in the previous Seven Years War. It catapulted him into power over the heads of more experienced politicians tainted by defeat. Yet curiously his father, who had coached him for the House of Commons, left him ill-equipped for the international stage. The Younger Pitt had no direct knowledge of foreign countries except for a six-week visit to France with his friends Eliot and Wilberforce in the autumn of 1783. This began in farce when their letters of introduction

166

for their stay in Rheims took them to a lowly grocer whom they found serving at his counter, but it ended on a high note at the French Court at Fontainebleau where, wrote Wilberforce, 'They all, men and women, crowded round Pitt in shoals; and he behaved with great spirit.' Pitt was, however, better educated in the classics than in contemporary languages. Wraxall noted that he was grammatically conversant in French but 'at twenty-five he spoke it imperfectly, and wrote in it without freedom or facility'. Though he subsequently improved, he was still insufficiently certain in 1797, when battling with his fluent cousin Grenville over overtures to France, to have his own proposed draft letter translated into French by the expert George Ellis.[2]

Nor was Pitt well informed by reading about foreign countries. Sir John Sinclair thought his principal defects as a statesman were that 'he was not much inclined to read anything but classical works, and greatly undervalued modern literature', and that 'he knew nothing of foreign languages, or of the characters of foreign nations, and did not seem desirous of receiving any information about them' (Sinclair had undertaken an extensive tour of the courts of northern Europe in 1786–7). Wraxall recalled a conversation with Pitt about the Spanish possessions on the Pacific Coast of America, during the Nootka Crisis in 1790, in which 'he owned to me that he had not only never read, but, he assured me, he never had heard of Commodore Byron's narrative of his shipwreck in the *Wager* on the coast of Patagonia – a book to be found in every circulating library'.[3]

He started with good intentions. The Foreign Secretary, Carmarthen, noted that while other Cabinet colleagues were inattentive to foreign affairs, Pitt 'for some time applied himself to the correspondence with great assiduity'. Nevertheless it was not until May 1784, after the parliamentary crisis was over, that the two met for a day's discussion on European politics. They agreed on the need to break France's ring of protective alliances and to form some counterbalancing system of their own, but they had no idea how to do so without becoming involved in an entangling alliance which might draw them into Continental quarrels and into a new war which Britain was in no condition to fight.[4] Moreover a beaten country with a new government of uncertain permanence scarcely presented itself as an attractive partner. Instead Pitt looked to restore the national strength by what his assistant, Grenville, later described as a policy of 'oeconomy, peace and commerce'. State finances would be brought back into balance, the National Debt would be reduced, economic revival would be stimulated, while the Irish Commercial Propositions were designed to re-establish by economic means the withering bonds of unity between the British Isles. 'Let this business of Ireland terminate well,' Pitt wrote in August 1785, 'let peace continue for five years, and we shall again look any Power in Europe in the face.'[5]

During the Irish debates, Pitt declared finance and the navy to be the 'two most important interests of this country'. His most controversial propositions allocated the surplus on the Irish hereditary revenue towards the costs of the navy and applied the British Navigation Acts in Ireland. His priority was to restore British naval power, shaken by the American war. Shelburne's vision of a liberal trading partnership with the former colonies was rejected in favour of protecting British-owned shipping, to increase the pool of trained seamen available to the navy. Pitt supported measures proposed by Jenkinson (from 1786 Lord Hawkesbury) at the Committee (from 1786 Board) of Trade that culminated in the 1786 Navigation Act, which established a registry of British shipping to prevent illegal trading and which Jenkinson introduced as 'a Bill for the increase of Naval Power'. Like his predecessors, Pitt regarded empire as necessary for the growth of British trade and shipping – and hence of its financial and naval power. American goods were excluded from the West Indies, Britain's greatest wealth-producing colonies, in order to build up Canada as alternative supplier, and Grenville's Canada Act of 1791 created two Canadian provinces with a form of representative government (involving a hereditary or life legislative council, akin to the House of Lords, to balance the elected assembly) intended to be less susceptible to revolution. In the East, Pitt's 1784 India Act, strengthening government control, was designed to consolidate Britain's position in its main eastern trading stronghold; rival French designs were trumped by the recovery of British influence over the Dutch and their East Indian bases in 1787; steps were taken to develop a Pacific whale fishery, provisioned by a new convict colony established at Botany Bay in 1788; and efforts were made to increase trade with the vast Chinese empire. A British embassy finally reached Peking in 1793–4. In 1790 Ministers threatened war with Spain to protect a new trading base established at Nootka Sound on the north-west coast of America.[6]

Amidst the expansion of British shipping and trade, Pitt gave particular attention to the navy. During a period of economy, he ring-fenced sufficient funds to repair and maintain the battle fleet. Expenditure on the navy in 1786 at £3,127,000 was £389,000 higher than the highest previous peacetime total in 1772. Whereas the navy reckoned that 10 ships had to be built or repaired each year to maintain a battle fleet of 100 ships of the line, Pitt procured parliamentary grants between 1783 and 1793 for the completion of 43 new ships, with 10 more ordered or on the stocks, and 85 repaired: an average rate almost two a year above the navy's basic requirements. Pitt himself took a personal interest in progress. The son of the Comptroller of the Navy from 1790 to 1794 later wrote that:

> It was no uncommon thing for Mr Pitt to visit the Navy Office to discuss naval matters with the Comptroller, and to see the returns made from the yards of the progress in building and repairing the ships of the line; he also desired to have a periodical statement from the Comptroller of the state of the fleet, wisely holding that officer responsible to him, without any regard to the Board.

Naval mobilisation was at the heart of the British response to diplomatic crises in 1787, 1790, 1791 and 1792–3, and the British ability to mobilise a sound battle fleet more quickly than its opponents was its major initial advantage in such confrontations.[7]

In the early years, however, only the new government's international impotence was apparent. The situation grew worse in 1785 with a new Dutch alliance with France, while Carmarthen's forlorn efforts to draw Austria and Russia into alliance with Britain were finally wrecked by George III's decision, as Elector of Hanover, to join with Prussia in a league of German princes opposing Austria's attempt to exchange its Belgian provinces for Bavaria. When Cabinet Ministers confessed their ignorance of and powerlessness to interfere with George's Hanoverian conduct, the Russian Empress Catherine II concluded that 'The foreign affairs of Great Britain are not really directed by the English minister, but by the spiteful King himself under the direction of his Hanoverian ministry.' In February 1786 the Sardinian envoy wrote that Pitt was only the organ of the Cabinet when he found himself sometimes obliged to speak on foreign affairs. Pitt even confessed to him that he was too inexperienced to meddle in them very much.[8]

Over the next two years, however, events thrust Pitt into the leading role in the direction of foreign policy. Carmarthen lacked energy and application but was unwilling to change post. Pitt urged him to seek Cabinet guidance, but Thurlow procrastinated over the drafting of treaties, Camden sat on papers put in circulation, and Richmond, a former Secretary of State, whose attendance Pitt specifically requested at Cabinets on foreign policy matters, oscillated between extremes and stayed away when he thought his advice would be rejected.[9] Consequently Pitt found himself by default Carmarthen's main support, and gradually assumed control of areas where the Foreign Secretary lacked interest, or weight, to carry policy forward himself. This happened first over commercial negotiations with foreign powers. Pitt was involved anyway as head of the Treasury and through his drive to expand commerce. After his 1785 Irish failure, Pitt shifted his commercial preoccupations abroad, assisted by Jenkinson, and more particularly by his cousin, Grenville, whom he made Jenkinson's Deputy at the Board of Trade.

It was Pitt, rather than the distrustful Carmarthen, who responded to French pressure to reactivate flagging trade talks by appointing the commercial expert, William Eden, as negotiator in December 1785. Thereafter the instructions sent under Carmarthen's name to Eden were settled between Pitt and Grenville and, according to the latter, mostly drawn by Grenville's hand. A commercial treaty was signed with France on 26 September 1786, at which time projects were also in negotiation with Portugal, Spain and Russia. Pitt was involved in all of these, in the Spanish case in particular composing or amending despatches and, with Jenkinson, drafting the treaty proposals. However, although nineteenth-century commentators hailed Pitt as the great precursor of their all-prevailing doctrine of free trade, Pitt, unlike his predecessor Shelburne, was more cautiously committed to freer rather than free trade, and always provided that it did not disadvantage the growth of British shipping. Whereas Shelburne desired speedy negotiation of a commercial treaty with the new United States, Pitt avoided any such treaty until appeasement of the Americans became necessary during the war with Revolutionary France in 1794. The 1786 French treaty provided for reciprocal treatment and reduced tariffs and tonnage duties to the rates each allowed to its most favoured trading partner, but it still managed to protect the London silk industry by maintaining the ban on importing French silks. This careful pursuit of a balance of advantages for shipping and trade, combined with the fear among other states of competition from the resurrecting British economy, actually made Pitt less successful in his commercial negotiations than were his European rivals. John Ehrman has shown that between 1783 and 1792 Russia and France made six treaties, all or partly commercial, and Spain four, whereas Britain negotiated for eight but only completed that with France. A former treaty was subsequently renewed with Russia in 1793, and, with Pitt's support, Grenville included liberal commercial terms with the United States, against Hawkesbury's opposition, in the 1794 Jay Treaty.[10]

The 1786 Anglo-French Commercial Treaty may have only succeeded because the French (who were in financial straits) and William Eden (who was in political straits) needed it to succeed. Nevertheless Pitt got the credit and popularity with British manufacturing and mercantile interests as it conspicuously expanded British trade with France. In the process he gained confidence in his ability to act on the international stage. He and Eden continued to correspond when the latter remained in France to oversee the implementation of the treaty. In December 1786 the British envoy to the United Provinces, Sir James Harris, also drew Pitt into private correspondence at the suggestion of Carmarthen, who was having difficulty in interesting King and Cabinet in Harris's scheme to build up a party behind the pro-British Dutch head of state, the Prince of Orange, to combat the dominant pro-French Patriot party. Harris's letter led Pitt to call on Carmarthen for a full briefing. The Foreign Secretary was delighted to find that Pitt's doubts related to means rather than the measure itself. Secret service funds for Harris were raised to £12,000 in January 1787, followed by a £70,000 loan to Orangeist provinces after Harris visited London to brief the Cabinet in May. Pitt met him privately and questioned him closely. He had doubts whether it was worth risking war and disturbing the growing national prosperity by such a major escalation of the stakes, rather than waiting some years till they were strong enough to match the French. Nevertheless he decided to take the gamble and his backing was crucial to winning the reluctant consent of the King.

Pitt's inexperience still showed in the way he disregarded Richmond's cautionary warning of the need to hire German mercenary troops in case war resulted. He failed to anticipate how quickly a crisis might occur, as indeed it did when the Princess of Orange manoeuvred the Patriots into arresting her at the end of June 1787 and then appealed to her brother, King Frederick William II of Prussia, and to the British to avenge her mistreatment. Prussia demanded satisfaction and assembled troops near the Dutch border, and the Patriots appealed for French support.[11] This sudden mid-summer crisis found Pitt in London while most of his Cabinet colleagues were scattered in their country homes. The Archbishop of Canterbury, noting that only Grenville and Richmond were at hand to advise him, expressed concern about his capacity to handle the situation and longed for the return to London of the war-experienced Stafford and Thurlow. Pitt possessed an honourable mind, fine understanding and prompt decision, but he was 'without experience, or, I fear, accurate knowledge sufficient of the true temper of other countries'.[12]

In fact Pitt kept his head remarkably well. After seeking financial information from Eden in Paris and interviewing the recently disgraced refugee French finance minister, Calonne, he increasingly felt that, because of its financial and political problems, France was 'neither inclined to extremities, nor prepared for them'. He sent Grenville to Holland to verify Harris's assertions that the Orangeists were now in a position to supplant the pro-French Patriots, and he used his cousin's reports to convince the King to adopt a firm line. British agents reported that French claims to be assembling troops at Givet on their northern border were a bluff. Was he prepared to call that bluff? If so he might overturn the Franco-Dutch alliance and win back the latter, whose navy could sway the balance in home waters and whose overseas bases while available to the French navy were a major threat to Britain's East Indian empire.[13] Pitt's problem was Britain's lack of a large army, for which it needed the services of a major Continental power. Prussia had assembled troops, but hesitated to use them while it was unsure how its eastern rivals Russia and Austria would react. Berlin's fears, however, were dispelled in early September when news arrived that Turkey had declared war on Russia, diverting Russian and Austrian attention and freeing the Prussians to advance into the United Provinces. It was widely believed in Europe that the British envoy at Constantinople, Sir Robert Ainslie, had incited the Turks to war, though Thurlow subsequently confided that 'They give us too much credit; we really tried to prevent it.'[14]

Pitt determined, by 7 August 1787, to back the Prussians if they would act. By the end of that month steps were taken to succour the Orangeists and hire Hessian troops. On 3 September, Prussia was offered a subsidy and naval support. Finally, after receipt on the night of 15 September of a French warning that they would support the Patriots if Prussia invaded, Pitt summoned Cabinet Ministers and his Treasury Secretary, George Rose, back to London. A meeting on the 19th agreed to mobilise the fleet and augment the army – after which Pitt went off to dine with Calonne to 'hear all the politics of France, which form no bad variety in the interval of our own'.[15] Grenville was sent to Paris to find a way for the French to withdraw with dignity, but in fact the rapid and total collapse of Patriot resistance to the Prussian advance presented Paris with a *fait accompli* which it was reluctantly obliged to accept.

It was in the Dutch crisis of August to September 1787 that Pitt took over control of British foreign policy. This was recognised abroad. In the following January, the French Foreign Minister described Carmarthen as 'only the proxy for Mr Pitt'. Pitt drafted many of the despatches to the Hague, Paris and Berlin himself, sent his own man Grenville to the two former and personally interviewed the French envoy in London (unsuccessfully since the friendly tone he adopted in his anxiety to preserve the benefits of the commercial treaty led the Frenchman to mistake his real determination to back the Orangeists and the Prussians).[16] Pitt rather than Carmarthen handled the King and informed absent Cabinet colleagues, acting decisively as the real leader of the government in contrast to the rather uncertain figure seen by Harris at the Cabinet meetings in May. He had achieved a remarkable diplomatic turnaround. Predominant influence over the Dutch was wrested back from France. Coming so soon after the disastrous American war, the outcome was, in the words of Camden, a miraculous escape 'from the most perilous situation we ever experienced'. Pitt received universal praise although, as he frankly admitted, 'it had turned out so fortunate for Britain rather from an extraordinary combination of circumstances than from any other cause'.[17]

Doubts still remained in Europe as to the permanency of Pitt's pre-eminence. His battles with Lord Chancellor Thurlow did not escape the ears of foreign envoys in London and the French in particular interpreted them as a battle for control of British foreign policy between Pitt on one side and the King, supported by a ministerial cabal led by Thurlow and Hawkesbury, on the other. The King still believed British intervention in Europe was premature and rejected Pitt's promptings of the need to restore peace in the Baltic by rescuing Sweden from Danish attack in the autumn of 1788. A looming quarrel was fortuitously averted by the British envoys in Denmark and Prussia, who negotiated an armistice on their own unauthorised initiative – though this raised questions whether envoys or government were running British foreign policy. The King's illness and the Regency Crisis followed to raise new doubts about Pitt's continued tenure of office and brought foreign policy to a complete standstill until the King recovered.[18]

. . .

PITT'S GRAND DESIGN

Hence it was only after the King's recovery in 1789, which confirmed Pitt in power and also led the convalescent Monarch temporarily to leave more to his ministers, that Pitt was in a position to take serious steps to resolve Britain's fundamental foreign policy problem. Pitt needed to safeguard his victory in the United Provinces against future French retaliation. He also wished to resume his policy of peaceful economic recovery. Yet an alliance for the former might endanger the latter, and for this reason he was reluctant to enter individual alliances as the Prussians proposed in 1788 and the Austrians in 1793. He still feared becoming embroiled in an entangling alliance, that would drag Britain into European quarrels, and preferred a general alliance of the great powers, to provide effective collective security. Nevertheless fear that Prussia might otherwise ally with France forced him into making a defensive alliance with Berlin during June to August 1788.[19] Since each also made defensive alliances with the Dutch, a Triple Alliance came into being. This soon threatened to realise all Pitt's worst nightmares, when the Prussians sought to exploit it to seek territorial aggrandisement as compensation for any advantage Russia and Austria might gain from their war with the Turks. For the next two years Pitt and Carmarthen (from 1789 Duke of

Leeds) struggled to discourage successive Prussian schemes for territorial exchanges which would enable them to acquire Danzig and Thorn from Poland. Without consulting London, in 1789 the Prussians encouraged Poland to break from Russian domination and negotiated with separatist movements within the Austrian dominions in Belgium (which declared its independence in January 1790) and in Hungary. In early 1790 they concluded a defensive alliance with the Poles and negotiated another with the Turks preparatory for war with Austria.

The experience confirmed Pitt in his belief that, if Britain was to involve itself in Europe, it should be as part of one great collective system which would guarantee European peace and security. It was a vision, in his own words 'to diminish the Temptation to wars of Ambition',[20] which had been attempted among his predecessors only by Stanhope in 1716–21 and Newcastle in 1748–55, with scant success. Pitt made his first attempt in 1790–1, proposing further schemes to the European powers in 1793, 1798 and 1805, though their eventual realisation had to wait until his disciple Castlereagh briefly implemented the essence of his design between 1815 and 1821.

Pitt's first opportunity came in 1790–1 because Britain was temporarily in a position to punch above its weight in European affairs, as a result of the collapse of France into Revolution in 1789 and the inability of the Russians and Austrians to end the eastern war in the face of unexpectedly vigorous Turkish resistance. He sought to assemble enough powers – Poland, Denmark, Sweden, perhaps Spain – around the Triple Alliance to enforce the re-establishment of the pre-1787 territorial position as the basis for a lasting peace which would avoid any scramble for compensatory aggrandisement. They would rescue Sweden's Finnish provinces, threatened by Russia when Stockholm rashly sided with the Turks in 1788. They would detach Austria from its Russian ally, by encouraging Vienna to look to them to mediate an end to the ruinously expensive Turkish War and the return of Belgium to Austrian rule, with former Belgian constitutional liberties guaranteed by the allies so as to avoid future revolt. And, lastly, they would compel Catherine the Great of Russia to make peace with the Turks on terms that surrendered Russia's direct conquests, but left it dominant over the Khanate of the Crimea, seized in 1783. Having isolated Russia by drawing Austria into the Triple Alliance orbit, they hoped that Catherine might then also be encouraged to escape from her isolation by associating with the alliance, and that all these powers would join in a mutual guarantee of each others' territories (including Turkey's European possessions), which they would defend against attack. If it worked, such an outcome would constitute a mammoth non-aggression pact that would suppress the ambitions of the two most aggressive powers, Russia and Prussia. It would set up Poland as a potentially attractive alternative trading partner for naval stores for Britain, which was having great difficulty in getting Russia to renew a commercial agreement that expired in 1788. By no means least, if France did not eventually accede to this system it would be left utterly isolated and impotent. The situation in the American War would be completely reversed.[21]

Pitt's opportunity for implementing his grand design was reliant on the temporary pressures debilitating France, Russia and Austria. The plan was breathtakingly ambitious – redolent of those comprehensive self-regulating permanent solutions (parliamentary reform, the Irish Commercial Propositions, the Sinking Fund) that he had attempted in domestic affairs in his early years. Luck as well as nerve was necessary for success, but whereas in the Dutch crisis he was aided by 'an extraordinary combination of circumstances', another less fortunate combination lost him control of the situation in 1790–1.

An unexpected development disrupted preparations and diverted British attention when news arrived in late January 1790 that the Spanish had arrested a British ship at Nootka Sound on the north-west coast of America. The issue of Spanish claims to a suzerainty of the Pacific was raised in a way in which neither country could afford to back down. Pitt quickly intervened to delay hostilities by toning down Leeds's aggressive response until further information was received. He then set about acquiring sufficient knowledge to take the matter further. It was at this time that Wraxall lamented Pitt's ignorance of Byron's book about the coasts of South America, but he added that, when he subsequently obtained a copy for the Premier, 'the rapidity and facility with which he acquired, digested, and converted to purposes of utility his knowledge was altogether wonderful'.[22] The arrival in early April of the entrepreneur who had established the Nootka base, with news that three ships had been seized and their crews mistreated, and asserting that he had claimed the land for Britain by agreement with the local Indians, then led Pitt to step up the pressure.

On 30 April 1790 the Cabinet resolved to demand immediate satisfaction and to mobilise the fleet. On 6 May Pitt asked the Commons for supplies, asserting that Spanish pretensions would prevent Britain from extending its navigation and fishery in the Pacific. The most experienced available envoy, Fitzherbert, was sent to Madrid to demand immediate reparations for the seizures and to seek a permanent solution by Spanish renunciation of their exclusive claims to Pacific navigation and to all unoccupied territory, so as to prevent any recurrence. War plans were also prepared to attack the Spanish Caribbean. With the Triple Alliance holding together, and agents sent to Paris to reassure the leaders of the French Assembly, Pitt thereafter stuck to his firm line, himself drafting or correcting Leeds's drafts of the most important instructions and sending their final ultimatum on 2 October. On the 28th the Spanish agreed to a Convention which restored Nootka and the seized ships to British possession with compensation, and which, while evading fixing definite borders for Spanish America, accepted the British right to settle in the areas beyond Spanish settlement on the north-west coast and to fish in the Pacific.[23]

The news was triumphantly received in London on 4 November, and a month later the delighted King offered Pitt the Order of the Garter. However the Nootka Crisis had distracted Ministers from events in Europe for nine months. While their refusal to assist Prussia in plundering Austria led the two German powers to settle their differences in July 1790, on terms broadly comfortable to Pitt's grand design, on 14 August Leeds had to write to Berlin asking the Prussians to delay an armed ultimatum to Russia while the Spanish confrontation continued, since Britain could not guarantee to send its promised supporting squadron to the Baltic.[24] With this the pressure on a beleaguered Russia began to slip away. On the same day, the Swedes unilaterally made peace with the Russians. The delay also enabled the Austrians to recover their composure, achieve a reconciliation with the Hungarians and in November send troops to reoccupy Belgium (without the allied guarantee of its liberties). As Vienna's position improved, it became less amenable to joining the pressure on its former Russian ally. Additionally, the Nootka Crisis made Spanish co-operation improbable, while in the Turkish war Russian troops at last broke the back of Turkish resistance with the capture of the fortress of Izmail in December 1790.

Pitt therefore returned to his grand design after Nootka in much altered circumstances. Overtures despatched on 8 January 1791, for support for a Triple Alliance ultimatum to Russia, met with a disappointing response. Sweden's terms were impossibly exorbitant; Denmark wished to remain neutral. Even the Dutch were lukewarm. Nevertheless Pitt pressed on. He was flushed by his Nootka success, swept along by his natural optimism, eager to grasp the chance of a comprehensive solution, and egged on by his envoys in St Petersburg, Stockholm, and particularly the usually well-informed Joseph Ewart at Berlin, that Russia would give way after a show of resistance and that this was the only way for Britain to retain its influence over Prussia and the lesser Baltic powers. When in mid-March Frederick William II pressed personally for an immediate ultimatum, backed by the Prussian army and a British fleet, the Cabinet, attended by Ewart who was home on leave, agreed to send a fleet to the Baltic and a squadron to the Black Sea. An ultimatum drawn up by Pitt himself was sent to Berlin for approval and forwarding to Russia, centred on Russian return to the Turks of the fortress of Ochakov, close to the 1787 Russo-Turkish frontier. Ochakov was believed to control the major river outlets into the Black Sea from Poland (with which Britain wished to develop trade), and its restoration would effectively mark a return to the former frontier which Pitt believed essential for restoring international stability by stemming demands from rivals for equivalents to any Russian gains.

When he sent off his ultimatum on 27 March 1791, Pitt was confident that Russia would give way to superior force,[25] but he soon found himself unable to muster such force to overawe the stubborn Russian Empress, whose nerve proved stronger than his former French and Spanish opponents. The Prussian request pre-empted his original intention to delay the ultimatum until Parliament was in recess,[26] and when he asked the Commons on 29 March for supplies to despatch the fleet, he failed to convince members of the necessity of the measure.

In the parliamentary debates, the incompleteness of his preparations caught up with him under Opposition attack. Distracted by the Nootka Crisis and his battle with Chancellor Thurlow, he had not sufficiently reappraised the situation. Leeds's Under-Secretary lamented on 9 March how long it had been since the Foreign Secretary 'had been honoured with any conversation by Mr Pitt'.[27] He had not collected precise information on Ochakov, which it subsequently transpired was neither as strong nor as strategically significant a barrier as he had believed. Questions remained on the capacity of the navy to operate in the Baltic or the Black Sea. He was still in negotiation with the powers who were supposed to back the Triple Alliance's ultimatum, and could not announce their support. He had as yet no commercial treaty with Poland which the scheme was designed to promote, and he could hardly say openly that his ulterior aims were to limit the aggressiveness of his Prussian ally and to draw Russia, which he was now trying to coerce, into a collective security system with the Triple Alliance. His defence of his policy was consequently less forceful than usual – Thurlow complained of Ministers being effectively 'gagged' – and his Commons majority, though still large, fell from 103 on 29 March to 80 on 12 April (when according to the French envoy he had been counting on 150) as his loyal supporters showed themselves increasingly lukewarm in their support for a confrontation which seemed remote from British interests.[28] After the 12 April debate Pitt complained that 'they can be embarked in a war from motives of passion [Nootka], but they cannot be made to comprehend a case in which the most valuable interests of the country are at stake'.[29]

With doubts even being voiced by some of the Cabinet, most vociferously by Richmond, but also by his closest confidant, Grenville, and above all fearful that he could not get a vote of credit from Parliament, Pitt opted on 31 March to send an express to Prussia to stop the ultimatum. On 16 April the Cabinet agreed instead to explore a Danish proposal for a compromise solution (in the event Catharine rejected it and made peace on her own terms). It was an unexpected and bitter blow for Pitt. He told Ewart 'with tears in his eyes, that it was the greatest mortification he had ever experienced'.[30] Yet his hopeful vision had been built on insecure foundations. Even if he had forced the Russians to make peace on his terms and induced Vienna and St Petersburg to join his collective security system, it remained to be seen whether such a system, created on the temporary weakness of Russia, Austria and France, would survive the recovery of any of them. Events following his failure showed how difficult it was to restrain Prussian and Russian acquisitiveness for long, and, if the Turkish route to their expansion was temporarily closed, there remained the weaknesses of Poland and France to exploit, with fatal consequences to the chances of concert among the European powers.

. . .

ORIGINS AND OUTBREAK OF THE GREAT WAR WITH FRANCE

The Ochakov humiliation abruptly halted Pitt's first heady excursions into the international arena. Leeds resigned, to be replaced by Grenville, and the two cousins reverted to the pre-1787 pacific isolationist policy of nursing domestic prosperity and national security which, further, might ensure constitutional stability at a time of rising domestic radicalism inspired by events in France. The French Revolution could be left to its internal preoccupations. Pitt treated the apocalyptic warnings of Burke lightly, and told the Commons that 'He did not think it was the business of that House to discuss what was the best constitution of government for France, for America, or for any foreign country.' In August 1791 Grenville avowed 'our determination of the most scrupulous neutrality in the French business', and in September the cousins refused to become involved in an Austro-Prussian proposal for international intervention to free the French Royal Family. When this appeared to come to nothing, Pitt declared in February 1792 that 'there never was a time in the history of this country, when, from the situation of Europe, we might more reasonably expect fifteen years of peace, than we may at the present moment'. Even the French declaration of war on Austria in April did not alarm him – they were likely to fight each other to quick exhaustion or, after Prussia joined Austria in July, France would be defeated and its recovery as a dangerous rival further delayed. Even after the French overthrew their monarch, declared a republic, and went on to repulse the Prussian invasion in the late summer, Grenville could still insist that Britain would keep 'wholly and entirely aloof'. It was only when, in November, the French unexpectedly drove the Austrians out of Belgium, opened the Scheldt in defiance of Dutch treaty rights, and promised fraternity and assistance to all oppressed peoples desiring liberty, that the British government was roused from its complacency in order to protect Holland. Suddenly confronted with a replay of the 1787 crisis, Pitt was sure that 'nothing but our shewing that we are firm can ward off the blow'.[31]

'It is indeed mortifying to be exposed to so many interruptions of a career the most promising that was ever offered to any Country,' he lamented as he contemplated being forced from his peace policy.[32] He was ready to bribe the victorious French general, Dumouriez, to negotiate a general peace, and he spoke directly to a senior French Foreign Office official, Maret, opportunely present in London, to make sure that the French were aware of British concern and determination to support the Dutch, to resist the Scheldt edict and to demand security against the Edict of Fraternity and Assistance. The French government, however, was receiving congratulatory addresses from British radical societies, and, believing Britain was on the verge of revolution, refused to give way. It instituted revolutionary government in occupied territories, and demanded in turn that Britain officially recognise the new French Republic, threatening to appeal directly to the British people over Ministers' heads if they threatened war.

Pitt's quick action to stimulate the loyalist Association Movement and call out the militia cleared his domestic difficulties sufficiently to enable him to keep up his pressure by securing parliamentary votes to augment the army and the navy. The evasive and threatening French reply, received on 27 December, led the cousins to adopt a Russian proposal to rally the neutral Powers behind Britain and Russia in an armed mediation to end the Continental war. If France rescinded its threatening decrees, withdrew within its own frontiers and pledged non-intervention in the affairs of others, Pitt and Grenville were prepared to seek an international pledge to recognise the Republic and not intervene in France's internal affairs. But, wary of encouraging French pretensions, they held back official communication of this latter offer until there were signs of French compliance with their demands. Wilberforce subsequently blamed

Ministers for thus failing to avert war,[33] but it is improbable that the French government would have seen such a pledge as sufficient to merit a withdrawal to France's former frontiers. The French public was fired by a vision of natural protective frontiers on the Rhine, and the fragile government of a revolutionary regime would not risk losing face at home by making the concessions required, particularly when it believed that foreign well-wishers would support the Revolution against their own governments.

With little sign of the French giving way, Pitt concluded by mid-January 1793 that war was inevitable and that, since British naval preparations were more advanced than those of the French, the sooner it began the better. France's colonies were vulnerable; he had a £2 million war-chest and expected an annual surplus of £600,000 on permanent revenue; and the other neutral powers seemed ready to join in a war in which France would be isolated.[34] The tables would be completely turned from the previous American War. His major concern was to ensure that public support did not collapse as over Ochakov.[35] From the end of December, Grenville was composing his despatches as much for an internal audience as for the French government (which was doing the same). The correspondence was published on 17 January. Anti-British speeches in the French Convention were publicised and, finally, the French were manoeuvred towards making the actual declaration of war by the expulsion of the Republic's representative, Chauvelin, dismissed on news of the execution of Louis XVI, ostensibly because his official accreditation was still as minister of the dead King and not of the unrecognised Republic and had consequently expired. The French National Convention readily declared war on 1 February 1793, and immediately invaded Holland.

The war, which was to continue with two brief intermissions for 23 years, broke out within barely two and a half months of the initial crisis, and Pitt was bitterly criticised thereafter by pacifists and sympathisers with the French Revolutionary ideals for having done so little to prevent it.[36] But however real or self-imposed the communication difficulties, there is no indication that either side had not got its view clearly across to the other. Their views, however, were incompatible. Existing international law was set against claimed natural law. Public concession was ruled out as a sign of weakness which might stimulate the other's pretensions and encourage internal opponents of each regime (such indeed had been the result of the French humiliation in 1787). The British were now alive to the international danger of the French Revolution being fed by success and exploding into Europe, whereas if it could be re-confined it might implode instead. French views were not dissimilar

about Britain's expanding imperial pretensions and domestic vulnerability. Ideological incompatibility, and national fears and hopes, were
focused by a confrontation postponed rather than avoided in 1787. Pitt
and Grenville always knew they might yet have to fight to preserve that
victory. Pitt had established and then lost an alliance system designed to
preserve it. Another protection for it was Austrian rule in Belgium,
whose independence from France Pitt described in 1789 as 'undoubtedly
worth the risk or even the certainty to this country of . . . a war'. In 1791
Grenville saw the only significant risk to their new isolationist peace
policy as French intervention in support of revolt in Belgium, followed
by playing the same game in Holland, in which case 'We must interfere.'
Ministerial policy was decided long before the threat became a reality in
November 1792.[37]

The French declaration of war opened the way for Pitt to demand a
more positive limitation of French power and ideology. The principles
of 'indemnification for the past and security for the future', behind
which he rallied widespread parliamentary support, covered very specific
ideas. The 'most prominent object of the war', Dundas explained, was
the safety of the United Provinces and, as a corollary to this, the maintenance of Austrian rule over Belgium as the only secure barrier against
French influence over the Dutch. Second, the seizure of the French
possessions in the East and West Indies was 'of infinite moment, both in
the view of humbling the power of France, and with the view of enlarging our national wealth and security'. Lastly, the termination of anarchy
and restoration of good order in France was 'certainly a material object',
but not to be put before the other two.[38] Ministers took a longer-term
view than the immediate danger from French Revolutionary doctrine
and looked to forcing a decisive conclusion to the century-long series of
wars between Britain and France. If France could be securely confined
in Europe, and its fleet destroyed by battle and assaults on the French
naval arsenals and prevented from resurrection by the loss of France's
booming colonial trade and shipping, the French would lose their power
to damage Britain, whatever their form of government, and Dundas
predicted that 'this country . . . may probably long rest in quiet'.[39]

To ensure such a lasting settlement, Pitt also looked for a stable
and lasting government in France that would honour the terms of the
intended peace treaty. The principles of the Jacobin regime that seized
power in France in 1793 seemed destructive to both internal and external
stability. So long as he was confident of Britain's ability to continue the
war (particularly in 1793–5 and in 1799), Pitt was adamant that he
would make no peace with a revolutionary Jacobin government.[40] After
an initial hesitation while Ministers gauged the strength of internal

feeling, royalist risings at Toulon and in the Vendée led them to recommend the re-establishment of Monarchy in a series of declarations to the French people in the autumn of 1793, specifying it as the only form of government whose supporters they were prepared to assist.

Unlike Burke and his disciples, however, Pitt was not in favour of a complete restoration of the French monarchy to its pre-Revolutionary absolutist position. He saw untrammelled Bourbon ambition as a cause of previous wars, and favoured 'monarchical government with proper limitations', to be achieved by returning to the 1788 position and making a new constitution which avoided the failings of those since tried.[41] Even this ideological prejudice was restrained by the Premier's habitual pragmatism. He would not rule out negotiation with any other form of regular government if it became solidly established. While providing guns, money and limited military assistance to the royalists within France, and financing emigrant royalist regiments and eventually paying pensions to the émigré royal princes outside the Republic, Pitt and Grenville would not recognise the Comte de Provence either as Regent or as Louis XVIII. After a briefing from Pitt in January 1795, Canning recorded that:

> it is not the *form* of the Govt. there, but its *power* and *will* to afford and maintain *security* to other countries, that we consider as *indispensable* – that about monarchy, or republicanism, or Revolutionary Committees, or this or that set of men or set of principles, we have no care or consideration – *further* than as they go to promise or to make improbable, the secure maintenance of peace, if on other grounds peace should be desirable.[42]

. . .

PITT AS A WAR MINISTER

After nine years of successful peacetime government, Pitt at last found himself engaged in a war. He was to become the longest wartime premier in British history – a longevity that is testimony both to his political skills and personal ascendancy but also to his inability to bring the war against Revolutionary France (1793–1802) and that which followed against Napoleon from 1803 to a successful conclusion.

The outbreak of war found Pitt at the height of his powers and he threw himself into the direction of the war with a gusto that contrasts strongly with his initial reticence about embarking on foreign affairs. This was in spite of his confession in 1794 that 'I distrust extremely any Ideas of my own on Military Subjects.'[43] He may have agreed with Dundas's assertion in the same year that 'All modern wars are a contention of purse, and . . . the Minister of Finance must be the Minister of War.'[44] Certainly the position of Dundas as executive director of war strategy (which fell to him through his office as Secretary of State for Home and the Colonies) gave the Premier the opportunity to participate fully in the evolution of policy while relying on someone he trusted to ensure its implementation. In negotiating the union with the Portland Whigs in 1794 he insisted on keeping the military supervision of the war in Dundas's hands, inventing a new office of Secretary of State for War for the purpose. Management of the war could not be left with Portland since Pitt could neither expect to establish the same relationships as with Dundas, 'nor . . . be content, on the other hand, to leave that department to his *separate* management'.[45]

Pitt insisted on personal involvement. He kept close control of war and foreign policy and planning through his close relationship with Dundas and Grenville, even personally deputising for them within their own departments when they were absent. In October 1793 when the Foreign Secretary was on holiday at Walmer, Pitt interviewed the Prussian envoy and told his cousin that 'You need have no scruple in sending me as much business as you please, as . . . I have at present nothing to do.' A year later the War Secretary was at Walmer, while Pitt sent a despatch to the Duke of York 'in the absence of Mr Dundas who has left his pen in my hands'.[46]

Pitt seems to have been the first head of the Treasury to have taken on himself the active co-ordination of the national war effort and this may have been another significant step in the evolution of the position of Prime Minister. The British system of war administration was the sum of the efforts of separate departments, many with independent representation in the Cabinet, and Pitt regarded his relationship with Dundas as essential for ensuring it functioned effectively. 'You know the difficulty with *other* Departments,' he told Grenville, 'even with the advantage of Dundas's turn for facilitating business, and of every act of his being as much *mine* as *his*.'[47] A truculent Richmond was kept in line by threat of dismissal when he seemed to be obstructing preparations for a West Indian expedition in September 1793.[48] Spencer at the Admiralty was cajoled into choosing a naval commander in chief for the great West Indian expedition of 1795 who could work with Dundas's choice of land commander, and in April 1798 into sending a fleet back into the Mediterranean in support of British foreign policy.[49] In the winter of defeat in 1794–5 Pitt even sacrificed his own brother in a purge of the heads of Admiralty, Ordnance and army in order to restore confidence and revitalise management of the war.

This co-ordinating leadership was exercised at a direct individual level rather than through the Cabinet. The Cabinet had proven a poor tool for managing crises in Pitt's first decade in office, and the dominating triumvirate considered it an impediment to the decision and despatch necessary in war. The needs of war administration and political management led Pitt to expand its membership from eight to an unwieldy 13. 'Our Cabinet is a pretty large society of men and it is pretty obvious that on this subject as little as any other it is likely we should not always agree,' responded Dundas, when Pitt told him in 1798 that Westmorland had requested discussion of his home defence plans.[50] While the informality of Cabinet procedures, devoid of agenda or minutes, usually enabled the triumvirate to push through their pre-concerted plans, they nevertheless sought to bypass it whenever possible. In 1797 Dundas obtained the King's authorisation to discuss a projected South American expedition only with Pitt, Spencer and the Admiralty Secretary, Nepean, and the Duke of York at the War Office. Later that year the 'outline and substance' of a secret solicitation of a bribe to make peace from individuals claiming connections within the French government was made known to the Cabinet, but the particulars were known only to the Secretaries of State and Chatham, and the names only to Pitt and Dundas. In 1799 Pitt proposed to Grenville to avoid a Cabinet by making despatches available to be read in the Cabinet room and only hold a meeting if anyone objected to them.[51] The Cabinet was called upon to adjudicate when the three disagreed, but otherwise it was not efficiently integrated into Pitt's system of war management – he felt he had greater control without doing so.

Pitt's war management highlighted many of the best and worst points in his habits of doing business. His active, enterprising, 'improving' spirit led him constantly to seek ways to carry the offensive to the enemy. He could not abide being 'condemned to a *wretched defensive*'. The enthusiasm he could generate by his direct involvement carried or drove colleagues along with him, and gave life to Britain's slow and cumbersome military bureaucracy.[52] He enjoyed the excitement of military operations, corresponding directly with Sir James Murray, Chief of Staff in Flanders, about the expedition against Dunkirk in 1793; travelling with Dundas to Southampton to see Abercromby's great West Indian expedition before it embarked in September 1795. Again with Dundas he went to Kent in August 1799 to inspect the troops and speak to Abercromby, commanding the initial landing force of the expedition to Holland, driving him forward against his doubts on the basis of Grenville's assurances of a Dutch rising. 'All military difficulties are completely overruled, and every step will be instantly taken for the immediate embarkation of the troops,' the Premier wrote to the Foreign Secretary.[53]

Pitt's desire to keep the pressure on France was a matter of calculation as well as inclination. If modern wars were 'a contention of purse' (and his own experience in the 1780s supported that common belief) then the surest and quickest way to victory was to exhaust the French means to resist. In April 1793 he outlined to the Duke of Richmond an evolving plan of multiple operations as Britain's small strike force mobilised: in Flanders, against the west coast of France, in the Mediterranean, and against the French West Indies. He was subsequently criticised by the King and some Ministers for not concentrating his effort – though they failed to agree where the concentration should be – and historians have been far more scathing. In practice the available strike force was too small to operate by itself anywhere except in seizing colonies or coastal raiding, and too small to be decisive even if added to the main armies of the German powers. Pitt preferred to break it into contingents which could encourage a greater number of potential allies to act simultaneously on different fronts: the Austrians in Flanders, the Russians (if they could be got) and royalists in western France, the Mediterranean powers and the royalists in the south of France. He told Murray in Flanders that, while he was very much impressed by his idea of bringing a respectable force to act on one point, the available confederacy did not preclude acting on that principle against many points at the same time and, 'if we can distress the enemy on more sides than one, while their internal distraction continues, it seems hardly possible that they can long oppose any effectual resistance'.[54]

The danger of this strategy, however, was in snatching after every opportunity that presented itself and consequently dispersing resources so far as to be strong nowhere. This was the trap that Pitt, in his enthusiasm, fell into at the end of 1793 in trying to pursue all his objects even though the numbers of trained troops available had not fulfilled his original expectations. Richmond, a veteran of two wars, had urged that he was going much too fast in his plans, which could not be executed in anything like the time proposed. A newly recruited army needed longer preparation and training, and, in Britain's case, if it was wasted it would be hard to replace. However Pitt's imagination was caught and he could not be shaken from his purpose. He made a few observations, 'rather disagreeing with me that troops might not be very tolerably fit for service almost as soon as raised when incorporated into old Corps, but seemed rather to consider this as a matter that must be and therefore not worth discussing or entering into'. 'What he so ardently wished he willingly believed,' said Grenville on another occasion, and Wilberforce thought him less sagacious than might have been expected of a man of his superior talents in his estimate of future events and sometimes in his judgement of character. To Wilberforce his deficiencies in such matters 'might probably arise from his naturally sanguine temper, which in estimating future contingencies might lead him to assign too little weight to those probabilities which were opposed to his ultimate conclusion'.[55]

Pitt's enthusiasm could be crucial at times in driving forward the British war effort, but it could also be dangerous. Unlike his father before him or Churchill later, who were equally prone to interfere in military matters, he lacked any military experience. Grenville complained of his presence at military conferences in 1801, that 'he has very little know-ledge of that detail, and still less habit of applying his mind to it, and his sanguine temper is very apt to make him think a thing *done* in that line when it has been shown that it *may be done* whereas unfortunately the difference is infinite'.[56]

Two problems particularly emerged. One was that his often ill-disciplined personal intervention clashed with the need for methodical procedures in complex undertakings. His well-intentioned wish to facilitate business led him into a direct correspondence with Sir James Murray, Chief of Staff of the British army in Flanders in 1793. It led him into opening letters addressed to George Rose from the commissary in Flan-ders, 'thinking they might contain something material to be attended to'.[57] But it confused established lines of communication which led to misunderstandings. He promised Murray in a private letter in July 1793 that he would investigate the utility of naval co-operation to besiege Dunkirk, but, amid the many other calls on his time, then failed to follow this up, while Dundas, who always felt it would be useful, was waiting for an official requisition from Murray – who must have thought that Pitt was already attending to it! In consequence Dundas was left scrambling for naval assistance too late in the operation.[58] Perhaps Pitt learned his lesson: after the unsuccessful campaign of 1793 he saw com-manders before they embarked, but ceased to correspond with them in the field.

The second problem was how far he was ready to take military advice as compensation for his own ignorance. The expedient of reinstating the experienced but aged Lord Amherst as Commander in Chief did not work, and he was discarded in early 1795. Richmond was consulted in early 1793, and again in 1794, but sidelined when he disagreed with the Flanders campaign and 'totally left out of all private consultation as to military service'. He was 'never consulted in the smallest degree' even in what concerned his own department in the preparation of the 1793 West Indian expedition, and from spring 1794 he effectively withdrew from the Cabinet. The return of Earl Cornwallis from India provided an alternative principal military adviser, and in February 1795 Pitt gave him Richmond's office and a place in Cabinet. Cornwallis's views carried some weight in 1794–5, but his self-confessed gloomy pessimism proved uncongenial to Pitt's mercurial temperament. By 1798 he too complained that he was never consulted 'in the smallest degree' on defence against invasion, and he later confided to a friend that his views were so little regarded, and he met with such discouragement on every occasion, that he felt the greatest disinclination to offer any opinions unless called for.[59]

Occasionally Pitt sought the opinion of military friends such as Lord Mulgrave,[60] but most often Pitt and Dundas chose the operation, either by themselves or from schemes suggested to them, and dealt directly with the commanders they appointed, who were invited to propose plans and state requirements. Relations were not always harmonious. Abercromby's son recorded that, when his father stated the difficulties of the 1799 Dutch expedition frankly and unreservedly, 'Mr Pitt, who was unacquainted with the details of military operations, and with the means that were required to afford a reasonable chance of success, could not repress his impatience, and on one occasion remarked, very pointedly, "There are some persons who have a pleasure in opposing whatever is proposed."'[61] Even Dundas came to fear that Pitt's enthusiasm might override military realities. Mindful of the way Pitt had jeopardised his West Indian expedition in order to throw troops into the disastrous Quiberon landing during his absence in 1795, he appealed to Pitt to listen to the military experts when another project for operations in western France was raised in his absence in December 1799: 'I perfectly trust the assurances you give me, that you will not permit the eagerness or the sanguineness of your temper to carry you beyond the result which an accurate investigation of the subject in detail actually presents to you.' This was 'a tendency which I think belongs to your disposition' and which was to be guarded against in examination and execution of military plans.[62] Pitt did defer to Sir Charles Grey and Col. Twiss.

Alongside these fallibilities, however, Pitt found deep resources throughout the 1790s in his irrepressible optimism, which enabled him to shrug off the worst misfortunes and continue the contest. Sir Gilbert Elliot found Dundas 'much dismayed' and Lord Chancellor Loughborough 'considerably depressed' when the British expedition against Dunkirk was bloodily repulsed in September 1793, but 'Pitt seemed to carry it off better than the rest, treating it as a misfortune, but as an occurrence to be looked for in all wars'. Pitt told George Rose that 'it ought only to have the effect of increasing, if possible, our exertions'. Within days news arrived of the surrender of Toulon and Wilberforce found him with 'a great map spread before him', his imagination fired with new schemes for an offensive from the South of France. Although this too failed when the French were able to concentrate forces at Toulon faster than Pitt and his allies, and recaptured it in December, and although in 1794 the French repulsed the Austro-British offensive in Flanders, and overran Belgium and Holland, yet Pitt still pressed upon the doubting Wilberforce that:

> He could not believe that it would be possible for the French government to find the immense amount of their expenditure both of men and money. How well do I remember his employing in private, with still greater freedom and confidence, the language which in a more moderate tone he used in the House of Commons, that the French were in a gulf of bankruptcy, and that he could almost calculate the time by which their resources would be consumed![63]

It was particularly in the adversity of the French wars that Pitt stayed true to his beliefs that patience was the greatest political virtue, and that all would come right in time. It so frequently had in his remarkable career. 'You know,' wrote Auckland to Mornington in April 1798, 'that (excepting perhaps during the [1797] naval mutiny) he never has inclined to despondency or even serious discouragement: at present he entertains strong hopes that all will somehow end well.'[64]

Yet he did not simply abandon himself to hope. 'We must endeavour to overcome all these impossibilities,' he told Grenville in discussing the obstacles to a new European Coalition. He suggested that Pretyman's sermon, at the St Paul's Thanksgiving after the naval victory over the Dutch at Camperdown in 1797, should 'prove that God, who governs the world by his providence, never interposes for the preservation of men or nations without their own Exertions'. He still had the same message in his last public speech, when he was toasted as the saviour of Europe at the Mansion House after another naval victory at Trafalgar in 1805: 'I return you many thanks for the honour you have done me; but Europe is not to be saved by any single man. England has saved herself by her exertions and will, as I trust, save Europe by her example.' These famous few words, which the Duke of Wellington thought 'one of the best and neatest speeches I ever heard in my life . . . nothing could be more perfect', typified the inspiration his own deep personal patriotism could arouse. At times Pitt could be depressed and racked by indecision, and the naval mutinies over pay and conditions in 1797 for the first time shook his certainty of the British patriotic spirit. But he had the capacity to regenerate his optimism. When he was not in the cellar he was in the garret, communicating to others his spirit of manly defiance of misfortune and conviction that salvation could be achieved by collective exertion. His cousin, Grenville, certainly had a more obstinate determination to uphold national honour by rejecting any thought of a patched-up compromise peace, but he could never have roused the House of Commons into singing the chorus 'Britons, strike home' as Pitt did at the rousing climax of his speech of 10 November 1797.[65]

Besides his habitual optimism and belief in patience, more material factors enabled Pitt to keep the war going despite defeat in Europe. The effort he had put in to strengthening the navy after the American War now paid off. Moreover, whereas he could put the fleet to sea in better repair at the start of the war than ever before, the French fleet was ravaged by the chaotic effect of the Revolution on discipline in the dockyards and afloat and by the loss of much of the *ancien régime* naval officer corps. French naval power never recovered from the loss of 22 ships of the line in the first two years of the war through the fall of Toulon and through battle and shipwreck, so that when the Dutch and Spanish navies changed sides in 1795 and 1796, the British navy, though pressed, was never run so close as in the American War. In 1797–8, despite the naval mutinies, it helped keep Pitt in power and prolonged the war by defeating in turn the Spanish at Cape St Vincent (February 1797), the Dutch at Camperdown (October 1797) and the French at the Nile (August 1798).

Mastery of the seas also enabled Dundas's much maligned strategy of colonial conquests to bring important pay-backs. In contrast to former wars, British overseas trade boomed in the 1790s. When the successes of the initial West Indies expedition were jeopardised by French-inspired rebellions in British islands, Dundas responded quickly by sending the biggest yet British overseas expedition (32,000 men) in 1795–6, which saved the islands and maintained the trade expansion that was so important to financing a prolonged British war effort. The operation destroyed Britain's last remaining strike force (half of which was killed by tropical diseases) but enabled the war to continue until the European Powers came forward once more.

Lastly, Pitt's political and financial skills were vital to keeping resistance to France going. He fought off attacks on his conduct of the war. His change of approach towards negotiations, from late 1795 to 1797, successfully put the blame for any failure to make peace on the French. His ability to maintain sufficient financial confidence enabled him to borrow to levels undreamed of before, and ultimately to persuade the propertied public to accept major new taxes.

. . .

THE QUEST FOR A WINNING GRAND ALLIANCE

Whatever Britain's own efforts, it lacked a large army to defeat the armed Revolution by itself. Pitt looked, in Dundas's words, to 'bring down every Power on earth to assist them against France'.[66] This was the traditional British method, which worked most famously in the Grand Alliance of William III and Marlborough that defeated Louis XIV. Moreover Pitt and Grenville hoped to tie all the allies together in a mutual guarantee of their possessions after the war, in a way similar to that envisaged in Pitt's earlier collective security scheme. France's aggressive behaviour played into Pitt's hands and, by summer 1793, the Revolutionary Republic had ranged against it Austria, Prussia, Britain, Holland, Spain and the princes of the German Empire and Italy. With French finances in disarray, and dissident federalist republicans and royalists alike in revolt against an increasingly dictatorial central government, governing by means of a Reign of Terror, it is not surprising that the directors of the British war effort were confident. Pitt declared that the war could not last more than a year, and the more cautious Dundas that it would be 'a very short war and certainly ended in one or two campaigns'.[67]

However when Pitt and Grenville sought to create a coherent alliance out of the Powers ranged against France, they realised how far they had lost control of the situation by their withdrawal from Continental politics in 1791. Austria and Prussia had agreed to recoup their costs in the French war through Prussia joining Russia in a new partition of Poland, and Austria exchanging Belgium for Bavaria. Grenville vainly protested at the plundering of a 'neutral and unoffending nation' in the east, and, to persuade Austria to remain in Belgium to provide a strong barrier to contain France, they had to promise military assistance to help the Austrians acquire French fortresses across the Flanders border. Their hands were thus tied diplomatically and strategically from the start. Pitt and Grenville sought to give a positive direction to the war effort by encouraging other Powers to seek indemnity from France, rather than from helpless neutrals like Poland, but found themselves faced with demands which would reduce France to the limits it had before Louis XIV's conquests in the previous century.[68]

In practice British efforts were self-defeating. By encouraging such pretensions in order to create unity, they instead aroused jealousies and disagreements which impeded the combined war effort, particularly when Britain proved so much more successful in conquering its indemnity in the West Indies than they did in France. Moreover, these designs clashed with Pitt's hope of an internal counter-revolution, since no patriotic Frenchman would willingly abet any crippling of French power. Royalists only sought British aid when they were on the verge of defeat, and then still endeavoured to evade British control, while the vast majority of the French people, fearful of being partitioned like Poland, rallied behind the Republic. In consequence French Revolutionary power developed faster than allied unity, and, before Pitt and his colleagues could find a means to rally a concerted allied effort behind an agreed programme of indemnities, French victories caused the coalition to collapse around them.

His efforts, however, made Pitt a central figure of French Revolutionary demonology, portrayed as offering British guineas – 'Pitt's gold' – to incite both the European Powers and internal traitors to destroy France and the Revolution. There was in fact less basis to this image than fear-distorted Revolutionary propaganda represented. Arms and money (mostly forged revolutionary *assignats*) were supplied to the French royalists, but the cousins were reluctant to see Britain become, in Grenville's phrase, the 'milch cow' of Europe. Ministers followed traditional paths in hiring troops from the German princes to swell their own small army. Offers of subsidies were made repeatedly to Russia, but Ministers refused to pay the exorbitant price Catherine demanded for the few troops she offered. Instead money was given, not to incite Powers to take up arms, but as glue to hold the Coalition together when allies seemed unlikely otherwise to continue. From 1793, £150,000 a year was paid to Piedmont-Sardinia, and this was followed by a £1.2 million subsidy to Prussia in 1794, and a guarantee for a £4.6 million Austrian loan from the London money market in 1795. Faced by a French field army whose numbers were swelled by the 1793 *levée en masse* to over 700,000, Pitt needed the assistance of the combined armies of all the great military powers of Europe (only in this way was Napoleon finally defeated in 1813–15). In these wars, he paid more and offered more than any of his predecessors in former wars, but far less than his successors.

His money, moreover, was unable to overcome the distraction to the Great Powers caused by the simultaneous extinction of Poland. Poland was an immense embarrassment for Pitt. He shared the public disgust, openly declaring the second partition 'odious' in 1793, and the third 'unjust' in 1796. 'But,' he argued, 'should we, because a partition was made of Poland, abandon that resource [the military assistance of the partitioning powers against France] without which we must fall a prey to the destruction levelled at all Europe, and particularly at Great Britain?'[69] His solution to the problem was to try to segregate events in the west from events in the east, and to have nothing to do with the latter. He and Grenville refused Prussia a guarantee of its spoils from the second partition in 1793, and they refused a subsidy to Russia to impose a settlement of the third partition which was distracting the Powers from the war with France in 1795. Such a distinction was not, however, one the eastern Great Powers could afford to make. A Prussian army, which Pitt agreed to subsidise in 1794, was held inactive on the Rhine when revolt broke out in Poland. The Austrians too abandoned their British-backed Flanders offensive when it was checked in May–June, in order to conserve forces for Poland. Russia refused to send troops to the west and focused on putting down the Polish revolt preparatory to a final partition. The campaign in the west came to a standstill while the Polish revolt was suppressed, and in the meantime Holland was overrun in the winter of 1794–5.

Pitt himself was prepared to make greater sacrifices to hold the anti-French coalition together than his intransigent cousin. He was prepared in 1793 to offer British East Indian acquisitions to the Dutch, when they demanded territory from Austrian Belgium as their war indemnity, and he urged a softer line than Grenville's stern refusal of Prussia's request for a subsidy. However, as in the military management of the war, his personal interventions were disruptive of the smooth course of diplomacy. After pressing negotiations for a Prussian subsidy to successful completion in early 1794, he then turned his attention to domestic treason and failed to ensure the prompt payment of the first instalment of that subsidy by the Treasury, providing the Prussians with a perfect excuse not to move.

Convinced that France was on the verge of financial collapse, Pitt was perpetually restless to keep pressure on the Republic. Twice in 1795 he went against his closest advisers in snatching after chances to pull victory from the jaws of defeat. Early in the year he determined to make another subsidy offer to Prussia, to recover Holland, refusing to accept Grenville's advice that differences over Poland meant that a choice had to be made between *either* Prussia *or* Austria and Russia, the latter of whom were more powerful and warmer towards the war. He only desisted when news arrived that Prussia had made peace. Then in the summer he committed British troops in support of an initially successful royalist landing in France at Quiberon, hoping that it might inspire a major royalist uprising and ignoring the impact on Dundas's great West Indian expedition. Again he only desisted when news arrived that the royalist landing had collapsed. Pitt seems always to have been more hopeful of the effect of internal royalist revolt than either of his two closest colleagues.

The European struggle was continued on the basis of a Triple Alliance of Britain, Russia and Austria (Carmarthen's original goal in 1784).

However, Russia was more concerned with its eastern interests and evaded military commitment, leaving the burden of containing the French to its partners. The tide of war swung the way of the French Republic as it forced the Dutch to join it in 1795 and the Spanish also, in 1796. Pitt had to consider seriously the prospect of making peace before all his allies left him, hoping to trade captured colonies for a French evacuation of Belgium. The proposal was finally put in autumn 1796 when Harris, now Lord Malmesbury, was sent to Paris in an unsuccessful attempt to seek a peace for Britain and Austria that would restore the Belgian barrier.

When Austria too was forced to make peace in 1797, Pitt abandoned even Belgium, and dragged a resistant Grenville into peace negotiations at Lille that might keep a minimum of colonial conquests as some small counterbalance to French success in Europe. He told his negotiator, Malmesbury, with whom he maintained direct contact, that he felt it 'my duty as an English Minister and a Christian to stop so bloody and wasting a war'. With only one ally, Portugal, remaining, with loans to finance the war only obtainable on ruinous terms and shaken by the outbreak of mutinies in the fleet, there was no successful conclusion to the war in sight. Pitt seems to have decided that if peace was obtainable, he could use it to rebuild British strength again to match French power, as he had after the American War, and that this was a better way forward than losing more lives in a fruitless prolongation of the present contest. Once his mind was made up he went all out for peace, against the instincts of both Grenville, who felt he was humiliatingly sacrificing national dignity, and Dundas, who was horrified that he was willing to return all the French colonies and retain only Dutch Ceylon and the Cape of Good Hope and Spanish Trinidad. Grenville verged on resignation and Dundas too reportedly contemplated resigning with a peerage at the peace. Pitt indeed told Malmesbury privately that he would even sacrifice Ceylon or the Cape if necessary, and he seriously considered solicitations from intermediaries claiming links with members of the French government for bribes of up to £2 million to obtain peace on such terms. When in 1801 Pitt threw himself as dramatically behind similar peace terms (without the bribe) negotiated by Addington, Dundas lamented his 'over-eagerness to aim at the object immediately in contemplation. He is either in a garret or a cellar.'[70]

Negotiations failed when hardliners seized power in Paris by a new coup in September 1797, and Pitt focused on internal financial and manpower means to enable Britain to continue the war alone. The interval in the European war, however, at least gave Pitt the chance to seek a general international agreement on future peace terms in advance of any new outbreak, instead of having to improvise unity as he had vainly attempted in 1793–4. Partly on the basis of some ideas suggested by the Duke of Brunswick, Grenville produced a design focused on a Quadruple Alliance of Britain, Russia, Austria and Prussia, as the ultimate guarantee of peace and stability, around which the smaller powers would gather. Rather than seek to restore the pre-1793 situation, which had failed to stop French aggrandisement, a system of stronger buffer states around France was proposed, to be supported by the four Great Powers, themselves strengthened by acquisitions carefully balanced to avoid jealousies and future wars over readjustments. The four would guarantee each others' rights and territories against all foreign attack, and this guarantee would be extended to other powers who wished to join and were admitted by common consent of the four. While experience since 1793 made the cousins more convinced, in Grenville's words, that 'Europe can never really be restored to tranquillity but by the restoration of monarchy in France',[71] this was kept out of the project put on the table.

The scheme, another revival of Pitt's 1789 grand design, was also the basis of Pitt's subsequent proposals for the foundation of any solid system of European security. The plan he offered Russia, seven years later in 1805, refined the concept of a double-line protective barrier of buffer states: in Italy Piedmont, backed by Austria; in Belgium Prussia backed by Holland, each expanded at the expense of smaller neighbours, with France confined to its former limits. For this Pitt was by then prepared to reduce British acquisitions to an absolute minimum – Malta or Minorca and the Cape of Good Hope – while again a Bourbon restoration in France, though desirable, was not essential. The Quadruple Alliance would guarantee the peace settlement by means of:

a Treaty to which all the principal Powers of Europe should be parties, by which their respective rights and possessions, as they have been established, shall be fixed and recognised; and that they should all bind themselves mutually to protect and support each other, against any attempt to infringe them:– It should re-establish a general and comprehensive system of public law in Europe, and provide, as far as possible, for repressing future attempts to disturb the general tranquillity; and above all for restraining any projects of aggrandisement and ambition similar to those which have produced all the calamities inflicted on Europe since the disastrous aera of the French revolution.[72]

This was the grand comprehensive solution that Pitt finally reached in answer to his conundrum of 1784 of how to link Britain into an alliance system that would not entangle it in future wars. But while he had an answer, it was still as hard to achieve it. In 1798–9 discord among the projected allies again thwarted the plan. This time Pitt was ready to provide subsidies from the outset, and allocated £2.5 million for this purpose. But Prussia, secure behind a line of neutrality which gave it a predominant influence over north Germany, refused to act, while Austria's refusal to honour what it considered to be a usurious loan raised by Pitt on its behalf in 1797, barred the way to concert with Vienna. Russia was more co-operative, and when the Continental war resumed in March 1799, the cousins were forced to rely on Russian influence to establish any allied unity, but this was always precarious because of the instability of the Russian Emperor, Paul. The so-called Second Coalition was thus even less concerted than the First, with quickly disastrous consequences. The proposed major thrust into France, through a British-subsidised Russian army in Switzerland, was ultimately dependent on Austrian support, but the Austrians became concerned when Grenville refused to reveal the ulterior intentions of a further expedition, scraped together to support a proposed revolt in Holland. Vienna feared a British attempt to seize and dispose of Belgium (which it still claimed). The Austrian army was consequently removed from the Swiss border to the middle Rhine as a precaution. Pitt belatedly pressed his cousin to be more conciliatory to the Austrians, but it was too late. The Russians in Switzerland, now unsupported, were defeated in September, while, when an Anglo-Russian army landed in Holland in August, a Dutch revolt failed to materialise. Although the Dutch fleet surrendered at its Texel base, the Allies failed to break out of the Helder peninsula and had to be withdrawn two months later.

Nevertheless the Austrians with Russian help had cleared the French from Italy, and Napoleon's November coup was seen as a sign of further instability in France which might bring the restoration of Monarchy closer. The end of 1799 saw Pitt avowing 'every reason to be persuaded, that one campaign, if our Confederacy *can any how* be kept together, will secure all we can wish'. He was not to know how quickly his hopes of the Powers of Europe would be again dashed and how soon he would be driven to the edge of his own resources and ability to manage the British war effort.

There was one further radical step that Pitt was prepared to take in support of the war. From the very start of his administration he had been conscious of the international weakness consequent upon the semi-autonomous position won by Ireland in the American War. The Lord Lieutenant, his friend Rutland, warned in 1784 that without a union Ireland would not be connected with Britain for twenty years longer. Pitt had sought economic unity through the Irish Commercial Propositions. The failure of this scheme and the opposite line taken by the Irish

Parliament in the Regency Crisis highlighted the fissure between the two Kingdoms, and in 1792 he voiced wistfully his long-term wish for a union.[73] He tried palliative measures of Catholic Relief, confessing in briefing a new Irish Chief Secretary in early 1794, that Ireland 'had been and must yet continue, a government of expedients', and hoped to get by. He told Camden before sending him to replace Richmond in 1795 that Ireland occupied little of his thoughts.[74] However his thoughts were soon focused by the impact of the war on increasing troubles in Ireland as the opponents of the Protestant Ascendancy turned to France for help. Attempted French invasion of Ireland at the end of 1796, followed in 1798 by an Irish uprising, highlighted Ireland as the Achilles' heel of the British war effort and resolved him to press his ultimate solution of Union. This he saw as solving the internal instability within Ireland which was a constant invitation to foreign intervention. Union would remove the power of the minority Protestant Ascendancy to mis-rule, and it would also ease their fears by subsuming the majority Irish Catholics within the wider Protestant majority of the two Kingdoms combined. And it would of course provide a united government capable of sustaining a consistent policy. Ministers looked forward to the impression this would create on Europe. 'We shall then be an Empire in reality and have it so much more in our power to give stability and security to . . . the other powers in Europe and to hold that balance which cannot be safely held by any other hands than our own,' wrote the British Minister responsible for relations with Ireland, the Duke of Portland.[75] Union was a foreign policy measure pressed through against all obstacles in 1799–1800 to help win the war and secure the future peace.

· · ·

NOTES AND REFERENCES

1   Add. MSS, 69,133, f. 3; A. von Arneth, *Joseph II und Leopold von Toscana, Ihr briefwechsel von 1781 bis 1790* (Vienna, 1872), pp. 149, 152.

2   R.I. and S. Wilberforce, *Life*, vol. 1, pp. 34–44; Wheatley (ed.), *Wraxall*, vol. 3, pp. 224–5; Leeds Central Library, Canning Papers, Canning Diary, 24–25 June 1797.

3   Sinclair, *Correspondence*, p. 90; Wheatley (ed.), *Wraxall*, vol. 3, p. 224.

4   Browning (ed.), *Leeds Memoranda*, p. 101; BL Egerton Mss, 3498, f. 40 Pitt to Carmarthen, 24 June 1784.

5   Add. MSS, 69,139, p. 10; *Pitt/Rutland Corresp.*, pp. 111–12.

6   *Parl. Hist.*, vol. 25, col. 389; Ehrman, *Pitt*, vol. 1, chs. 12–14.

7   P. Webb, 'The rebuilding and repair of the fleet 1783–93', *BIHR*, vol. 50 (1977), pp. 194–209; Ehrman, *Pitt*, vol. 1, pp. 313–14, 517; NRS, *Letters*

and Papers of Admiral of the Fleet Sir Thomas Byam Martin G.C.B. (ed.)
R.V. Hamilton, vol. 3 (1901), p. 381.

8 The best account of British foreign policy in Pitt's first ten years is J. Black,
British Foreign Policy in an Age of Revolutions 1783–1793 (Cambridge, 1994).
See also Blanning, '"That horrid Electorate"', pp. 311–44; Ehrman, *Pitt*,
vol. 1, pp. 467–77; J.W. Marcum, 'Voronstov and Pitt: The Russian Assess-
ment of a British Statesman, 1785–1792', *Rocky Mountain Social Science Journal*, vol. 10, no. 2 (1973), p. 50; J. Black, 'The Marquis of Carmarthen and
relations with France 1784–1787', *Francia*, vol. 12 (1985), p. 285.

9 Olschki (ed.), *Relation du Cordon*, pp. 33–4; BL Eg. Mss, 3498, Pitt to
Carmarthen 24 June, 15 Oct., 16, 24 Nov., 1, 7 Dec. 1784, 8 Aug., 13 Nov.,
26 Dec. 1785, Richmond to Carmarthen 16 Nov. 1785.

10 Add. MSS, 69,141; J. Ehrman, *The British Government and Commercial Negotiations with Europe 1783–1793* (Cambridge, 1962), summarised in Ehrman,
Pitt, vol. 1, ch. 16.

11 The 1787 Dutch crisis can be followed in Black, *Age of Revolutions*, Ehrman,
Pitt, vol. 1, ch. 17 and A. Cobban, *Ambassadors and Secret Agents. The diplomacy
of the first Earl of Malmesbury at the Hague* (1954).

12 Hogge (ed.), *Auckland Corresp.*, vol. 1, p. 441.

13 Add. MSS, 34,427, ff. 52–3, Pitt to Eden, 15 June; Black, *Age of Revolutions*,
p. 147 *et seq.*; Ross (ed.), *Cornwallis Corresp.*, vol. 1, pp. 334–6, Pitt to
Cornwallis, 2 August 1787.

14 PRO, PRO30/29/1/15 to Stafford, 17 Oct. 1787. The accusation is dis-
counted in J. Black, 'Sir Robert Ainslie: His Majesty's Agent-provocateur?',
European History Quarterly, 14 (1984), pp. 253–83. Carmarthen had hoped
in the previous December to fan Russo-Turkish differences to divert French
attention from Holland but he did not intend war. Rather than war in the
east, Pitt in August 1787 hoped to exploit Austrian suspicions that France
was fomenting disputes in Belgium to make the other eastern powers more
sympathetic to Prussian intervention in Holland (Ross (ed.), *Cornwallis
Corresp.*, vol. 1, p. 336). The Turks had ample reasons of their own to fight
Russia without the insinuations of a British envoy who could offer them no
assistance from his government.

15 Browning (ed.), *Leeds Memoranda*, p. 118; Stanhope, *Pitt*, vol. 1, p. 346.

16 Cobban, *Ambassadors and Secret Agents*, p. 162.

17 Ehrman, *Pitt*, vol. 1, pp. 531, n. 1, 534, 536; Malmesbury (ed.), *Diaries*, vol. 2,
pp. 303–6 for the May Cabinets; J.H. Rose, 'Pitt and the Triple Alliance',
Edinburgh Review, vol. 211 (1910), p. 66; Wheatley (ed.), *Wraxall*, p. 55.

18 J. Black, 'Anglo-French relations in the age of the French Revolution
1787–1793', *Francia*, vol. 15 (1987), p. 417; T. Blanning and C. Haase,
'George III, Hanover and the Regency Crisis', in Black (ed.), *Knights Errant*,
pp. 135–50.

19 Rose, 'Pitt and the Triple Alliance', pp. 65–9; Black, *Age of Revolutions*,
pp. 167–8, 173–9.

20 PRO, PRO30/8/195, f. 49, Notes relating to the Ochakov episode.

21 This and the following paragraphs summarise much complicated diplomatic manoeuvring which can be followed in Rose, 'Pitt and the Triple Alliance', pp. 70–84; J.H. Rose, *William Pitt and the National Revival* (1912 edn.), chs. 21–3, 26–7; Ehrman, *Pitt*, vol. 1, pp. 544–53, vol. 2, ch. 1; P.W. Schroeder, *The Transformation of European Politics 1763–1848* (Oxford, 1994), ch. 2; and especially Black, *Age of Revolutions*, pp. 179–224, 257–328. Much of the final plan was unveiled in despatches to the relevant Courts on 8 January 1791.

22 Wheatley (ed.), *Wraxall*, vol. 3, p. 224.

23 Black, *Age of Revolutions*, pp. 233–56; Ehrman, *Pitt*, vol. 1, pp. 553–71.

24 PRO, FO64/18, Leeds to Ewart, 14 Aug. 1790.

25 Rose, *Pitt and the National Revival*, p. 610, to Auckland on the effect of an Anglo-Dutch fleet in the Baltic.

26 Ehrman, *Pitt*, vol. 2, pp. 14–15.

27 Browning (ed.), *Leeds Memoranda*, p. 148.

28 *Ibid.*, p. 159; Black, *Age of Revolutions*, pp. 300–14.

29 Rose, *Pitt and the National Revival*, p. 617, Ewart to Jackson, 14 April 1791 (see Ehrman, *Pitt*, vol. 2, p. 25, n. 1 for when it was said).

30 *Ibid.* The Ochakov crisis can be followed in Ehrman, *Pitt*, vol. 2, ch. 1 and Black, *Age of Revolutions*, ch. 6.

31 *Speeches*, vol. 2, p. 36; *C.C.GIII*, vol. 2, pp. 222–4; Ann Arbor, Mich., Pitt Papers, Pitt to Dundas, 27 Nov. 1792.

32 Ann Arbor, Mich., Pitt Papers, Pitt to Dundas, 15 Nov. 1792.

33 R.I. and S. Wilberforce, *Life*, vol. 2, pp. 12–13. Something of this concession had in fact been hinted to the French via an intermediary, William Miles, on 29 November. C.P. Miles (ed.), *The Correspondence of William Augustus Miles on the French Revolution* (1890), vol. 1, p. 357.

34 Malmesbury (ed.), *Diaries*, vol. 2, pp. 501–2.

35 P.I. Bartenev (ed.), *Archives Woronzow* (Moscow, 1870–95), vol. 9, p. 285.

36 For the contemporary debate see J. Cookson, *The Friends of Peace* (1982).

37 Add. MSS, 28,068, f. 358; HMC, *Fortescue*, vol. 2, pp. 171, 177. The best studies of the origins of the war are J.T. Murley, 'The origin and outbreak of the Anglo-French War of 1793', Oxford DPhil thesis, 1959; L.M. Porter, 'Anglo-French relations 10 August 1792 to 1 February 1793', York PhD thesis, 1973; T. Blanning, *The Origins of the French Revolutionary Wars* (1986), ch. 5; J. Black, 'The coming of the war between Britain and France, 1792–1793', *Francia*, vol. 20, no. 2 (1993), pp. 69–108.

38 *Parl. Hist*, vol. 30, col. 715, Pitt's speech, 25 April 1793; BL Loan, 57/107, Dundas to Richmond, 8 July 1793; *L.C.GIII*, vol. 2, p. 58.

39 PRO, HO50/455, 'Hints suggested by the perusal of Lord Mulgrave's letter', 27 Aug. 1793; P. Kelly, 'Strategy and counter-revolution: the journal of Sir Gilbert Elliot, 1–22 September 1793', *EHR*, vol. 98 (1983), pp. 340, 346. For a fuller explanation of the rationale of this strategy see M. Duffy, *Soldiers, Sugar and Seapower: The British expeditions to the West Indies and the War against Revolutionary France* (Oxford, 1987), ch. 1.

40 *Speeches*, vol. 2, pp. 161, 174–5, 218, 263–71; Leeds Central Library, Canning Papers 30, Pitt to Canning, 3 Dec. 1799.

41 HMC, *Fortescue*, vol. 2, pp. 438–9 (letter of 21 Sept., misdated to 5 Oct.). See also J. Mori, 'The British government and the Bourbon Restoration: the occupation of Toulon, 1793', *HJ*, vol. 40 (1997), pp. 699–719. Contrary to Dr Mori both Pitt and Grenville were resolutely opposed to any acceptance of the Constitution of 1791 as wanted by the Toulonais (FO72/28, Grenville to St Helens, no. 26, 4 Oct. 1793).

42 HMC, *Fortescue*, vol. 2, pp. 438–9; Jupp (ed.), *Canning Journal*, pp. 194–5.

43 *Windham Papers*, vol. 1, p. 246, to Windham, 21 Sept. 1794.

44 Aspinall and Smith (eds.), *Eng. Hist. Docs.*, vol. 11, pp. 123–4, Dundas to Pitt, 9 July 1794.

45 HMC, *Fortescue*, vol. 2, p. 595.

46 *Ibid.*, p. 436; *Windham Papers*, vol. 1, p. 246. See also *L.C.GIII*, vol. 2, p. 9, no. 839; Baring (ed.), *Windham Diary*, p. 345.

47 HMC, *Fortescue*, vol. 2, p. 595.

48 BL Loan, 57/107, Pitt to Richmond, 24 Sept. 1793.

49 NRS, *Spencer Papers*, vol. 1, pp. 172–3, 177–8, vol. 2, p. 433; HMC, *Fortescue*, vol. 4, p. 595; P. Mackesy, *Statesmen at War: The strategy of overthrow 1798–1799* (1974), pp. 17, 20.

50 John Rylands Library, Eng. Mss 907 no. 19, to Pitt 31 May 1798; see also PRO, PRO30/8/140, Grenville to Pitt, 11 April 1800.

51 *L.C.GIII*, vol. 2, p. 537; Stanhope, *Pitt*, vol. 3, appendix, p. viii; HMC, *Fortescue*, vol. 6, p. 36.

52 HMC, *Fortescue*, vol. 2, p. 593. For his part in such preparations see M. Duffy, ' "A particular service": the British government and the Dunkirk expedition of 1793', *EHR*, 91 (1976), pp. 529–54; and for his personally pushing forward the new head of the Transport Board over the 1795 West Indian expedition see Ann Arbor, Mich., Melville Papers, Pitt to Dundas, Wednesday [30 Sept. 1795].

53 HMC, *Fortescue*, vol. 5, p. 224.

54 PRO, PRO30/8/101, Pitt to Murray, 19 July 1793.

55 PRO, WO30/81, Minutes of conversation with Mr Pitt, 10 April 1793; Stanhope, *Pitt*, vol. 3, p. 391; A.M. Wilberforce (ed.), *Private Papers*, pp. 71–2.

56 Quoted in Mackesy, *Statesmen at War*, p. 5, from Bucks RO, AR 41/63, to Thomas Grenville, 3 Aug. 1801.

57 Harcourt (ed.), *Rose Diaries*, vol. 1, p. 127.

58 PRO, PRO30/8/102, f. 214, Pitt to Murray, 19 July 1793; PRO, WO6/7, pp. 202–3, Dundas to Murray, 29 Aug. 1793, Private.

59 BL Loan, 57/107, no. 21, Richmond to Dundas, 24 Sept. 1793; Ross (ed.), *Cornwallis Corresp.*, vol. 2, p. 336, vol. 3, p. 174.

60 *Windham Papers*, vol. 1, p. 246.

61 Lord Dunfermline, *Lt-Gen. Sir Ralph Abercromby, K.B., 1793–1801: a memoir by his son* (Edinburgh, 1861), pp. 148–9.

62 John Rylands Library, Eng. Ms 907, Dundas to Pitt, 4 Jan. 1800.

63 Kelly, 'Strategy and counter-revolution', pp. 341–2; Harcourt (ed.), *Rose Diaries*, vol. 1, p. 128; R.I. and S. Wilberforce, *Life*, vol. 2, pp. 45, 91–2.

64 *The Wellesley Papers* (1914), vol. 1, p. 55; See also Pitt's own letter to Mornington of 23 April in Lord Rosebery, *Pitt* (1892), pp. 208–9.

65 HMC, *Fortescue*, vol. 4, p. 152; Ashbourne (ed.), *Pitt Chapters*, p. 345; Stanhope, *Pitt*, vol. 4, pp. 346–7; G. Festing (ed.), *John Hookham Frere and his friends* (1899), p. 11. Pitt's war speeches were republished at a low point of the First World War in 1915 in the hope that they could do the same then (R. Coupland (ed.), *The war speeches of William Pitt the Younger*, Oxford, 1915).

66 *Parl. Hist.*, vol. 30, col. 378 (Dundas's words, 12 Feb. 1793).

67 Baring (ed.), *Windham Diary*, p. 386; R.I. and S. Wilberforce, *Life*, vol. 2, pp. 10, 391.

68 Kelly, 'Strategy and counter-revolution', p. 346.

69 *Parl. Hist.*, vol. 30, col. 718, vol. 32, col. 1128.

70 BL, Althorpe Mss, G221, Dundas to Spencer, 17 Nov. 1801.

71 HMC, *Fortescue*, vol. 5, p. 243.

72 Despatch to Russia, 19 Jan. 1805, see C.K. Webster (ed.), *British Diplomacy 1813–1815* (1921), p. 393.

73 *Pitt/Rutland Corresp.*, p. 19; Salomon, *Pitt der Jüngere*, p. 559, Pitt to Westmorland, 18 Nov. 1792.

74 Bickley (ed.), *Glenbervie Diaries*, vol. 1, p. 35; PRO, PRO30/8/326, Camden to Pitt, 6 May 1796.

75 Portland to Wickham, 29 April 1800, quoted in Wilkinson, 'The Fitzwilliam episode', *Irish Historical Studies*, vol. 29 (1995), p. 339, n. 108, from Hants RO, Wickham Mss, 38M49/8/21/1.

Chapter 8

'ENOUGH TO KILL A MAN':
THE EROSION OF POWER

. . .

'THE DOUBT OF BEING EQUAL
TO ALL I WANT TO DO'

Between early 1798 and mid-1800 Pitt stood at the height of his power and prestige. He actually seemed to have fulfilled his disappointed hope, when North fell in 1782, of 'presenting to the eyes of the world, what he had read with rapture, but almost despaired of seeing – a patriot King, presiding over a united people'.[1] He persuaded the King to set an example by heading the donations to the great patriotic subscription to pay for the war, which the nation enthusiastically followed. The public flocked to join volunteer regiments against the menace of invasion. Militia regiments volunteered their services to go to Ireland to suppress the revolt which broke out in 1798, and in 1799 many thousands of militiamen enthusiastically volunteered to join the regular army for the invasion of Holland. The Irish revolt, though locally alarming, was never as widespread as many had feared and was quickly suppressed. Most of the remaining rump of Opposition MPs absented themselves from Parliament, facilitating Pitt's success in pressing through such extremely sensitive measures as the income tax in 1799 and Union with Ireland in 1800. All Pitt needed to elevate his reputation above all his predecessors was victory when war broke out again on the Continent in March 1799. But again victory eluded him. Instead his powerful position eroded in a process of virtually irretrievable decline.

Without a victorious and decisive end to the war to sustain him, a combination of private and public problems conspired to produce his unexpected fall from office in February 1801. After so many years in power, both he and his leading colleagues had lost their resilience in the face of continuing pressures of business. Pitt particularly became stressed by the increasing loneliness of his power. During 1796 he became enamoured of the 20-year-old Eleanor Eden, daughter of Lord Auckland, but in early 1797 he rejected any idea of marriage, asserting decisive and insurmountable obstacles in his personal situation. Certainly his desperate financial situation prevented him from making any settlement on a wife against the event of his death. He was moreover already and irremovably married to business, and he later told his niece, Hester Stanhope, that no man should marry who could not give a proper share of his time to his wife.[2]

However, having committed himself to a life of bachelorhood, he found his earlier bachelor friendships, particularly with the two who accompanied him on his French holiday, dropping away. Wilberforce's religious awakening led him to oppose the continuance of the war in 1795 and to pursue single-mindedly the campaign against the slave trade in the face of Pitt's more pragmatic restraint. The friendship revived, but never regained the intimacy of the early 1780s. Much more devastating to Pitt was the loss of Edward Eliot in 1797. Eliot was his oldest and closest Cambridge friend, and if there was any man that Pitt loved it was this self-effacing and loyal companion. On the eve of Eliot's marriage to Pitt's favourite sister, Harriot, Pitt secured for him the sinecure office of Remembrancer of the Exchequer (worth £1,400 p.a.), expecting to be 'a great deal abused . . . I think not justly, tho' perhaps a little plausibly, but which I shall have abundant reason to endure with patience'. The couple moved in with Pitt, and, after Harriot's death in 1786, Eliot continued to live with the Premier in Downing Street, 'like brothers', in the words of their former tutor Pretyman. The two also spent time together at their out-of-town residences – at Eliot's villa at Battersea Rise in Clapham, and at Holwood and Walmer. When Eliot arrived while Wilberforce was visiting Pitt at Walmer in October 1792, Wilberforce recorded that 'Affection glistened in his countenance, when he came in to Pitt. I stole off to bed at 11, and got off early on Saturday morning, thinking no further object of sufficient magnitude would be attained by my staying, to balance a quiet instead of an unsabbatical Sunday.' Eliot was still living with Pitt in Downing Street when the young Jenkinson and Canning supped with them in April 1794. There is no evidence that their mutual affection was in any way sexually consummated, but their closeness was important to Pitt, and he was devastated by Eliot's sudden death in September 1797. Rose, who was with him, told Wilberforce that 'he never saw, and never expects to see anything like it'. 'To Pitt, the loss of Eliot is a loss indeed,' added Wilberforce. The Premier was a much lonelier man thereafter.[3]

Pitt's friendship with Grenville too was never quite so close after the latter married in 1792 and looked to spend more time with his wife at their new house at Dropmore. The grinding discipline of running a major department efficiently eventually led Grenville to thoughts of retreat. In 1794 he was already hinting that he might wish to retire at the end of the war. Dundas too was becoming weary. In 1797 he talked of retirement and a peerage. In November 1799 and again in April 1800 he asked to be allowed to resign, pleading failing health and sleeplessness, but Pitt declared he could not afford to let him go. Worse, by 1800 Pitt found his two closest colleagues, trapped in their posts by an exasperating and seemingly endless war, sniping at each other as for the first time serious differences emerged within the triumvirate over war strategy. Grenville urged that safety had to be found through co-operation with European allies, and Dundas that it should be found by securing British interests overseas.

Pitt struggled desperately to contain these squabbles within his formerly close team, but the failure of the grand strategic offensive plan of 1799, and the subsequent withdrawal of Russia from the war, left him for much of 1800 wavering over what strategy to pursue. He failed to provide either a lead himself or the co-ordination to back the policy of either of his closest colleagues. Plans were raised, debated, dropped, and the initiative passed from the war-planners in London. In consecutive letters to Grenville on 1 and 2 June, Pitt departed from one plan in favour of another and then reverted back again as new intelligence arrived.[4] The consequence was that divisions increased. By October Dundas described the Cabinet as split five ways on peace policy and four ways on strategy. Moreover none of those managing the war effort could be sure that they could rely on the Premier. As war with the neutral Baltic Powers threatened in July, when a Danish frigate resisted its convoy being searched, Grenville worked the Cabinet up to a firm line, but still had his Under-Secretary, Hammond, write to the latter's friend, Canning, to beg him to implore Pitt to be inflexible on the issue. When a temporary naval armistice with France was under consideration in September, the distraught Secretary of the Admiralty, Nepean, appealed via his friend Huskisson to the latter's superior, Dundas, not to take his intended recuperative holiday in Scotland where he would be in no position to influence the vacillating Premier.[5]

Pitt was now showing clear symptoms of suffering from stress. Some who knew him thought that his health was first visibly affected in the autumn of 1793, after the Dunkirk disaster. The strain was much clearer in 1795, when Canning noted that the convivial parties in Downing Street had become much less frequent. In 1795, too, the cartoonists began to focus on the Premier's spells of lonely boozing with the amenable Dundas at Wimbledon. And in 1795 for the first time he called upon the physician Sir Walter Farquhar to attend him for general debility. Farquhar attributed it to the excess of public business and urged relaxation from the arduous duties of office in order to regain his strength. Pitt told him this was impossible.[6] In February 1797 the Archbishop of Canterbury noted that 'The Premier seems to live much out of sight, and is always rêveur.' He was hoarse, his face swollen, and 'not like health'. In September 1797, Eliot's death, the collapse of the peace negotiations and need for a new financial system to continue the war produced his first stress-related breakdown. He confided to Canning that 'At present (between ourselves and strictly so) tho' I am materially better, and without any complaint that is itself serious, I am unwell enough at moments to feel uncomfortable from the doubt of being equal to all I want to do.'[7]

It may have been stress which produced the bitter words, and his refusal to retract them, that led to his duel with George Tierney, in May 1798. Within a week he was 'seriously ill' and, though he quickly recovered, he told Pretyman that 'I still feel the effects, which you know but too well, of having been so long making exertions beyond my real strength; and the knowing that I am not equal to doing all that at such a moment I wish is probably what most retards my progress'. In October he was ill again and convalesced for three weeks at Addington's country home at Woodley, after which Grenville wrote to their mutual friend, Mornington, that 'Pitt has recovered from his actual illness but his constitution is evidently shaken by his excessive labour; and I feel it is in vain to hope he will enjoy for the future the same active and vigorous health of *body* that he has hitherto been blessed with'.[8]

Although at the height of his authority, in every autumn from 1797, excepting the more hopeful 1799, 'mental anxiety upon public affairs' and the prospect of the load of parliamentary business in the new session, caused his health temporarily to collapse. Autumn 1800 saw his worst collapse yet, and he was again nursed back to health at Addington's.[9] The strain accentuated some of his worst habits – his drinking (though he made efforts to restrain this when he was ill), and his tendency to avoid tackling unpleasant business until the last minute when he would rush through it. It also led him into lying late in bed in the mornings, which drew sarcastic complaint from his colleagues about being able to do a morning's work 'before the day breaks in Downing Street'. It was surely about Pitt's later years that Addington, long after, recalled that he 'sat late at table, and never rose till eleven, and then generally took a short ride in the park', and Dundas that 'He was by disposition extremely indolent, as much so as Charles Fox. He would sleep for ten or twelve hours. He did not begin business till 12 or one o'clock in the day. In business he never attended to *details*, other persons went through that part, and he took only the results.'[10]

At Westminster, 1800 found a tired and harassed Ministry suffering from Pitt's growing lethargy and inattention to detail, and beginning to make mistakes. A bill to remedy defects in the income tax, introduced hurriedly by George Rose, had to be taken back in April because of defective drafting. Pitt took it over personally, but only got it through in May in an emasculated form. In June, Pitt encouraged Hawkesbury to introduce a bill to increase competition in the flour trade by chartering a London Flour Company, but was then absent when some of his own junior office-holders joined with the Opposition to bring it close to defeat. In November 1800 Ministers forgot to renew the Seditious Meetings Act before it expired.[11]

Pitt's resilience became largely contingent on the situation of the war. In September 1799, Grenville could write delightedly that 'Pitt's health and spirits are revived by this tide of success in every quarter'. Even when the Russians left the war shortly after, Pitt still hoped for victory through the more efficient Austrian army, only to have his hopes shattered in June 1800 by Napoleon's narrow but nevertheless decisive victory at Marengo. He had had money at hand for one more Continental campaign and that had now failed. George Rose reported the Premier as bearing the news 'with fortitude', yet just over a month later and with famine adding to Pitt's problems, Rose was declaring him unwell and that Pitt's physician Farquhar agreed with Rose's view, that his illness arose more from his mind than anything else.[12]

Nevertheless Pitt still remained a formidable politician. Repeatedly in the autumn of 1800 he rallied himself to show that he had lost none of his skills at political in-fighting, nor the tactical astuteness with Parliament and people that had raised him to undisputed Premier and national leader. He at last came to a decision and took the lead on war strategy. With fresh peace negotiations probable in the near future, he determined to improve Britain's bargaining position by forcing through Dundas's project to drive the French from Egypt, in the face of vociferous opposition from Grenville and Windham, and the hostility of the King. Admittedly now manipulation and guile were employed rather than the 'firmness and temper' used in 1797. Lord Liverpool subsequently recalled that:

Lord Grenville complained that Pitt had authorized him to give assurances to Vienna and other courts of military co-operation, which he afterwards suffered to be overruled by the Cabinet; that Pitt, finding Lord Liverpool was for the Egyptian plan, called out (contrary to custom) for Liverpool's opinion – 'I wish to hear Lord Liverpool's sentiments'; that on voting those who gave an opinion were nearly equal, but Pitt, summing up, counted those of three members who had not given any opinion and so the matter was decided.[13]

Domestic crisis also loomed with another bad harvest and food rioting on a scale he had not before encountered. He confided to Addington, on 8 October, that the question of peace or war was not half so formidable as that of the scarcity, 'for the evils and growing danger of which I own I see no adequate remedy'. 'These are uncomfortable speculations,' he added, 'and I am not the better for brooding over them during the confinement and anxiety of some weeks past.' Two days later, however, he had decided to acquiesce to the public pressure to recall Parliament, and after three weeks' recuperation at Addington's Berkshire country seat, he was ready to defy Grenville's and Portland's free-market urgings by having a Commons committee steer through a package of moderate interventionist measures. It was a fudge which staved off famine but failed to lower prices, so that in the ensuing months industrial depression followed, demands to end the war spread and eventually organised extra-parliamentary opposition sprang up again. However the rioting temporarily eased, and confidence was restored among the propertied classes in the localities who hesitated to obey calls to maintain law and order without any relief programme to conciliate the discontented.[14]

While Pitt seemed as dominant as ever in Cabinet and Parliament, however, his influence was crucially weakening with the King. He should have attended to the warning signals. Pitt's very success against Fox had made the King feel less fearful of the latter and more independent of his Minister. The King did little to restrain criticisms in the Lords by his son, the Duke of Clarence, of measures supported by Pitt: the bill to restrain the slave trade on the Sierra Leone coast in 1799; a divorce bill in 1800. Pitt himself commented on the great appearance of hostile Court influence in the former case, and Lord Bathurst detected a potentially troublesome attempt to establish 'a sort of princely influence' in the Lords in the latter.[15] In the summer of 1800 the King himself became increasingly restless at his Ministry's handling of the war. He particularly disliked proposals for a naval armistice in order to join with Austria in peace negotiations, and when, without prior consultation, he was presented with a Cabinet minute to attack Ferrol in late July, he initially rejected it. Lord Malmesbury later learned that when the King summoned him and Windham to Weymouth in August, he was contemplating appointing

Windham First Minister and Malmesbury Foreign Secretary because he had 'for a long time since been dissatisfied with Pitt's, and particularly Grenville's "authoritative manners" towards him'. Instead, however, George contented himself with grumbling at the Egyptian expedition.[16]

. . .

THE CATHOLIC QUESTION AND THE FALL OF THE MINISTRY

This was hardly the atmosphere for Pitt to present the Monarch with his most radical constitutional proposal yet: to repeal the religious Test Acts and replace them with a political test against Jacobinism, but this is what he attempted in his desire to achieve a comprehensive settlement of the Irish problem. Formerly he had looked to achieving Catholic Emancipation in Ireland by degrees over a longer term, but the needs of the war and probable armed peace after it, now led him to accelerate this process which would, as he eventually explained to the King:

> conciliate the higher orders of the Catholics, and by furnishing to a large class of your majesty's Irish subjects a proof of the good will of the United Parliament, afford the best chance of giving full effect to the great object of the Union, – that of tranquillizing Ireland, and attaching it to this country.[17]

The Union, however, made any repeal of the Test Acts a United Kingdom measure, not just one for Ireland. When Ministers discussed the issue in late September and early October 1800, they all anticipated trouble from the King, the Church and probably the Law.[18] This was a powerful combination, and Pitt was aware 'how very large a part of England the Church of England Party were, [and] how great a value they attached to this question'. He thought it 'comparatively speaking of very little importance', and an earlier Irish secretary noted after a briefing that 'Mr Pitt seems to think the Christian religion more in danger than the overthrow of Protestantism by Popery'. His earlier opposition to repeal of the Test Acts had avowedly been on grounds of expediency, and expediency likewise led him to drop the measure from the original terms of the Union treaty in order to ensure Irish Protestant support.[19] When, however, this failed to produce an Irish parliamentary majority in 1799, the Lord Lieutenant was authorised to indicate Cabinet favour for an enactment, after the Union, if this was necessary to attract Catholic support. Although Cornwallis and his Chief Secretary Castlereagh ultimately managed without a formal promise, they felt themselves sufficiently committed to urge Pitt to adopt the measure when Union finally passed, and Pitt expected the issue to be raised when the first meeting of the Union Parliament took place at Westminster at the beginning of 1801. In view of the state of the war, it was not the time to have Ireland blowing up in his face.[20]

To overcome the expected storm of opposition, Pitt and his closest colleagues assembled a package of measures which they hoped would meet all concerns. Repeal of the Test Acts, commutation of tithes to rent payments and endowments to provide salaries for Irish Catholic and Dissenting clergy would complete the conciliation of non-Anglicans. The latter provision also had the advantage of making such clergy more dependent upon and controllable by the State and consequently might be hoped to placate Anglicans. The Church of England would be provided with additional protections by a clause in the new oath binding office-holders to support the Establishment in Church and State, and by new measures strengthening the authority of the Church hierarchy over their clergy, and increasing the pay of the poorest clergy, whose poverty in-hibited their residence in their parishes. Emphasis would be turned from the danger from Catholicism to that from Jacobinism, and a new oath, applicable to office-holders, Catholic and Dissenting preachers and all schoolteachers, would require specific rejection of the doctrine of the sovereignty of the people.[21]

The King had already shown his deep-rooted opposition to repeal of the Test Acts when he remonstrated against Fitzwilliam's proposals in 1795, which he declared as 'beyond the decision of any Cabinet of Ministers' and highly dangerous to encourage without previous concert with the leading men of every order of the State. In 1798 he warned that no further indulgences should be given to the Catholics, and in 1799 that he would be an enemy to Union if he thought it would be attended by any change in the situation of the Catholics.[22] When those ministers available in London discussed this obstacle in September 1800 during the absence of the King at Weymouth, Pitt 'undertook to speak to him on it the moment He returned and in the meantime to sound the Opinions of considerable Persons in the Country and use every means in his Power to put the Question in the best Shape'.[23] This he failed to do. Ill-health, the dispute over the Egyptian expedition, famine and food riots and the emergence of a Russian-inspired Armed Neutrality of the Baltic Powers to resist British restrictions on neutral maritime trade, all conspired to divert the Premier's attention, and it was not until January 1801 that the imminent assembly of the Union Parliament brought his focus back to the Catholic question.

Several of his colleagues subsequently blamed him for failing to prepare the King. Camden loyally attributed this to Pitt's realisation of the need to ensure the backing of the majority of the Cabinet in order to sway him, though he criticised Pitt's neglect of his relations with the King, instancing that he had regularly been six weeks in London without attending the royal Levée. Despite the warning signals, the Premier was seemingly beginning to take his influence over the King for granted. Even on the Catholic issue, the King had reluctantly conceded Irish Catholics the vote in 1793, and his opposition in 1795 seemed to suggest he might be moved if the leading men of every order of the State agreed. Pitt may not have realised how far he had since convinced himself that it was contrary to his Coronation oath. On other measures dear to his heart, the King had eventually given way to pressure from his Ministers, sacrificing the smaller German states in 1796, and accepting negotiations with France in 1796, 1797 and 1800. In 1800 his opposition was also overborne in relation to the expeditions to Ferrol and Egypt.

Pitt's victories had been largely won by showing that he had a united Cabinet behind him.[24] On this occasion, however, the Cabinet was divided. Lord Chancellor Loughborough, Liverpool and Westmorland, subsequently followed by Portland and Chatham, all indicated opposition. In January 1801 Pitt tried to manoeuvre an appearance of unity by the sort of tactics Windham had complained of in 1799: creeping informal Cabinet discussion which avoided a vote and, by holding out the prospect of further discussion, evaded the point where opponents might make a formal stand until the opportunity to do so had passed. He declared a meeting on 11 January to be preliminary, and another on the 25th (summoned at only a day's notice) was drawn into a bare statement of individual opinions in the absence of a number of opponents or doubters – Liverpool (who was ill), Chatham (not summoned by Pitt from his regiment because 'you seemed from our last conversation to have no decided bias on your mind'), and especially the Chancellor, whose views several of those present felt should be heard. Pitt, according to Camden, promised to see the Chancellor and summon another Cabinet for the next day, so that opinions were given without qualifications or arguments for or against. Pitt subsequently declared that he thought the understanding was that he should see the Chancellor and call another meeting if the Chancellor wished it. When the Chancellor did not wish it, he felt he had the requisite Cabinet approval to take the matter forward.[25]

Pitt in fact interpreted his straw poll of opinions at the Cabinet on the 25th as providing the majority to proceed to the requisite next step of gathering the backing of 'the leading men of every order in the State', and at dinner afterwards he authorised the Irish Secretary, Castlereagh, to inform the Irish Chancellor, Lord Clare, of the government's deliberations and decision. Presumably he was trying to build up a momentum in which the leading men of the State would follow the government's lead, and the rest of the Cabinet would then swing behind a unanimous official minute to the King, to which he might be expected on past precedent reluctantly to concede. He told the King on 31 January that he concurred in what appeared to be the prevailing sentiment of the majority of the Cabinet.

If this was so then the plan was thwarted when the decision was leaked to the King before Pitt was ready. Two of the Cabinet opponents of the measure, Loughborough and Westmorland, were subsequently suspected of being the leakers and tainting the King's mind.[26] If so, they may have seen it as the only way of defeating Pitt's Cabinet artifices. At the Levée on 28 January the royal wrath exploded on the unfortunate Dundas (Pitt was again absent), culminating in a declaration, loud enough to be overheard and with echoes of 1783, that 'I will tell you, that I shall look on every man as my personal enemy, who proposes that Question to me,' adding that 'I hope all my friends will not desert me.'[27]

Taken unawares, Pitt called an emergency Cabinet meeting the same day. Following the tactics he had adopted when the King initially rejected the Ferrol expedition, six months before, Pitt determined on a calm statement of his case to the King and told colleagues that he must go out if his measure was not carried. He and Grenville undertook to put on paper the heads of the plan proposed, which should be shown to the Cabinet next day, and then taken by Pitt to the King. Again the King forestalled him by appealing to the Speaker of the Commons, Addington, to use his influence to dissuade Pitt from agitating his scheme. Addington called on Pitt next morning as intermediary for the King, and in the changed situation the Cabinet never met – indeed thenceforth Pitt acted without consulting Ministers as a body. A minimum of information was supplied to Ministers who called on him and a little more was opened to Grenville, and probably Dundas, but he largely decided the fate of his Ministry by himself.[28]

Addington's initial report to the King indicated hopes of a satisfactory outcome, and Windham, calling on Pitt on the 30th, found that all had changed from the last Cabinet and that he conceived he must give way.[29] Perhaps Pitt intended the mutual abstinence from lobbying on the issue that he put in his letter to the King on the 31st. But before that letter was written he received further information, confirming the extent of the King's opposition and which led him to a firmer stance. Possibly this was news of the assiduous lobbying by those around the

King, which induced the Primate of Ireland to withdraw support for the replacement of the vociferously anti-emancipation MP for Armagh by a pro-Catholic sympathiser.[30] In a letter to the King on 31 January (of which Pitt told his colleagues only after it was sent),[31] the Premier pressed the case for emancipation at length, offered to avoid agitating the subject in Parliament while the King considered his case, but asked to be allowed to resign if the King then continued to disapprove. With domestic unrest continuing, and the result of expeditions to the Baltic and to Egypt pending, he would not desert his post if the King thought his exertions useful. He was willing to continue until 'the chief difficulties of the present crisis' were surmounted or materially diminished, and even for longer if it was necessary to prevent agitation or discussion of the Catholic question, though he reserved the right to state his principles at an appropriate time, and (as in 1785 over parliamentary reform) he urged the King to discountenance use of his name to influence the issue in the interval too.

The King consulted Addington on the frame of his reply and pressed the Speaker to head his government if agreement could not be reached with Pitt. The royal reply on 1 February declared his absolute opposition to Catholic Emancipation, 'from which I never can depart'. He urged Pitt not to resign, and agreed to abstain from talking on the Catholic Question, though he declared his inability to stop others guessing at his opinions, which he had never disguised. To Pitt the response, particularly this last statement, was unacceptable, and on the 3 February he wrote his letter of resignation to the King, having first assured Addington of his full support if he took over the government.[32]

Contemporaries were stunned at Pitt's sudden withdrawal from office after so many years and when he was seemingly still at the height of his power. He himself admitted to his brother on the 5th that 'I did not foresee the extent of the consequences to which within this week the question has led.'[33] Many looked for some secret explanation such as the wish of Ministers like Dundas to resign, or Pitt's desire to rid himself of difficult colleagues like Grenville, Spencer or Windham.[34] More plausibly, Lord Malmesbury accused him of seeking an excuse to resign because he could neither win the war nor make peace. But, writing to Canning on 10 January, Pitt had looked forward hopefully to making peace when the Baltic and Egyptian expeditions were successfully accomplished, and he offered in his letter to the King on the 31st to continue in office until the crisis was over.[35]

Both Grenville and Dundas stressed that the Catholic issue was indeed the real reason.[36] While to them it was primarily a matter of conviction, honour and principle, Pitt also had his eyes on the power-politics implications of the crisis. To his brother he stressed not only their opposition of views with the King, but 'the industry already used on the question . . . [and] . . . the imprudent degree to which the King's name was committed on a question not yet even regularly submitted to him'. After seeing Pitt, Canning told Malmesbury that 'if on this particular occasion a stand was not made, Pitt would retain only a nominal power, while the real one would pass into the hands of those who influenced the King's mind and opinion out of sight', and again, later, that 'Mr Pitt told him that he went out, not on the Catholic Question simply as a measure in which he was opposed, but from the manner in which he had been opposed, and to which, if he had assented, he would, as a Minister, have been on a footing totally different from what he had ever before been in the Cabinet.'[37]

Perhaps victory in war might have made Pitt unstoppable (though it would also have made the measure less necessary), but failure to win the war made his cause unwinnable. The continuing crisis prevented him from trying to force his proposals through, for fear of destabilising the country at such a delicate time. Castlereagh explained to the Lord Lieutenant that to try the question now would only pledge people against it, they had no chance of success in the Lords, and, even if carried through both Houses, the King would still refuse his assent. To force it through would deprive it of its supposed benefits of creating a more United Kingdom. Afraid that pressing the issue in Parliament would only stir up the Irish Catholics, Pitt urged restraint upon them as the best path to long-term success.[38] However he felt that he could not afford to submit to the methods brought against him. This was where the situation differed from the earlier similar dialogue with the King over parliamentary reform, when there were not others so obviously working on the King against him. Moreover, once the King found an alternative in Addington, with whom he had been developing a warm relationship, Pitt could not blackmail the Monarch that his threat of resignation might let in Fox. Since he could not defeat his opponents at Court and inside government by either persuading the King or taking his battle into Parliament, resignation seemed the only option.

. . .

PITT OUT OF OFFICE –
THE PURSUIT OF 'CHARACTER'

The King began his letter concluding their correspondence (on the only occasion he ever addressed him as 'My Dear Pitt') with the words: 'As you are closing, much to my sorrow, your political career'. Pitt's banker, Coutts, concerned at his desperate financial plight, urged a quick return to the Bar, which might yield £3,000 a year at once and the Lord Chancellorship in a few years' time.[39] Where did Pitt himself see his future? While some might have welcomed the chance of retirement and repose after over 17 years as head of government, no one else had ever faced this prospect at the age of 41, and there is no indication that he ever regarded his political career as over. The exercise of power was in his blood, and his actions betoken a man expecting to return again, sooner or later, as Prime Minister. He was at pains to ensure his reputation for patriotic political virtue by urging Addington to accept the King's choice, with the promise of his full support. He also persuaded many of his Ministry to continue under Addington.

Pitt claimed to his brother that he had long thought that the Speaker was the person to whom the King would resort when need arose. Indeed Pitt himself had contemplated Addington temporarily replacing him in 1797. It is not improbable that he regarded this family friend, whose political career he had fostered, as a temporary stopgap now. He was certainly looking ahead on 24 February, when he told Pretyman of his intention to pledge himself never to come into office without full permission to raise the Catholic Question again. He was, however, quickly shaken from this resolution by a sudden recurrence of the King's derangement, which delayed the transfer of power.

The King blamed Pitt for his relapse, and in early March Pitt assured the Monarch through his doctors (and authorised George Rose to confirm in writing some months later) 'that during his reign he would *never* agitate the Catholic question . . . whether *in* office or *out* of office'. Here was a strong implication of remaining in, or returning to office, and, indeed, before he finally handed back his Seals of Office on 14 March, he succumbed to promptings from Dundas, Camden and others for Addington to be informed that if he and the King wished the former government to be restored, then Pitt was willing to discuss it. When Addington made clear his determination to continue, Pitt quickly repudiated the feeler.[40]

It was when Addington developed a liking for his new position that Pitt found how far he had boxed himself into a long waiting game. Having promised his support to Addington, to try to oust him would be an act of betrayal. He required both Addington's and the King's consent to take office again, and only felt justified in looking for this if he was called upon by the country to come forward. But he resisted Canning's desire to stir up a such a call. He wished to avoid 'the aspect of caballing and intriguing for power', and told his over-zealous acolyte that 'I stand pledged; I make no scruple of owning that I am ambitious – but my ambition is *character*, not office. I may have engaged myself inconsiderately, but I am irrecoverably engaged.'[41] It was perhaps disingenuous of him to distinguish pursuit of character from pursuit of office because the former had always been the only sure path to office for a politician without party, and was even more necessary for a statesman looking to be called back as Prime Minister.

There was a heavy price to be paid for waiting, for his perennial inattention to his private finances now caught up with him. Deprived of the profits, prestige and protection of high office, he found his creditors unwilling to wait any longer for payment. His resignation left him with an income of £3,000 a year as Warden of the Cinque Ports, whereas, when George Rose was called in to examine his accounts in 1800, he found debts and unpaid bills totalling £46,000. Yet anxious to maintain his political independence, he gratefully declined the King's offer of £30,000 towards the payment of his debts, and likewise an offer from Addington of the sinecure Clerkship of the Pells. All he would accept, as a loan, was a subscription of £11,700 from close friends and supporters. He sold his gifts, from foreign princes and from civic corporations, for another £4,000. He also sold his expectations of the reversion of his mother's pension (she was shortly to die in 1803) and of the parliamentary grant to the earldom of Chatham (his brother was childless), but it was not enough to stop his beloved Holwood having to go too, auctioned off for £15,000 in 1802. He lived austerely in rented accommodation when in London, and journeyed the City in a common chaise. Pretyman remembered that for three years he could not afford to entertain company to dinner in London, and received only a few close friends at Walmer Castle. It was not, however, a lonely life, for he was a welcome guest among his circle of friends, and in 1803 he enlivened his household by taking into his protection his Stanhope nephews, seeking refuge from an inflexible father, and also their spirited elder sister, Hester, who became companion, housekeeper and hostess for his last years. Nor was his retrenchment total, as his compulsive bent for 'improvement' led him to rent and landscape land adjacent to Walmer in 1802. Nevertheless his life out of office was one of self-imposed gentlemanly poverty.[42]

There were initially compensations for retirement. Canning described him as 'really as full of spirits in his new idleness as a boy just come home for the holidays'.[43] For a while he acted as adviser to the new Ministry, particularly when peace negotiations were opened with France, and he energetically canvassed friends to support the preliminaries signed in London in October 1801. Many were aghast that all the British overseas conquests except Trinidad and Ceylon were returned, and he admitted privately that he would have liked the Cape as well, but never-theless he accepted the outcome as the best that could be got in circum-stances when a period of peace was necessary to restore the national prosperity and government finances.

Ironically the peace, which Pitt helped to secure, released Addington from dependence upon him. Between the signing of the preliminaries and the final Treaty of Amiens in March 1802, the two dined together only twice. As the consultations grew less frequent, Pitt became increas-ingly frustrated and disillusioned with the policies of his former protégé. When Napoleon showed no signs of restraining his ambition, Pitt became critical of what he considered to be the Ministry's weak performance in finalising peace terms at Amiens. He felt Addington did not sufficiently defend the reputation of the former Ministry against the attacks of the old Opposition. An inquiry into Navy Board affairs initiated by Addington's independently-minded First Lord of the Admiralty, Earl St Vincent, could not but be construed as criticism of their management under Pitt. He was offended at not being told by Addington when his old ally, Dundas, was offered and accepted a peerage as Lord Melville. And he was horrified at the extensive borrowing to which Addington resorted in his first peace-time budget. Severe ill-health in the autumn of 1802 – the first major occurrence of the affliction that was to kill him – laid him low and kept him at Walmer and then convalescing at Bath, rather than attending Parliament (for which he was criticised by the government-sponsored *The Times*), but he now determined to evade all further attempts of the Ministry to draw him into confidential consultations.

As deteriorating relations with France threatened renewal of war, Addington and his followers felt the need to strengthen the Ministry to face the new crisis and in early 1803 at last turned to Pitt. Each side played hard. Addington proposed a position of equality under a figurehead First Lord of the Treasury; Pitt initially protested his ill-health and then finally came out with an insistence that he could only return as First Lord of the Treasury and Prime Minister. When this was reluctantly conceded by Addington and his Cabinet, Pitt overplayed his hand by insisting that former colleagues such as Grenville, Spencer and Windham, who had become bitterly critical of the conduct of Addington and his Min-isters, as well as Melville, should re-enter the Ministry, with Addington moving to Secretary of State and a new role as Speaker of the Lords, and others, including the Premier's ally Hobart, retiring. All this should be at the Cabinet's request and at the expressed desire of the King. Not surprisingly, Addington's ministerial colleagues baulked at such a humiliating surrender and the talks collapsed.[44]

Pitt's ideal for his return to power was to re-create his former long-lived Ministry by general agreement. In this way he might re-establish his powerful position of the late 1790s, while, through his promise on Catholic Emancipation, avoiding the denouement of 1801. It was an optimistic vision which ignored the Cabinet splits of his last years in power (perhaps he intended a reshuffle of offices to avoid them), and also how far the political situation had changed since then. His passive strategy for returning to office by pursuing 'character' – as the virtuous and patriotic statesman standing above politics and waiting for the call – had lost him the initiative. At his request, many of his former government had stayed on with Addington and negotiated the peace. Five ministers, Dundas, Camden, Grenville, Spencer and Windham, had followed him out of office, but while the first two loyally accepted his support for the peace preliminaries, the other three bitterly attacked them, so that his former supporters had effectively split into three. The breach widened when, after the failure of his overtures to Pitt in early 1803, Addington turned to the former Opposition for help and drew Pitt's old adversary Tierney into government as Treasurer of the Navy. Moreover Addington had called a general election on the initial popularity of the peace in 1802, so that the Parliament with which Pitt now had to deal was of Addington's making, rather than his own.

Consequently the Addington Ministry proved more resilient than Pitt had ever imagined, and, even after war with France was resumed on 18 May 1803, it took another year to get it to agree to give up office – another year in which Pitt's hopes of a triumphant restoration of his former Ministry were dashed as its one-time members fell apart over the conduct of the war. Pitt sought desperately to stay above the political infighting by a patriotic advocacy of the war. Attending Parliament at its outbreak for the first time in over a year, he delivered one of his greatest speeches on 23 May – 'an electrifying peroration on the necessity and magnitude of our future exertions', in the words of one of his listeners.[45] The limitations of this approach were shown, however, when he was crushingly defeated in trying to shelve an Opposition motion of censure on 3 June, when government, Opposition, and even some of his own supporters combined to vote against him.

Nevertheless he was still resilient enough to bounce back by his energetic promotion of the war effort. He was eager to make the war a people's contest. When the country faced invasion in July, he forced Ministers to agree to a mass arming of volunteers, setting a lead himself by forming three battalions of Cinque Port volunteers and accepting the colonelcy of the Trinity House volunteers. By the end of the year 380,000 volunteers had been enrolled for home defence. Whatever its military value, the national call to arms stimulated a patriotic upsurge, and Pitt had put himself again in his favoured role as Patriot leader of a movement of national unity. For a time it restored all his old vitality. His niece described how 'Mr Pitt absolutely goes through the fatigue of a drill-sergeant. It is parade after parade, at fifteen or twenty miles distant from each other. I often attend him; and it is quite as much, I can assure you, as I am equal to, although I am remarkably well just now.' She noted, in January 1804, that 'his most intimate friends say they do not remember him so well since the year Ninety-Seven'. Yet again his optimism was fired into ambitious dreams for the future. Wilberforce described him as 'rampant about setting Europe to rights, etc. after vindicating our own safety'.[46]

Pitt now expected to return to office in the near future and had his eyes fixed on the best circumstances in which he could do so to ensure his power. He was attracted by the prospect Grenville put to him, of a patriotic government of national unity – a political equivalent of the volunteers, which included 'All the Talents' from all sides of Parliament, and which it was believed would make the greatest impression on Europe of British resolve in the war. Only the untalented Addington and his followers, whose languid and uncertain management of the war infuriated him, would be excluded. However Pitt was wary of alienating the King, whose support he also needed, but who was still attached to Addington, and whose hostility to Fox was unabated. Hence he refused to enter into a formal United Opposition with Grenville and Fox to bring Addington down.[47]

His continued pursuit of the ideal solution, in the event, left him the worst of all worlds. He was unable to deter the combined Grenville–Fox attack on Addington, but when the Ministry faltered but did not fall, he decided not to wait for the spontaneous call of his country. His anxiety at the resultant disruption to the war effort eventually led him to join the attack to force a quick end to the impasse. As his majorities crumbled, Addington's nerve finally failed and he resigned on 29 April 1804, leaving the King no alternative but to ask Pitt to form a Ministry.

·   ·   ·

THE FLAWED VICTORY OF 1804

Two vital differences marked Pitt's return to power in May 1804 from the situation in which he first acquired it 20 years earlier. One was his relationship with the King; the other was the recurrently debilitating state of his own health.

The King had no wish to drop his Prime Minister, who had loyally responded to his call for help in 1801. Though he eventually accepted the change with an appearance of grace, his hand had nevertheless been forced. Gracious words to Pitt could not hide his reluctance to make the personal sacrifices necessary to provide the new Ministry with strength. As a last resort, he would accept Grenville and other leaders of the United Opposition, but on no account would he admit Fox to the Cabinet. Pitt tried to ease the situation by writing to the King to explain his reasons for finally attacking the Ministry, by reassuring him on the Catholic Question, and by determining not to force him to accept the hated Fox into a Cabinet of All the Talents. But he had too much ground to make up from his total detachment from the Monarch since his resignation. He had declined George's wish that he might continue to see him on the grounds that this might be misconstrued. His Chathamite prejudices against secret influence determined him to avoid such accusations being made against him, but he carried this scrupulousness to excess, and never saw the King at all from when he left office until he resumed it.[48] In consequence the 'real affection' George III had expressed for Pitt in his first Ministry was little expressed in his last. The King's unwillingness to make sacrifices to his new Premier's needs was most clearly shown, not in his instinctive refusal of Fox, but in the new Royal Household appointments that he carried through independently of Pitt's patronage needs, and which included both the dismissal of Pittites such as Lord Amherst (for voting at the last against Addington) and the appointment of Lord St Helens, whom Pitt regarded as an unfriendly influence.[49]

Moreover, even supposing he could regain the King's full confidence, the fact that George III was twenty years older than in 1784 and suffered yet another mental relapse in March, made the royal backing a much less influential factor for a Prime Minister than formerly. Pitt's old ally, Melville, admitted in April 1804 that it was almost impossible for any government to be strong and permanent that rested solely on the health and life of the King. The Duke of Richmond too pointed out that, with the King aged 66 and in bad health in body and mind, whereas the Prince of Wales was 42, many would be inclined 'in such a precarious state of things to pay early court to the rising sun'.[50] Pitt made unavailing efforts to overcome this handicap by offers of office to the Prince's supporters and, in the autumn, by an abortive attempt to achieve a reconciliation between the Monarch and his son.

In consequence Pitt's freedom of action in Parliament was very limited. While his future could only be assured by gathering a powerful support that could make him independent of the declining Monarch, his immediate dependence on the King made it impossible to do anything that might upset the Monarch's precarious health. He hoped that Fox would agree to a proposal, which had royal approval, to earn later entry by undertaking the St Petersburg embassy to woo Russia into the war. However, Fox's friends refused to enter office without him, whereupon Grenville and his group considered themselves honour bound to their United Opposition allies to stay out also.

The result was that Pitt was unable to assemble the powerful administration that might rally the country and impress Europe. The faithful George Rose identified three particular difficulties: a want of weighty Cabinet Ministers, a lack of able spokesmen in the Commons and a shortage of firm supporters in Addington's Parliament. The situation was not dissimilar to that Pitt had faced when he first came to power at the end of 1783. Indeed the words of the new Foreign Secretary, Lord Harrowby (Pitt's former faithful Commons subordinate, Dudley Ryder), echo those of Carmarthen and Sydney in 1783. He confided to Malmesbury that 'he was in a situation he by no means coveted, but his friendship for Pitt made him not hesitate in accepting it. Neither his health nor his habits were calculated for it, and he had for three years been totally inattentive to public business.' The new Cabinet included only five members of Pitt's former Cabinet, of whom the only heavyweights, Melville (First Lord of the Admiralty) and Portland (Lord President), were now spent forces. The new Secretary for War, Camden, declared Melville in October to be 'by no means unshaken' by the pressure and anxiety of business, and he was shortly to prove a political liability, while Portland was in failing health. Camden admitted himself not up to 'taking a very matured and decided line on general measures'. In the absence of heavyweights from the Opposition, Pitt was obliged to include old friends, Mulgrave and Montrose, and to add Hawkesbury and Westmorland to those already marked to be kept on from Addington's ministry (Eldon, Portland, Chatham and Castlereagh).[51]

Of the Cabinet only Castlereagh, an indifferent speaker, sat with Pitt in the Commons. The Premier's ablest vocal support, Canning, was a disappointed advocate of a junction with Grenville. He reluctantly accepted office as Treasurer of the Navy to back his mentor, but he found it hard to resist baiting the ex-Addingtonians in the Ministry and Pitt nearly had to offer his head in June to placate and retain the upset Home Secretary, Hawkesbury. Canning's friends, Granville Leveson-Gower and Lord Morpeth, declined to join the Ministry, and Pitt's second tenure of the Premiership was marked by a failure to attract able younger members to his side: significant perhaps of attitudes to Pitt's uncertain long-term prospects, as well as of his recent long absences from the Commons which had limited his opportunities to talent-spot.

The parliamentary session which continued to the end of July 1804 was thus one fraught with anxiety. Pitt's Additional Force Bill to recruit an offensive army was assailed both by the United Fox–Grenville Opposition and by the Addingtonians, and at one point the government majority fell to 28 (less than Addington's when he resigned) before rallying to 42 to get the measure through the Commons.

In 1784 Pitt had risen triumphantly above such difficulties virtually single-handedly, through his own energetic efforts, backed by the resolute support of the King. He tried to do the same on this occasion without the King's active assistance and under the handicap of the physical affliction that was shortly to kill him. His appointment of the inexperienced and diffident Harrowby and Camden to the Secretaryships of State controlling the war effort showed his intention to keep its management in his own hands.[52]

It was a much lonelier position than earlier, deprived of the jovial relief of the company of many of his old friends. Grenville was now in opposition. His old court jester, Pepper Arden, now Lord Alvanley, died in March 1804. Relations with Dundas, cooler since his peerage from Addington, had deteriorated to the point that Wilberforce declared them as 'scarcely on speaking terms'. Wilberforce described a dinner with Pitt and some of his remaining friends in July as 'a dull day. Pitt not in spirits'. The painter Lawrence was present at a dinner attended by Pitt and other members of the Ministry in November 1804, and 'noted how high above the rest Mr Pitt appeared to be in the consideration of the whole party. It did not prevent social conversation, but all seemed to be impressed with an awe of him. At times it appeared like Boys with their Master.'[53] If over the course of time the Prime Minister came to rely on Hawkesbury and Castlereagh (Secretary for War from July 1805) as the efficient Secretaries of State, like Grenville and Dundas in his former Ministry, the relationship was different. William Napier has left a graphic eyewitness description of a meeting between them, with the two 'bending like spaniels' and Pitt, head thrown back, eyes fixed immovably 'as if reading the heavens, and totally regardless of the bending figures near him', listening and interjecting short observations, and dismissing them 'with an abrupt stiff inclination of the body, but without casting his eyes down'.[54]

Pitt accepted this position of isolated pre-eminence almost out of defiance. Lord Chancellor Eldon recalled his indignant reaction to Grenville's refusal to join him without Fox, that 'he would teach that proud man that, in the service and with the confidence of the King, he could do without him, though he thought his health such that it might cost him his life'.[55] The strain the effort imposed upon him was later typically described by his impressionistic niece:[56]

in town, during the sitting of parliament, what a life was his! Roused from his sleep (for he was a good sleeper) with a despatch from Lord Melville; – then down to Windsor; then, if he had half an hour to spare, trying to swallow something:– Mr Adams with a paper, Mr Long with another; then Mr Rose: then, with a little bottle of cordial confection in his pocket, off to the House until three or four in the morning; then home to a hot supper for two or three hours more, to talk over what was to be done next day:– and wine, and wine! – Scarcely up next morning, when rat tat-tat – twenty or thirty people one after another, and the horses walking before the door from two till sunset, waiting for him. It was enough to kill a man – it was murder!

For relief Pitt turned to the rejuvenating company and horseplay of the younger members of his entourage, Hester Stanhope, her teenage brothers and their friend William Napier. He also turned to the bottle. Napier described how he would 'come home to dinner rather exhausted and seemed to require wine, port, of which he generally drank a bottle, or nearly so, in a rapid succession of glasses; but when he recovered his strength from this stimulant he ceased to drink'. Hester Stanhope too reported how he drank 'a good deal too much wine at dinner' and 'considerable quantities' of wine and water at night.[57]

For a while in 1804 it seemed to work in the old way. The Additional Force Bill was forced through. A new attempt was made to tackle the Civil List debts by increasing its income and transferring more expend-iture to the Consolidated Fund.[58] Pitt's Treasury Minute of 19 August 1805, made possible by the long-awaited death of the nonagenarian chief clerk Thomas Pratt, completely restructured the organisation and supervision of Treasury business, and established continuity at the top through the first permanent, non-political 'Assistant Secretary and Law Clerk'.[59] When the attempted reconciliation between the King and the Prince of Wales failed, Pitt bounced back to outmanoeuvre his rivals in December by his own reconciliation with Addington. Although obliged to double his offer of Cabinet posts to include both Addington and the latter's friend Hobart (now Earl of Buckinghamshire), they were kept out of executive positions. Addington was persuaded to take a peerage as Lord Sidmouth to remove his alternative influence in the Commons. Other Addingtonians received lesser office, but others still were fended off by promises of posts when vacancies occurred. Boosted by the addition of Addington's 40 MPs, government support swelled when Parliament reassembled in January 1805, with majorities against Opposition motions of 207 on 11 February, 146 on the 21st and 140 on 6 March.

Pitt likewise brought his perpetual offensive spirit to the war effort. An approach to Russia on 26 June 1804 was followed on 24 July by overtures to Austria, Prussia and Sweden. In September, he resolved on a pre-emptive strike against Spain by ordering the seizure of the incoming Spanish bullion ships from Mexico, so as to disrupt the reported Spanish naval rearmament and payment of subsidies to France. Their interception in October resulted, on 12 December, in a Spanish declaration of war. But there was now the prospect of new allies, as well as new enemies, as his wooing of St Petersburg, building on the previous efforts of the Addington Ministry, at last bore fruit, aided by Napoleon's flagrant disregard for international law in kidnapping and executing the Bourbon Duc d'Enghein. In November 1804 a Russian envoy arrived in London to explore the possibilities of concert.

The negotiations were conducted by Harrowby, until incapacitated by a fall, and then by his successor Mulgrave, but there is evidence enough of Pitt's controlling influence behind the scenes.[60] What Pitt now added to British policy was a willingness to offer financial assistance on a grand scale for efforts on a grand scale. He would provide £5 million in subsidies for a new Continental campaign. Hitherto subsidy payments had only exceeded £1 million a year in 1794 (£2.5 million) and in 1799 (£1.5 million) and 1800 (£2.5 million). But the yields on the new incomes tax (improved by Addington) and the continued growth of British trade enabled him to override former constraints, and his concept of a people's war in which very large-scale forces would be needed to defeat France, led him to abandon the former more conditional and selective subsidy policy. If Russia could by these means secure the assistance of Austria and Prussia, he envisaged assembling 500,000 men against France. His willingness to think big was carried into his vision of a future resettlement and long-term security pact for Europe. His famous state paper for the Russians, of 19 January 1805, used ideas developed with Grenville in 1798 and new suggestions by Lord Mulgrave, but the concepts can be traced back to his collective security ideas of the late 1780s, and the drafts for the final paper were his own.[61]

. . .

'TOO LATE FOR ANYTHING':
THE TRAGEDY OF 1805

If 1804 brought hope, 1805 brought failure as Pitt's combinations unravelled. The year began with a furious row with the King, who refused to accept his nomination of his old tutor Pretyman for Archbishop of Canterbury. George III regarded Pretyman as both ecclesiastically and socially lightweight, and, without consulting Pitt, hastened to appoint the Bishop of Norwich. Pitt took this as a personal slight, indicating to the world the limits of royal confidence in his Ministry. For the first time his icy decorum in the royal closet deserted him and those outside heard voices raised in anger.[62] Pitt stormed in vain, however, as the King resolutely stuck to his decision.

Meanwhile the surprise union with Addington, and the price paid, shook the confidence of his supporters in his judgement and tactics. Pitt lost the Marquis of Stafford, son of his former Cabinet colleague, who, with his wife the Countess of Sutherland, influenced the return of at least six MPs. Despite Canning's and Hawkesbury's entreaties, Pitt failed to conciliate Stafford, did not inform him of the reconciliation with Addington and ignored his request for the Garter. His lack of explanation even alienated supporters whose friendship dated back to their Cambridge days: George Villiers, and William (now Lord) Lowther who had inherited the nine Lowther constituencies.[63] Moreover the advantages gained from the junction with Addington were soon blasted by a legacy of the latter's Ministry, when its Committee of Naval Inquiry published its tenth report in March 1805, accusing Melville, when Treasurer of the Navy in Pitt's first Ministry, of allowing the Paymaster, Alexander Trotter, to speculate with public funds. Melville himself had borrowed money from Trotter, and he also appropriated naval moneys for other purposes which he refused to divulge for reasons of state. Pitt was alert to the danger. 'He evidently thinks that it may shake the government,' noted Wilberforce, who was with him when his copy of the report arrived, and never forgot 'the way in which he seized it, and how eagerly he looked into the leaves without waiting even to cut them open'. He stood by Melville, being 'quite sure that there was no real pocketing of public money in him'.[64] Melville's honour and that of Pitt's first Ministry were at stake. But the honour of the Addingtonians who had set up the Committee of Naval Inquiry was also at stake on the other side, so that the new government coalition was split apart.

The Melville affair split the Opposition too, as Grenville was embarrassed by the motion of censure quickly brought forward by Whitbread and the Foxites on 8 April. But Pitt spoke miserably. Harrowby subsequently reported him very ill in the week of the debate, and Camden described him as victim of a bad bilious attack.[65] Wilberforce took the high moral ground and spoke against him, reportedly swaying 40 votes, so that the result was tied at 216 each, and Pitt again in his career lost on the Speaker's casting vote. Pitt's only hope for damage limitation was to try to gain time for passions to cool. Melville had to resign from the Admiralty on the 9th, and from the Privy Council a month later, but Pitt fended off demands for prosecution by reference to a Commons committee of inquiry, chosen by ballot, and eventually manoeuvred the charge to be adjudicated by impeachment in the Lords (which acquitted Melville in 1807) rather than by criminal prosecution before a common jury. Pitt too had to fend off an attack on his own high-handed handling of naval funds, in the eleventh report of the Committee of Inquiry, again using a balloted Commons committee, which accepted his explanations.

The union with Addington was finally wrecked when Pitt appointed Melville's chief naval adviser, the octogenarian Sir Charles Middleton, as his successor at the Admiralty, with a peerage as Lord Barham. Sidmouth and his friends claimed to have been promised the next appointment and threatened resignation. For a while Pitt held him by assurances that Middleton's appointment was only temporary, but the continuing attack on Melville by Sidmouth's supporters ultimately determined Pitt to exclude them from office, so that Sidmouth and his followers finally broke with the government on 4 July. Again Pitt showed his adeptness at damage limitation, holding on to them until only eight days before the end of the parliamentary session when the breach might have least immediate impact – much to Fox's chagrin![66]

The end of the session gave Pitt six months to strengthen his Ministry before the recall of Parliament in January. Camden, who replaced Sidmouth as Lord President of the Council, believed that 'without assistance in the Cabinet as well as in the House of Commons, he cannot go on with success'. Pitt had already begun to put out feelers to Grenville, and in mid-September he went down to Weymouth to make a further attempt to persuade the King to allow him to negotiate a coalition with the Opposition. This time, however, he encountered adamant opposition from the ailing but obstinate Monarch, not only to Fox but also to Grenville, which put negotiation out of the question. With his own health failing, Pitt desperately needed front-bench assistance in the Commons, but now had to fall back upon bringing two of his present supporters, Canning and Yorke, into the Cabinet.[67]

As the pressures on his famous skills as a political survivalist increased, the only chance of a rapid escape from his troubles was through dramatic success in the war. The high hopes of January had stalled on Russian reluctance to see British sea power enhanced still further. Pitt strenuously resisted their attempts to secure a British evacuation of Malta, captured in 1800 but not restored at the peace, but with the summer campaigning season approaching, he was on the point of surrendering that strategic base when French ambition came to his rescue. Napoleon's creation of a Kingdom of Italy with himself as King in March, followed by French annexation of Genoa in June, at last convinced both Russia and Austria that France must be resisted. Russia abandoned its demands on Malta and an Anglo-Russian agreement was finally ratified on 28 July, with Austria acceding to it on 8 August. In September war was renewed in earnest on the Continent.

Pitt's political future, as well as Europe's, now depended on a Continental campaign which, for all his efforts, he was virtually powerless to influence. All arrangements with Austria were made by Russia, leaving the British envoy in Vienna unused and uninformed. The British contribution to the combined war effort was in money, with £2.5 million destined to Vienna (it wanted £6 million!), £1 million each to Russia and to Prussia, if the latter could be persuaded to come forward, and half a million pounds to hire troops from lesser states. Britain also contributed the example of the crushing naval victory over the Franco-Spanish combined fleet at Trafalgar on 21 October. But what Pitt lacked was a large British strike force to act with effect in the land campaign. His success in recruiting an immense volunteer citizen army for home defence had inhibited recruitment for the regular army available for offensive operations. Pitt's attempted solution, his 1805 Additional Force Act, proved even less successful than Addington's 1803 Army of Reserve Act which he had so strongly criticised. Each sought to create a reserve pool from which general service regulars might be recruited. Addington, using the ballot, raised 45,492 (37,136 effectives) of whom 19,533 volunteered for general service. Pitt resorted to parish quotas, backed by the threat of parish fines, but produced less than half his target – only 13,000 men. In February 1805 the disappointed Pitt turned back to seeking to recruit regulars from the militia.[68]

The regular army was thus undermanned. In May 1806, Pitt's War Secretary, Castlereagh, declared its home establishment 47,500 short and colonial garrisons 10,000 deficient. Small strike forces could only be mobilised from it slowly and then landed where the enemy were at their weakest, but this was inevitably too distant to influence the main theatre of operations. In April 1805, 4,000 were sent to the Mediterranean to form part of a force of 5,000 landed along with 11,000 Russians in Naples in November. In June 6,500 sailed to seize the Cape of Good Hope, and in October 11,000 Anglo-German troops were sent to North Germany, followed by 12,000 more in December. Nevertheless the autumn of 1805 was the final Indian summer of Pitt's hopes and dreams.[69]

With optimistic reports that Prussia too was stirring, Pitt despatched Harrowby to Berlin in October with an offer of £2.5 million to field 200,000 men. Plans were laid to build up 65,000 British and mercenary troops in North Germany in the course of 1806 to co-operate with Russian, Swedish and hopefully Prussian forces. Malmesbury's son remembered a walk with Pitt in the park in November: 'He was naturally of a sanguine disposition. His plans were vast and comprehensive, and held out to his powerful mind the hope of establishing a European Confederacy, that should crush French ascendancy.'[70]

The bottom crashed out of his dream-world on Sunday 3 November, when a Dutch newspaper was received with details of the capitulation of the Austrian advanced corps at Ulm. With the public offices empty, Pitt and Mulgrave anxiously sought out Malmesbury to translate it for them. 'I observed but too clearly the effect it had on Pitt,' he noted, 'though he did his utmost to conceal it.' On the night of the 7th came the news of Trafalgar, joy at which was cloyed by the death of Nelson, which left Pitt for once unable to sleep – he got up even though it was three in the morning. Despite Trafalgar, the situation was now drifting away from him.[71] His desperate bid to encourage Prussian intervention led him into financial pledges way beyond his original intentions – totalling £7–8 million – but even this failed to move Berlin. Russia found a way to move the Prussians, but it involved the cession of Hanover to Berlin, which Pitt at once declared totally impossible and sought to hide from the King. Lastly, on 3 January 1806 news was received of the crushing French defeat of the Austro-Russian army at Austerlitz on 4 December.

An air of tragic inevitability surrounds the final year of Pitt's last ministry. An ailing Premier, he was struggling with little support against unexpected eventualities which were really beyond his effective control. The two strong men who had backed him through his first ministry, Dundas and Grenville, each in their own way fatally undermined his position in 1805. The future strong men, Premiers such as Perceval, Hawkesbury (Liverpool) and Canning, and essential ministers such as Castlereagh, were still serving their apprenticeship in his final Ministry. The way the Ministry rapidly collapsed after Pitt's death showed how far it had depended on him. He still showed flashes of his tactical mastery, but he was now so recurrently unwell that he no longer had the sustained energy, or decisiveness, to secure his position as he had 21 years before. He had always been prone to spasms of procrastination when he was reluctant to make up his mind on issues, and Wilberforce complained in June 1805 that procrastination in Pitt 'has increased to such a degree as to have become absolutely predominant'.[72] It was only when Castlereagh became a Secretary of State that Pitt's long-promised Order in Council to stop the slave trade to captured colonies was at last issued in September 1805.

Another friend, Pretyman, consoling George Rose on their respective disappointments, declared in February 1805 that:

I am persuaded that his lying so late in bed in a morning prevents his seeing and talking with many persons to whom he might otherwise be able to show attention. He is too late for anything. Business presses which *must* be done. Whatever can be put off is put off, and by this procrastination, many things, which, though they belong to no particular day, ought to be done soon, are never done at all. I lament this disposition more than I can express . . . Perhaps he may not feel all the energy which he did twenty years ago; and even conversation upon matters of business and explanation of conduct may grow in some degree fatiguing to him. I really believe it does, and that he finds solitude and entire rest sometimes necessary to him.[73]

His physician, Sir Walter Farquhar, recorded that from 1803 until the autumn of 1805 'every public event of importance which crowded on Mr Pitt's mind produced a corresponding effect upon the body'. Farquhar urged him to retire, but he refused, asserting that 'his country needed his services, and he would rather prefer to die at his post than desert it'. Yet his illness left his government vulnerable. Rose warned the King, in September 1805, that he 'was perfectly convinced, if Mr Pitt should be confined by the gout, or any other complaint, for only two or three weeks, there would be an end of us'. In October and November he suffered pains in his stomach and head, loss of appetite and additional 'flying pains' in his feet and limbs. In December he went to take the waters at Bath in a bid to restore his health preparatory to meeting Parliament in January. Early signs of improvement were followed by a relapse, made worse by news of Austerlitz, and he decided to return to London.[74]

He had been unable to strengthen his Ministry to compensate for Sidmouth's defection, and would soon have to tell Parliament of millions spent without effect, a war lost and expeditions recalled. As he took his farewell of Melville in Bath, he declared bitterly, 'I wish the King may not live to repent, and sooner than he thinks, the rejection of the advice which I pressed on him at Weymouth.' Emaciated and exhausted, he got as far as the house he had rented since 1803 for a retreat just out of town on Putney Heath. George Rose saw him there on 15 January, 'lying on a sofa, emaciated to a degree I could not have conceived . . . His countenance was changed extremely, his voice weak, and his body almost wasted, and so indeed were his limbs.' His health had now gone completely, and on 23 January he died. Reportedly his last words, credible for the Patriot statesman he had always aspired to be, were: 'Oh, my country! how I leave my country.'[75]

His physician told Malmesbury 'that Pitt died of *old age* at forty-six, as much as if he had been ninety'. Whether it was the strains of government, of which he refused to divest himself, that directly killed him, or whether it only hastened his succumbing to what Farquhar regarded as gout, and modern medical opinion has posited might have been cancer of the bowel or a gastrointestinal lesion, is not known.[76] It is an irony that he died 25 years to the day after he first took his seat in the Commons. He had headed the government for 18 years and 11 months of those 25 years.

. . .

NOTES AND REFERENCES

1 *Parl. Hist.*, vol. 22, col. 1190: speech of 13 March 1782.
2 Lord Rosebery (ed.), *Letters relating to the love episode of William Pitt together with an account of his health by his physician Sir Walter Farquhar* (1900), pp. ix, 1–5, 12–15; Meryon, *Hester Stanhope*, vol. 1, p. 180.
3 Stanhope, *Pitt*, vol. 1, pp. 312–13; *L.C.GIII*, vol. 1, p. 187; R.I. and S. Wilberforce (ed.), *Correspondence*, p. 8; R.I. and S. Wilberforce, *Life*, vol. 1, pp. 217, 366, 369–70, vol. 2, pp. 86, 234, 236; Jupp (ed.), *Canning Journal*, p. 77.
4 HMC, *Fortescue*, vol. 6, p. 242; P. Mackesy, *War without Victory*, chs. 3–6.
5 Add. MSS, 40,102, State of the Cabinet, 22 Sept., State of the Cabinet as to disposable force, 1 Oct. 1800; Leeds Central Library, Canning Papers, Bundle 76, Hammond to Canning, 29 July 1800; SRO GD 51/1/726/1, 2, Nepean–Dundas correspondence, 7, 9 Sept. 1800.
6 Rosebery (ed.), *Love episode of William Pitt*, pp. 32, 39.
7 Hogge (ed.), *Auckland Corresp.*, vol. 3, pp. 377–8; Leeds Central Library, Canning Papers, Bundle 30, 'Holwood Saturday'.
8 R.I. and S. Wilberforce, *Life*, vol. 2, p. 284; Ipswich and E. Suffolk RO, Pretyman Mss T108/42, Pitt to Pretyman, 19 June 1798; Add. MSS, 70,927, f. 25v.
9 Rosebery (ed.), *Love episode of William Pitt*, p. 32; Mackesy, *War without Victory*, pp. 168, 174–5.
10 Leeds Central Library, Canning Papers, Bundle 63, Grenville to Canning, 'Monday morning ½ p. 9' [Jan. 1800]; Pellew, *Sidmouth*, vol. 1, p. 152; Cave (ed.), *Diary of Farington*, vol. 9, p. 3458.
11 Ehrman, *Pitt*, vol. 3, pp. 266–7, 284–5; HMC, *Fortescue*, vol. 6, p. 373.
12 Add. MSS, 70,927, f. 34, Grenville to Mornington, 27 Sept. 1799; HMC, *Fortescue*, vol. 6, p. 52; Stanhope, *Pitt*, vol. 3, p. 208; Suffolk RO, Pretyman Mss T108/44, Rose to Pretyman, 25 June, 30 July 1800.
13 Bickley (ed.), *Glenbervie Diaries*, vol. 1, pp. 159–60.
14 Pellew, *Sidmouth*, vol. 1, p. 263; Stanhope, *Pitt*, vol. 3, pp. 247–50; Wells, *Wretched Faces*, pp. 181–4.
15 PRO, PRO30/8/101, f. 144, Pitt to Chatham, 29 May 1799; *Wellesley Papers*, vol. 1, p. 129, Bathurst to Wellesley, 28 May 1800.

16 Mackesy, *War without Victory*, pp. 112, 120, 125–33, 138–40, 167–8; *L.C.GIII*, vol. 3, pp. 376, 382–7, 424; Malmesbury (ed.), *Diaries*, vol. 4, p. 22.

17 Stanhope, *Pitt*, vol. 3, p. xxvi.

18 Camden's memorandum in R. Willis, 'William Pitt's resignation in 1801: re-examination and document', *BIHR*, vol. 44 (1971), pp. 239–357, at p. 250.

19 Jupp (ed.), *Canning Journal*, p. 98; Bickley (ed.), *Glenbervie Diaries*, vol. 1, p. 36; Ehrman, *Pitt*, vol. 2, p. 66, vol. 3, p. 177.

20 Ehrman, *Pitt*, vol. 3, pp. 175–92, 496–7; Willis, 'Pitt's resignation', p. 249.

21 Stanhope, *Pitt*, vol. 3, pp. xxv–xxvi; *C.C.GIII*, vol. 3, pp. 128–31, Grenville to Buckingham, 2 Feb. 1801; HMC, *Fortescue*, vol. 6, pp. 435–6, Grenville to Carysfort, 6 Feb. 1801; Jupp, *Lord Grenville*, pp. 272, 277.

22 Stanhope, *Pitt*, vol. 2, p. xxv, vol. 3, p. xvi; *L.C.GIII*, vol. 3, p. 186, n. 2.

23 Willis, 'Pitt's resignation', p. 250.

24 E.g. *L.C.GIII*, vol. 3, p. 376.

25 HMC, *Fortescue*, vol. 6, pp. 306–7; Kent RO, Chevening Mss, Pitt Papers 733, Pitt to Chatham, 5 Feb. 1801; Willis, 'Pitt's resignation', pp. 250–2; Add. MSS, 37,924, Windham diary entries 11, 25 Jan. 1801.

26 Loughborough had already, on 13 Dec. 1800, given the King a copy of the paper he had circulated among Ministers opposing emancipation, Pellew, *Sidmouth*, vol. 1, pp. 501–2; Malmesbury (ed.), *Diaries*, vol. 4, p. 5.

27 Willis, 'Pitt's resignation', p. 252.

28 *L.C.GIII*, vol. 3, p. 383, n. 1, 476; Add. MSS, 37,924, Windham diary entries, 28, 30 Jan. 1801; Willis, 'Pitt's resignation', pp. 253–4.

29 *L.C.GIII*, vol. 3, p. 477; Pellew, *Sidmouth*, vol. 1, p. 287; Add. MSS, 37,924, Windham diary, 30 Jan. 1801.

30 HMC, *Fortescue*, vol. 6, p. 434; *L.C.GIII*, vol. 3, pp. 474–5, 477–8; Willis, 'Pitt's resignation', pp. 254–5.

31 HMC, *Fortescue*, vol. 6, p. 434; Add. MSS, 37,924, Windham diary, 1 Feb; *L.C.GIII*, vol. 3, p. 499; Harcourt (ed.), *Rose Diaries*, vol. 1, p. 304.

32 The correspondence between Pitt and the King is in Stanhope, *Pitt*, vol. 3, pp. xxiii–xxxi; Pellew, *Sidmouth*, vol. 1, pp. 287–9; Harcourt (ed.), *Rose Diaries*, vol. 1, p. 286.

33 Kent RO, Chevening Mss, Pitt Papers 733, Pitt to Chatham, 5 Feb. 1801.

34 Bickley (ed.), *Glenbervie Diaries*, vol. 1, pp. 159, 262, 295, 375.

35 Malmesbury (ed.), *Diaries*, vol. 4, p. 39; Leeds Central Library, Harewood Mss, Canning Papers, bundle 30; Stanhope, *Pitt*, vol. 3, p. xxvii.

36 Add. MSS, 70,927, Grenville to Wellesley, 20 Feb. 1801; R.J. Mackintosh (ed.), *Memoirs of the Life of Sir James Mackintosh* (1835), vol. 1, p. 170.

37 Kent RO, Chevening Mss, Pitt Papers 733, Pitt to Chatham, 5 Feb. 1801; Malmesbury (ed.), *Diaries*, vol. 4, pp. 4, 75.

38 Ross (ed.), *Cornwallis Corresp.*, vol. 3, pp. 335–6.

39 Stanhope, *Pitt*, vol. 3, p. xxxii; *L.C.GIII*, vol. 3, p. 487, n. 1.

40 Aspinall and Smith (eds.), *Eng. Hist. Docs.*, vol. 11, p. 164, Pretyman [not Rose], 25 Feb. 1801; Ehrman, *Pitt*, vol. 3, pp. 528–32; Harcourt (ed.), *Rose Diaries*, vol. 1, pp. 360, 426–8; Colchester (ed.), *Abbot Diary*, vol. 1, pp. 258–9.

41 Malmesbury (ed.), *Diaries*, vol. 4, pp. 38, 75–6, 78; Harcourt (ed.), *Rose Diaries*, vol. 1, p. 335.
42 Rosebery (ed.), 'Tomline's estimate', *Monthly Review*, August 1903, pp. 32–4; Pellew, *Sidmouth*, vol. 1, p. 499n.; Ehrman, *Pitt*, vol. 3, pp. 534–45.
43 *L.C.GIII*, vol. 3, p. xiv.
44 Harcourt (ed.), *Rose Diaries*, vol. 2, pp. 22–3, 27–8, 30–40; Pellew, *Sidmouth*, vol. 2, pp. 114–16; R.I. and S. Wilberforce, *Life*, vol. 3, p. 219.
45 Stanhope, *Pitt*, vol. 4, p. 48 (J.W. Ward).
46 Stanhope, *Miscellanies, 2nd Series* (1872), pp. 68–9, 72; R.I. and S. Wilberforce, *Life*, vol. 3. p. 110.
47 R.I. and S. Wilberforce, *Life*, vol. 3, p. 147; HMC, *Fortescue*, vol. 7, pp. 210, 222.
48 Harcourt (ed.), *Rose Diaries*, vol. 2, p. 244; Lord Mahon (ed.), *Secret Documents concerned with Mr Pitt's return to Office in 1804* (1852), p. 44.
49 *L.C.GIII*, vol. 4, p. 164, n. 1, 181, n. 1; Olson, *Radical Duke*, p. 231.
50 Mahon (ed.), *Secret Documents*, p. 19; Olson, *Radical Duke*, p. 232.
51 Harcourt (ed.), *Rose Diaries*, vol. 2, pp. 119–20; Malmesbury (ed.), *Diaries*, vol. 4, p. 311; Ehrman, *Pitt*, vol. 3, pp. 669–74, 717–18.
52 Suffolk RO, Pretyman MSS T435/44, Rose to Tomline, 12 May 1804.
53 R.I. and S. Wilberforce, *Life*, vol. 3, pp. 187, 219–20; Garlick and Macintyre (eds.), *Diary of Farington*, vol. 6, p. 2436.
54 *Windham Papers*, vol. 2, p. 264; H.A. Bruce, *Life of General Sir William Napier* (1864), vol. 1, pp. 31–2.
55 Twiss, *Eldon*, vol. 1, p. 449.
56 Meryon (ed.), *Hester Stanhope*, vol. 1, pp. 65–6.
57 Bruce, *Life of Napier*, pp. 30–3; Ehrman, *Pitt*, vol. 3, p. 549.
58 Reitan, 'Civil List 1782–1804', *Procs. Cons. Rev. Europe* (1981), p. 136.
59 H. Roseveare, *The Treasury. The evolution of a British institution* (1979), pp. 154–5.
60 There are draft notes of the final 19 January proposal in Pitt's hand in the Dacres Adams Mss (formerly PRO30/58), and a letter from Mulgrave to Vorontsov on the following day is endorsed 'written by Mr Pitt' (PRO, FO 181/5).
61 J.M. Sherwig, *Guineas and Gunpowder, British foreign aid in the wars with France 1793–1815* (Cambridge, Mass., 1969), pp. 148–55, 365–6. E. Ingram, 'Lord Mulgrave's prospects for the reconstruction of Europe', *HJ*, 19 (1976), pp. 511–20 presses the new Foreign Secretary's contribution. There is further discussion in G.B. Fremont, 'Britain's role in the formation of the Third Coalition against France', Oxford DPhil thesis, 1991, ch. 7.
62 Stanhope, *Pitt*, vol. 4, p. 252.
63 J. Sack, *The Grenvillites 1801–29* (Urbana, Ill., 1979), p. 81; Thorne (ed.), *Commons*, vol. 4, p. 455; Ehrman, *Pitt*, vol. 3, pp. 746–7.
64 R.I. and S. Wilberforce, *Life*, vol. 3, pp. 217–20.
65 HMC, *Bathurst*, pp. 45, 48.
66 *L.C.GIII*, vol. 4, p. 340n.

67 HMC, *Bathurst*, pp. 49–50.
68 Cookson, *British Armed Nation*, pp. 114–16; R. Glover, *Peninsular Preparation. The reform of the British Army 1795–1809* (Cambridge, 1963), pp. 215–16, 230–40.
69 C.D. Hall, *British Strategy in the Napoleonic War* (Manchester, 1992), pp. 8, 115–26.
70 Malmesbury (ed.), *Diaries*, vol. 4, p. 346n.
71 *Ibid.*, pp. 340–1n.
72 R.I. and S. Wilberforce, *Life*, vol. 3, p. 324.
73 Harcourt (ed.), *Rose Diaries*, vol. 2, p. 91.
74 Rosebery, *Love episode of William Pitt*, pp. 36–7; Harcourt (ed.), *Rose Diaries*, vol. 2, p. 199.
75 Stanhope, *Pitt*, vol. 4, p. 369; the disputed last words are discussed by Ehrman, *Pitt*, vol. 3, p. 829, n. 2.
76 Malmesbury (ed.), *Diaries*, vol. 4, p. 246; Ehrman, *Pitt*, vol. 3, pp. 549–51.

FURTHER READING

What follows is necessarily a short selection from among many works consulted in the preparation of this volume. Pitt's career has always caught the imagination of historians and public. A.D. Harvey's *William Pitt the Younger 1759–1806. A Bibliography* (1989) lists 40 biographical books and articles, and even this omits some character sketches, while more work has appeared since he wrote. Dominating them all is John Ehrman's magisterial survey, *The Younger Pitt*, volume one of which, *The Years of Acclaim* (1759–89) was published in 1969, volume two, *The Reluctant Transition* (1790–6), in 1983, and volume three, *The Consuming Struggle* (1797–1806) in 1996. There is also still much of use in the other multivolume biographies: John Holland Rose's *William Pitt and the National Revival* (1912) and *William Pitt and the Great War* (1911) for matters of foreign policy, war and empire, and Lord Stanhope's four-volume *Life of the Right Honourable William Pitt* (1861–2) for a treasure-trove of original correspondence and contemporary anecdotes. Among single-volume studies that of Robin Reilly, *Pitt the Younger 1759–1806* (1978), stands out as the most complete. Shorter still, Eric J. Evans, *William Pitt the Younger* (1999), summarises well, while R.G. Thorne, 'Hon. William Pitt', in R.G. Thorne (ed.), *The House of Commons 1790–1820* (1986) and J. Mori, 'William Pitt the Younger', in R. Eccleshall and G. Walker (eds.), *Biographical Dictionary of British Prime Ministers* (1998) provide stimulating brief sketches, even if the present author would beg to differ from some of their interpretations.

The eighteenth-century political background from which Pitt emerged to power is well covered in Paul Langford, *A Polite and Commercial People. England 1727–1783* (Oxford, 1989), the articles in J. Black (ed.), *British Politics and Society from Walpole to Pitt 1742–1789* (1990), and J. Brewer, *Party Ideology and Popular Politics at the Accession of George III* (Cambridge, 1976). Other works put Pitt in a wider perspective carrying into the nineteenth century: I.R. Christie, *Wars and Revolutions. Britain 1760–1815* (1982); J. Derry, *Politics in the Age of Fox, Pitt and Liverpool* (1990); and F. O'Gorman, *The Long Eighteenth Century. British Political and Social History 1688–1832* (1997).

Marie Peters, *The Elder Pitt* (1998), provides an excellent survey of the career and attitudes which so much influenced his doting son's career. John Norris, *Shelburne and Reform* (1963), remains the best study of another early influence on Pitt. Jennifer Mori boldly attempts to dissect 'The political theory of William Pitt the Younger' in *History* (1998) and J.J. Sack, *From Jacobite to Conservative: Reaction and Orthodoxy in Britain c.1762–1832* (Cambridge, 1993) is good on the reality and the subsequent representation of Pitt's political beliefs, which he also expresses succinctly in Sack, 'The memory of Burke and Pitt: English conservatism confronts its past 1806–1829', *Historical Journal*, vol. 30 (1987). A pragmatic view is taken by F. O'Gorman, 'Pitt and the "Tory" Reaction to the French Revolution', in H.T. Dickinson (ed.), *Britain and the French Revolution 1789–1815* (1989). Much can still be gained from reading W.S. Hathaway's collection of *The Speeches of the Right Honourable William Pitt in the House of Commons* (4 vols, 1806), always with the caution that these are a selection of summarised reports of particular speeches delivered to a particular audience on particular occasions.

All biographies of George III disappoint after 1784. The best discussion is in the introductions and notes to A. Aspinall, *The Later Correspondence of George III* (Cambridge, 1962–70), while R. Pares, *George III and the Politicians* (1953), still remains the most stimulating study of that relationship. The revived prestige of the Crown is covered in L. Colley, 'The apotheosis of George III: loyalty, royalty and the British nation 1760–1820', *Past & Present* (1984) and M. Morris, *The British Monarchy and the French Revolution* (New Haven, Conn., 1998), though each largely neglects the part played by Pitt in this process.

There are solid recent biographies of Pitt's two closest colleagues in Peter Jupp, *Lord Grenville 1759–1854* (Oxford, 1985) and M. Fry, *The Dundas Despotism* (Edinburgh, 1992). M. Duffy has explored relationships within the Triumvirate in the 1790s more fully in 'Pitt, Grenville and the control of British foreign policy in the 1790s', in J. Black (ed.), *Knights Errant and True Englishmen* (Edinburgh, 1989). Pitt's third assistant of the 1780s, Charles Jenkinson, still waits for a biographer to penetrate the screen of his inscrutability. Pitt's internal rival, Thurlow, has an indifferent biography in R. Gore-Brown, *Chancellor Thurlow* (1953), and an excellent analytical sketch by G.M. Ditchfield, 'Lord Thurlow', in R.W. Davis (ed.), *Lords of Parliament* (Stanford, 1995). Two colleagues from whom Pitt hoped much, but who eventually disappointed him, are covered by A.G. Olson, *The Radical Duke* [Richmond] (Oxford, 1961) and P. Ziegler, *Addington* (1965). The relationship between Pitt and his closest acolytes is well shown in Dorothy Marshall, *The Rise of George Canning* (1938) and in Canning's own words by Peter Jupp (ed.), *The Letter-Journal of George Canning 1793–1795* (1991).

The role of the Cabinet in government, and the impact of Pitt upon it, are shown in A. Aspinall, 'The cabinet council 1783–1835', *Proceedings of the British Academy*, vol. 38 (1952); I.R. Christie, 'The Cabinet in the reign of George III, to 1790' in Christie, *Myth and Reality in Late Eighteenth Century British Politics* (1970); and Richard E. Willis, 'Cabinet Politics and Executive Policy-Making

Procedures, 1794–1801', *Albion*, vol. 7 (1975). That Pitt's methods of government management influenced his most successful disciple can be seen by comparison with the methods shown in Boyd Hilton, 'Lord Liverpool: the art of politics and the practice of government', *Transactions of the Royal Historical Society*, 5th series, vol. 38 (1988). Also useful is J. Derry, 'Governing temperament under Pitt and Liverpool', in J. Cannon (ed.), *The Whig Ascendancy* (1981). The operation of the offices of the Secretaries of State under Pitt is examined in R.R. Nelson, *The Home Office, 1782–1801* (Durham N.C., 1969) and C.R. Middleton, *The Administration of British Foreign Policy 1782–1846* (Durham N.C., 1977). The operation of patronage in government is revealed in D.J. Brown, 'The Government of Scotland under Henry Dundas and William Pitt', *History*, vol. 83 (1998).

The circumstances in which Pitt came to power and his difficult early learning period in government are covered in John Cannon, *The Fox–North Coalition: Crisis of the Constitution, 1782–1784* (Cambridge, 1969), and in Paul Kelly's articles stemming from his 1971 Oxford PhD thesis: 'British Politics, 1783–1784: the emergence and triumph of the Younger Pitt's administration', *Bulletin of the Institute of Historical Research*, vol. 54 (1981); 'The Pitt–Temple Administration, 19–22 December 1783', and 'British Party Politics, 1784–1786', both in *Historical Journal*, vol. 17 (1974); 'Radicalism and Public Opinion in the General Election of 1784', *Bulletin of the Institute of Historical Research*, vol. 45 (1972); 'Pitt versus Fox: the Westminster Scrutiny, 1784–5', *Studies in Burke and His Time*, vol. 14 (1972–3); and 'British and Irish Politics', *English Historical Review*, vol. 90 (1975) – on which see also David R. Schweitzer, 'The failure of William Pitt's Irish Trade Propositions 1785', *Parliamentary History*, vol. 3 (1984).

Pitt's attitude to economic reform is lucidly explored in P. Harling, *The Waning of 'Old Corruption'. The politics of Economical Reform in Britain, 1774–1846* (Oxford, 1996). Significant articles on the subject include J.R. Breihan, 'The Abolition of Sinecures, 1780–1834', *Proceedings of the Consortium on Revolutionary Europe*, vol. 11 (1981) and 'William Pitt and the Commission on Fees, 1785–1801', *Historical Journal*, vol. 27 (1984); E.A. Reitan, 'The Civil List and the changing role of the Monarchy in Britain 1782–1804', *Proceedings of the Consortium on Revolutionary Europe*, vol. 11 (1981). For his handling of finance see J.E.D. Binney, *British Finance and Administration 1774–94* (Oxford, 1958), and for the impact of war on financial policy see P.K. O'Brien, 'Public Finance in the Wars with France', in H.T. Dickinson (ed.), *Britain and the French Revolution 1789–1815* (1989) – summarising work begun with his authoritative 1967 Oxford DPhil thesis, 'Government Revenue, 1793–1815 – a study in fiscal and financial policy in the Wars against France'; R. Cooper, 'William Pitt, taxation, and the needs of war', *Journal of British Studies*, vol. 22 (1982) – based on his 1976 University of North Carolina PhD thesis, 'British Government Finance, 1793–1807. The development of a policy based on war taxes'; and A. Hope-Jones, *Income Tax in the Napoleonic Wars* (Cambridge, 1939).

For the Commons which Pitt worked with and upon see P.D.G. Thomas, *The House of Commons in the Eighteenth Century* (Oxford, 1971) and the Introductions to L. Namier and J. Brooke (eds.), *The History of Parliament. The House of Commons 1754–1790* (1964) and R. Thorne (ed.), *The History of Parliament. The House of Commons 1754–1790* (1986). Curiously the operation of the Lords has been more closely studied, above all in M.W. McCahill's excellent *Order and Equipoise. The Peerage and the House of Lords 1783–1806* (1978), but see also A.S. Turberville, *The House of Lords in the age of Reform 1784–1837* (1958), and the essays in C. Jones and D.L. Jones (eds.), *Peers, Politics and Power: the House of Lords 1603–1911* (1986).

The attractions and shortcomings of Pitt's major public opponent are well exposed by L.G. Mitchell, *Charles James Fox* (Oxford, 1992). The fate of his Party is discussed in L.G. Mitchell, *Charles James Fox and the Disintegration of the Whig Party, 1782–1794* (Oxford, 1971); J.W. Derry, *The Regency Crisis and the Whigs, 1788–1789* (Cambridge, 1963); and F. O'Gorman, *The Whig Party and the French Revolution* (1967). The split in the Opposition is also examined in D. Wilkinson, 'The Pitt–Portland coalition of 1794 and the origins of the "Tory" party', *History*, vol. 83 (1998). The suspicions of Pitt retained by one prominent member are shown in E.A. Smith, *Whig Principles and Party Politics: Earl Fitzwilliam and the Whig Party, 1748–1833* (Manchester, 1975), while the co-operative response of the former Opposition leader is developed in David Wilkinson, 'The Political Career of William Henry Cavendish-Bentinck, Third Duke of Portland, 1738–1809', University of Wales, Aberystwyth, PhD thesis, 1997.

The nature of the public to which Pitt principally addressed himself is admirably presented by Paul Langford, *Public Life and Propertied Englishmen 1689–1798* (Oxford, 1991). Pitt's place in the parliamentary reform movement is set in context in J. Cannon, *Parliamentary Reform in England, 1640–1832* (Cambridge, 1973), and I.R. Christie, *Wilkes, Wyvill and Reform* (1962). Much remains to be written on the connections between the politics of the City of London and national politics in the Pitt era, but the attitudes of the big City institutions can be seen in C.H. Philips, *The East India Company 1784–1834* (2nd edn., 1961) and Sir J. Clapham, *The Bank of England. A History* (Cambridge, 1970). While Pitt was not a man of strong religious beliefs himself, he was all too aware of the significance of religion in public opinion. The religious theme in politics is pressed most strongly by J.C.D. Clark, *English Society 1688–1832: Ideology, Social Structure and Political Practice during the Ancien Regime* (Cambridge, 2nd edn, 2000). More balanced views are provided in G.M. Ditchfield, 'The Parliamentary Struggle over the Repeal of the Test and Corporation Acts', *English Historical Review*, vol. 89 (1974), and R. Hole, *Pulpits, Politics and Public Order in England 1760–1832* (Cambridge, 1989). Pitt's attitude to the problems of poverty in the 1790s is discussed in J.R. Poynter, *Society and Pauperism* (1969).

The debate on the imminence of revolution in Britain in the 1790s is set out, for, in Roger Wells, *Insurrection. The British experience 1795–1803* (Gloucester, 1983), and against, in I.R. Christie, *Stress and Stability in Late Eighteenth Century Britain* (1984), arguments encapsulated by each author in articles in M. Philp (ed.), *The French Revolution and British popular politics* (Cambridge, 1991).

H.T. Dickinson, *The Politics of the People in Eighteenth Century Britain* (1995) provides consideration of the popular support on each side, and another overview is provided by Clive Emsley, *British Society and the French Wars 1793–1815* (1979). Different aspects of the domestic problems facing Pitt are discussed in E.P. Thompson's formative *The Making of the English Working Class* (1963, revised edn., 1968); A. Goodwin, *The Friends of Liberty. The English Democratic Movement in the Age of the French Revolution* (1979); H.T. Dickinson, *British Radicalism and the French Revolution, 1789–1815* (Oxford, 1985); Roger Wells, *Wretched Faces: Famine in Wartime England 1793–1801* (Gloucester, 1988); J. Bohstedt, *Riots and Community Politics in England and Wales 1790–1810* (Cambridge, Mass., 1983); J. Stevenson, *Popular disturbances in England 1700–1832* (2nd edn., 1992); J. Stevenson, 'Food Riots in England, 1792–1818' in Stevenson (ed.), *Popular Protest and Public Order* (1974); J. Cookson, *The Friends of Peace. Anti-War Liberalism in England 1793–1815* (Cambridge, 1982). Imperial problems are frequently detached but had a significant bearing in charging the atmosphere of the domestic situation. See M. Elliot, *Partners in Revolution. The United Irishmen and France* (New Haven, Conn., 1982) and *Wolfe Tone. Prophet of Irish Independence* (New Haven, Conn., 1989) – Wolfe Tone's was perhaps the most extreme reaction against Pitt's notorious failure to answer letters! M. Duffy's 'War, revolution and the crisis of the British empire', in Philp (ed.), *French Revolution and British popular politics*, adds the Caribbean to the Irish dimension. Jennifer Mori, *William Pitt and the French Revolution 1785–1795* (Edinburgh, 1997) juxtaposes domestic with foreign policy in the valuable longer context which provides a more balanced view of Pitt as reformer or oppressor. The repressive legislation of the 1790s and its impact are also considered by Clive Emsley, 'An aspect of Pitt's "terror": prosecutions for sedition in the 1790s', *Social History*, vol. 6 (1981) and 'Repression, "Terror", and the Rule of Law in England during the Decade of the French Revolution', *English Historical Review*, vol. 100 (1985).

The various impulses to counterrevolution and loyalism which Pitt so skilfully drew upon and continually worked to channel (more so than some authors indicate) have been plentifully examined, most significantly recently by R.R. Dozier, *For King, Constitution and Country. The English Loyalists and the French Revolution* (Lexington, Mass., 1983); J. Caulfield, 'The Reeves Association: A Study of Loyalism in the 1790s', Reading PhD thesis, 1988; M. Duffy, 'William Pitt and the origins of the loyalist association movement of 1792', *Historical Journal*, vol. 39 (1996); J. Cookson's excellent *The British Armed Nation 1793–1997* (Oxford, 1997), and his articles 'British Society and the French Wars, 1793–1815', *Australian Journal of Politics and History*, vol. 31 (1985), and 'The English Volunteer Movement of the French Wars, 1793–1815: Some contexts', *Historical Journal*, vol. 32 (1989); A. Gee, 'The British volunteer movement, 1793–1801', Oxford DPhil thesis, 1990; L. Colley, *Britons. Forging the Nation 1707–1834* (New Haven, Conn., 1992); D. Eastwood, 'Patriotism and the English state in the 1790s', in Philp (ed.), *French Revolution and British popular politics*; and H.T. Dickinson, 'Popular Loyalism in Britain in the 1790s', in E. Hellmuth (ed.), *The Transformation of Political Culture: Germany and England in the Late Eighteenth Century* (Oxford, 1990).

There have been some valuable local study dissertations in recent years: A. Booth, 'Reform, Repression and Revolution: Radicalism and Loyalism in the North West of England, 1789–1803', Lancaster PhD thesis, 1979 (part summarised in 'Popular loyalism and public violence in the north-west of England, 1790–1800', *Social History*, vol. 8 [1983]); M. Pottle, 'Loyalty and Patriotism in Nottingham 1792–1816', Oxford DPhil thesis, 1988; N.E.J. Strange, 'Manchester Loyalism, 1792–1798', Manchester MPhil thesis, 1990; and S. Poole, 'Popular Politics in Bristol, Somerset and Wiltshire 1791–1805', Bristol PhD thesis, 1992.

The fullest recent overview of international relations is Paul W. Schroeder, *The Transformation of European Politics 1763–1848* (Oxford, 1994). The British perspective under Pitt is covered by J. Black, *British Foreign Policy in an Age of Revolutions 1783–1793* (Cambridge, 1994); M. Duffy, 'British War Policy: the Austrian Alliance 1793–1801', Oxford DPhil thesis, 1971, and 'British Diplomacy and the French Wars 1789–1815' in H.T. Dickinson (ed.), *Britain and the French Revolution 1789–1815* (1989); and J.M. Sherwig, *Guineas and Gunpowder, British foreign aid in the wars with France 1793–1815* (Cambridge, Mass., 1969). Among other useful accounts of the origin of 'the Great War with France' are J.T. Murley, 'The origin and outbreak of the Anglo-French War of 1793', Oxford DPhil thesis, 1959; L.M. Porter, 'Anglo-French relations 10 August 1792 to 1 February 1793: a study of Great Britain and France in the six months prior to the outbreak of war', York PhD thesis, 1973; and T. Blanning, *The Origins of the French Revolutionary Wars* (1986). Pitt's attitude towards the French royalists is well set out in M. Hutt, *Chouannerie and Counter-Revolution. Puisaye, the Princes and the British Government in the 1790s* (Cambridge, 1983).

Aspects of Sir J.W. Fortescue's highly critical account of the direction of the war in his *British Statesmen of the Great War, 1793–1815* (Oxford, 1913) and *History of the British Army*, vol. 4 (1915), have been largely superseded by M. Duffy, '"A particular service": the British government and the Dunkirk expedition of 1793', *English Historical Review*, vol. 91 (1976), and *Soldiers, Sugar and Seapower. The British expeditions to the West Indies and the War against Revolutionary France* (Oxford, 1987). Contrasting explanations of the failure of the Second Coalition are provided by P. Mackesy in *Statesmen at War. The strategy of overthrow 1798–99* (1974) and P.W. Schroeder, 'The Collapse of the Second Coalition', *Journal of Modern History*, vol. 59 (1987). Pitt's war record during his second Ministry is evaluated in C.D. Hall, *British Strategy in the Napoleonic War 1803–1815* (Manchester, 1992); G.B. Fremont, 'Britain's Role in the Formation of the Third Coalition against France', Oxford DPhil thesis, 1991; and V.R. Ham, 'Strategies of Coalition and Isolation: British War Policy and North-West Europe, 1803–1810', Oxford DPhil thesis, 1977.

Irish issues are well surveyed by R.B. McDowell, *Ireland in the Age of Imperialism and Revolution 1760–1801* (Oxford, 1979); G. O'Brien, *Anglo-Irish Politics in the Age of Grattan and Pitt* (1987); and T. Bartlett, *The Fall and Rise of the Irish Nation. The Catholic Question 1690–1830* (1992). There are differing explanations of Pitt's resignation in R.E. Willis, 'William Pitt's resignation in 1801: re-examination and document', *Bulletin of the Institute of Historical Research*, vol. 44 (1971); P. Mackesy, *War without Victory. The downfall of Pitt, 1799–1802* (Oxford, 1984); and C.J. Fedorak, 'Catholic emancipation and the resignation of William Pitt in 1801', *Albion*, vol. 24 (1992). A less than flattering view of Pitt compared with his successor is provided by C.J. Fedorak, 'The Addington Ministry and the Interaction of Foreign Policy and Domestic Politics 1800–1804', London PhD thesis, 1990, and the consequences of his inaction when out of power are presented in R. Willis, 'Fox, Grenville and the Recovery of Opposition 1801–1804', *Journal of British Studies*, vol. 11 (1972). Pitt's career after his 1801 resignation is set in a wider context by A.D. Harvey, *Britain in the Early Nineteenth Century* (1978).

INDEX

Transport Office created   95

Treasonable Practices and Seditious
     Meetings Act (1795)   149, 151, 192,
     205

Trinity House Volunteers   159, 216

Triple Alliance   67, 192

Turkey   172, 174

Ulm, allies defeated at   226

Union with Ireland   94, 95, 125, 195–6,
     201

Union Parliament   208

United States of America   93, 170

Vansittart, George   122

Vansittart, Nicholas   115, 122

Vaughan, Benjamin   22

volunteer companies   125, 155, 158–9,
     201, 216, 225

Vorontsov, Simon   88

Wales, Prince of   15, 43, 44, 58, 112,
     123

Walpole, Horace   37
  commentator on Pitt   5, 6, 14, 26,
     99–100

Walpole, Sir Robert   31, 81, 104, 108,
     112, 132

war administration, British   183, 184

War of American Independence   3, 5

Ways and Means Committee   113, 118

West India Dock Act (1799)   122

West Indian expedition (1793)   62, 186

West Indian expedition (1795)   36, 184,
     189

West Indies, trade   168

Westminster scrutiny   143

Westmorland, Lord   46, 63, 64, 66, 69,
     210, 219

White's Club   113

Wilberforce, William   91, 92, 122, 123,
     142, 143, 154, 202
  commentator on Pitt   74, 75, 77, 78,
     90, 103, 109, 116, 124, 185–6,
     226
  friendship with Pitt   4, 5, 77, 166,
     202

Willis, Dr   44

Windham, William   37, 87, 206, 216
  appointments   63, 66, 70, 117
  commentator on Pitt   67, 90, 102,
     140

wine duty   34, 81, 108

Woodfall, William   140

Worsley, Sir Richard   111

Wraxall, Nathaniel   33, 100, 102, 114,
     141, 167, 175

Wyvill, Rev. Christopher   6, 7, 27, 33,
     116, 131, 135
  breaks with Pitt   136

York, Duke of, Frederick   36, 59, 64

Yorke, Charles   115, 118, 119, 224

Yorke, Sir Joseph   41

Yorkshire Association   27, 131

Young, Sir William   138